# THE PET PROFITEERS

By the same author:
*How to Bring Up a Child without Spending a Fortune*

# THE PET PROFITEER$
## The Exploitation of Pet Owners— and Pets—in America

### LEE EDWARDS BENNING

QUADRANGLE / THE NEW YORK TIMES BOOK CO.

Copyright © 1976 by Lee Edwards Benning.
All rights reserved, including the right
to reproduce this book or portions thereof in any form.
For information, address:
Quadrangle/The New York Times Book Co.,
10 East 53 Street, New York, New York 10022.
Manufactured in the United States of America.
Published simultaneously in Canada by Fitzhenry & Whiteside,
Ltd., Toronto.

**Library of Congress Cataloging in Publication Data**

Benning, Lee Edwards, 1934–
   The pet profiteers.

   Includes index.
   1. Pet industry—United States.  2. Pets.  I. Title.
SF414.7.B46       338.1′7′608870973      75-36266
ISBN 0-8129-0622-5

To Albert Ingalls Edwards
>friend
>father
>concerned dog breeder
>dog-club and federation officer

whose name is proudly printed, even if in invisible ink, on the cover and every page of this book

# CONTENTS

|      | *Acknowledgments*                         | ix  |
|------|-------------------------------------------|-----|
|      | *Preface*                                 | xi  |
| I    | Pet Shops                                 | 3   |
| II   | Kennel/Cattery Mail Order                 | 21  |
| III  | Adoption Agencies/Charities               | 33  |
| IV   | Vets                                      | 51  |
| V    | Food                                      | 61  |
| VI   | Accessories                               | 75  |
| VII  | Grooming                                  | 88  |
| VIII | Boarding                                  | 102 |
| IX   | Basic Training                            | 114 |
| X    | Breeding                                  | 123 |
| XI   | Utility                                   | 131 |
| XII  | Competition                               | 144 |
| XIII | Registries                                | 159 |
| XIV  | Lost and Found                            | 174 |
| XV   | Death                                     | 180 |
| XVI  | Postdeath                                 | 188 |
|      | *Appendix I   Purebred Dog and Cat Prices* | 199 |
|      | *Appendix II   Dog Breed Popularity Chart* | 201 |
|      | *Index*                                   | 205 |

# ACKNOWLEDGMENTS

Few are the books that can be said to be entirely one person's work. This is certainly not one of them.

It is the work of many, and you will hear their voices throughout the book. They include dog and cat lovers from every state, every age bracket, every walk of life. A recitation of their names would take pages for there were literally hundreds of them. But they and I know who they are and that without their help this book could never have been written.

Nor would it exist without the help of the man who swears to this day that sandwiched in among love, honor, and cherish was the word edit. And edit he did—adding, subtracting, questioning, and shaping this work into what it is. My thanks to him, my husband, Arthur, who takes the word helpmate literally.

Thanks, too, to Audrey Mather, who typed and typed and typed into the wee hours and beyond.

Special acknowledgment should be made of the knowledge imparted by two Ladys, one a mostly German shepherd and the other a purebred English springer spaniel; and by our official AKC champions and their champion get; and by our unofficial but still champion mousers, Smokey, Mother Cat, Pink Cat, et al.

To all, my thanks.

*I thank you for your voices, thank you,*
*Your most sweet voices.*

*Coriolanus,* II, iii, 179

# PREFACE

> Truth's a dog must to kennel; he must be whipped out,
> when Lady the brach may stand by the fire and stink.
>
> *King Lear,* I, iv, 125

Big dogs, little dogs, purebreds, mongrels—they're all going to hell in an orange crate or, to be more accurate, in a lettuce crate. And their feline cousins are close behind.

Today owning a pet is not simply a national pastime, something done for the kids' or your own pleasure. Today it's a national resource, one included in our annual gross national product. It is the sole support of a multibillion-dollar industry that deals in America's newest type of livestock. This, the product of puppy mills and pet farms, is shipped to pet shops all over the country like so many heads of lettuce.

Pet shops are proliferating at a rate that is surprising in view of mid-seventies economic conditions. This, in turn, spurs the growth of puppy mills, particularly in Midwestern states. As more and more ill-bred puppies are cranked out with inherent genetic problems and shorter prospective lifetimes, the whole pet industry benefits financially from what is nothing more than planned obsolescence in pets.

Veterinarians, as a result, are reaping a bonanza. And although surgical operations are standardized, fees are not. Thus one vet may charge one price while another may charge three to five times as much, or more.

The boarders, groomers, and accessorizers are keeping their prices in tune with, or perhaps ahead of, the times. And the gigantic dog- and cat-food industry goes merrily along making foods that sound and look good to people but, frequently, are not good for the pet's nutritional needs.

Buy a purebred dog or cat today for, say, $200, and you're likely to spend another $4,000 on it in the next twelve years. That's if you aren't susceptible to the come-ons for clothing, shows, vacations, jeweled collars, and fancy burials complete with memorials and perpetual care. If you want to go the whole route, you can easily line the pockets of the pet-business entrepreneurs with ten times that amount.

And for this, the chances are growing every day that you'll wind up with a dog that has a crippling hereditary disease, a sour disposition, and fake papers, or a cat less healthy than its barnyard relative.

There are other serious problems with pets. Overpopulation is more than just serious; it is nearing disaster proportions. Overpopulation has turned the entire animal-welfare-shelter industry into a gigantic killing machine rather than the "house of adoption" of a decade ago. It has our metropolitan areas up in arms about piles of feces in the streets and other health problems. And stray dogs, roaming in packs and living in abandoned buildings, constitute a growing menace for people and their pets.

Stolen dogs are now a fact of life. Dogs are being kidnapped for resale in pet shops, for the claiming of rewards, for dog fighting matches, for hunting trips, and you name it. And the so-called lost-dog registries will gladly take your money, but they surely can't guarantee you much in the way of results because of lack of cooperation among registries, including the American Kennel Club (AKC).

Who is doing something about the sad state of affairs in the dog world? Not too many, although there is plenty of talk. Not the AKC, the largest and most powerful force in purebred dogs. Not the breed clubs around the country, which are riddled with intraclub spats and petty jealousies. Not the state legislators, who, with few exceptions, have preferred to ignore pleas for pet-animal legislation. And most certainly not the pet shop/puppy mill combination that is contributing so much to the degeneration of the species and the runaway prices.

If this book merely makes you sad, instead of mad, it will have failed. Read it and run, don't walk, to your telephone, your writing desk, a speaker's podium. Do something, please. Or, if you can't, do nothing constructively. Remember, money talks. If you refuse to buy, to pay, to support, to patronize, to let this national disgrace go on, it will stop. Withholding your dollars can do what moral outrage can't, what legislation can't, what humane societies can't, and what books like this by themselves can't, and that's put America's human pet parasites out of business.

# THE PET PROFITEERS

# I  PET SHOPS

> The commercial puppy business—based on "puppy farms" or "puppy mills"—has been growing largely unchecked for twenty years. "It's an industry which has got out of control. It's out of hand," says one of the Midwest's most knowledgeable dog experts.
>
> DAVID ANABLE, staff correspondent of
> *The Christian Science Monitor*

It is December 31, 1974—New Year's Eve. A night of endings and beginnings. A most symbolically melodramatic time to begin a novel. But this is not melodrama. This is not even fiction. This story is true. The names have not been changed to protect the innocent. The only innocent involved is Jay Jay, a four-and-a-half-month-old Afghan puppy who was that day purchased from a pet shop in Connecticut. It could as easily have been in Wisconsin. Or Texas. Or California. For Jay Jay, like too many others, is the product of a $300 million-plus annual retail business. He is a pet-shop pup. He is not unique. This is why I tell his story.

And his story, like all the others in this book, must be told. As an animal lover, dog breeder, and chosen companion to nine lovable, garden-variety cats, I have no choice but to speak out. To protest against and attempt to halt the misuse and abuse of Americans' famed love of animals by those who look upon pets as a new kind of "livestock," the pet industry's own euphemism for dogs and cats.

Within the next year, more than six million animal lovers will put out their good, hard-earned money—more than half a billion dollars of it—to acquire what is truly the only love money can buy. Unfortunately, many, if not most, of these Americans will wake up to find that they've been had. That instead of love, they've bought an enormous heartache, not to mention a financial headache. The result is tragic for owner and pet alike: sooner or later, after one vet bill too many, the animal must go. Abandoned, surrendered to an adoption agency, or euthanized at the vet's.

And then, as you and I and the pet industry know, that soft-hearted animal lover will try again with a new pet and, most likely, a new problem. All because of mercenary commercial breeders, unscrupulous sellers, uncaring adoption agencies. And worst of all, the unknowledgeable, impetuous people who lose their hearts, not use their heads, when acquiring a pet. Would you believe that most prospective pet owners spend less time choosing what is to be a new member of the family than they do choosing a new pair of shoes?

One would think they were buying a toy. And that, to me, is the worst possible crime against pets. For a pet—be it purebred, mongrel, or stray—is not a four-legged, living toy to be discarded when it breaks down or proves unsatisfactory. Nor should owning a pet be considered a right. It is a privilege—more than that, a responsibility to be taken only after due consideration and seriously debated, if not out of love of animals or concern for the pet's impact on the family youngsters, then at least for the sake of the family finances. Today, there is no aspect of pet ownership that is inexpensive, much less cheap. It is practically a privilege reserved for the rich. Especially since more and more entrepreneurs see in America's vast pet population a gold mine to be milked and milked and milked some more for their own benefit, not that of the pet or its owner.

We could close down and seal one vein of that gold mine immediately if more people, when they saw a pet-shop pup for sale, would harden their hearts, think at least twice, and remember Jay Jay.

On that last day of December 1974—the last day of the holidays, when the biggest of Christmas bows look bedraggled and the glitteriest tinsel tawdry, even the Christmas puppies seemed dejected. There were some thirty of them sprawled in their cages at the H & M Pet-A-Rama. But only one was an Afghan. This was the dog Joan C. Freda had come expressly to see. She had heard he was there.

When she entered the shop, a few of the pups raised their heads expectantly, still not discouraged for having been passed over time and again in favor of some more irresistible pup. Jay Jay did not. He simply lay there in his cage. It was an adequate size for sleeping in, but not for romping or playing. Like the other pups, he lay on wire mesh. It was coarse mesh, about 2 by 2 inches, to allow the feces to fall through.

"When I went over to the cage," says Joan Freda, "he was totally disinterested. I got the salesgirl to open it, but he still didn't get up. He didn't give a damn what happened. She took him out and had to stand him up. He couldn't do it by himself. Finally, he stood there

*Mary Kay Hasseman/Pennsylvania SPCA*
Jay Jay at 4½ months, top, is a 12-pound bag of bones. After 6 months of extensive, expensive care he is still but a shadow of a normal 10½-month-old Afghan pup shown below.

straddle-legged, balanced precariously like two playing cards leaning against each other."

They wanted $350 for him, according to the salesgirl, but a second salesgirl, up front, said he was on sale. So, for $200, Joan Freda bought herself another Afghan; she already had ten healthy ones. What did she get for her money? A normal, healthy pup of his breed, at that age, should weigh between twenty-five and thirty pounds. Jay Jay weighed twelve.

There was no doubt about his physical structure. It was there to be seen, protruding through his skin, which was not a rosy pink, but a sickly oyster white, especially around the abdomen. His coat, if one could properly call it that, was sparse and dull. In fact, the few tufts of hair he did possess on his shoulders fell out the first time they were brushed.

His first visit to a vet had to be delayed because of the holiday, but vitamin supplements and special high-protein foods were started immediately. Just as quickly the problems began. Joan Freda awoke that night to a terrible racket. In the next room, Jay Jay was pounding his head on the wall in pain. The insides of his ears looked like red tapioca. Jay Jay was so severely debilitated, he was allergic to nourishment.

The vet, after examining Jay Jay, reported:

> The recently purchased Afghan puppy presented for examination was anything but a picture of good health. He was extremely thin, malnourished, showed an unkept, unhealthy coat, exhibited conjunctivitis, and a cough, and had evidence of diarrhea. [Note: so bad was this that his anus protruded three-fourths of an inch outside his body.] The front feet were "splayed" and the pasterns were "down," giving the impression of chronic malnutrition (with or without disease involvement). Further examination revealed a visible anemia. This animal was suffering from heavy ascarid [worm] infestation (+ + + on fecal exam), and also coccidiosis, which unquestionably was responsible for the severe diarrhea with blood (hemorrhagic enteritis). A moist cough was present, both tonsils were fiery and enlarged, and lungs were raspy. Cervical, prescapular and popliteal lymph glands were greatly enlarged, which would indicate a generalized systemic infection. This is the clinical picture of a puppy that was sold as "being healthy" only a few days previously.

Not only was he sold as being healthy, he also came complete with health-certificate-type papers. There were not one, but two signed certificates from local veterinarians. However, a close reading of them discloses that the vets were only certifying that the dog had been innoculated, not examined. One might wonder how one, much less two vets could give a shot to a sick pup without noticing his debilitated condition. One shouldn't be surprised, I guess. After all, neither vet was right about Jay Jay's sex—both having certified that he was a female.

The other paper, properly filled in and signed, was a guarantee! Pet-A-Rama's own Life Time Conditional Guarantee guaranteeing Jay Jay "for life against any and all diseases." Again, a close reading reveals that any and all diseases covers only "distemper, hepatitis, leptospirous [sic] or hard pad disease." Moreover, it specifically does not cover the afflictions that Jay Jay was suffering from: "H & M Pet-A-Rama shall not be responsible for any veterinary expenses arising from the treatment of such self limiting diseases as worms, coccidiosis, cold, coughs, laryngitis or tonsillitis nor shall these contitute [sic] grounds for return of this animal." The veterinary expenses now total hundreds of dollars and are still mounting. These expenses, plus the initial price, add up to a sum more than double the purchase price of a private breeder's top show-quality prospect.

Jay Jay, like most pet-shop pups, not only wasn't born on the property of H & M Pet-A-Rama, he wasn't even born in the state of Connecticut. Before he reached that pet shop, he had been through several hands. How many, we're still trying to determine. Since he hadn't been tattooed, we don't even know if the papers that accompanied him were truly his own. However, those papers would have us believe he was born on August 18, 1974, at the large commercial kennels of Sandi and John Dahm in New Sharon, Iowa.

On October 7, at seven weeks of age, he was—again according to his papers—sold to a Class B kennel, that of brokers Fritz and Barbara Brandt. Their kennel? Snow Peak Kennels, Avoca, Iowa, which is better than many, but not equipped to keep dogs any longer than the one calendar day required by law. (At one time, Snow Peak Kennels was so antiquated, they had to dip water out of the creek to water their stock.) The next documentation of Jay Jay's past is the sale some thirty-five days later to a pet shop in Connecticut. Then, another fifty days later, the sale of #862, a male, fawn-colored Afghan, to Joan Freda.

By all odds, Jay Jay should never have lived this long. Instead, today, he is happy and lighthearted. Although permanently stunted, he is not a bad-looking Afghan. In fact, one breeder of Afghans has admitted seeing worse in her lifetime. Of course, considering his original price, his veterinarian bills, and his diet of special foods, vitamins, and supplements, he may well be, ounce for ounce, the most expensive Afghan around.

That record may be matched by a komondor puppy bought from a nationwide chain of pet stores. The owner paid an even stiffer original price and got another Jay Jay. At three and a half months, the pup weighed twelve pounds. A healthy, normal komondor should weigh at least thirty pounds at that age. This pup, too, has cost its weight in vet bills and special diets.

The most expensive pet-shop pup of all time may be a Siberian husky bought as a pup for $250. It is now costing its owner a minimum of $40 a month in drugs and special food to keep the dog alive. And it will continue to do so for the rest of its life. The cause? A chronic digestive ailment to which huskies seem particularly susceptible.

But at least these puppies lived. A $350, eight-week-old, eighteen-ounce Yorkshire terrier didn't fare as well, even though it eventually became the property of a veterinarian. In spite of the owner's knowledge, expertise, and medications, the dog went into convulsions. He was too small, too sick, too weak to survive. He had been with his new master for less than twenty-four hours before he was dead. Dead of an easily preventable disease. One for which there is a vaccine. But the breeders of this $350 pup hadn't bothered to spend the few dollars necessary to save the dog from distemper.

I could go on citing example after example, including everything from rare breeds to mixed breeds to man-made breeds (such as the peke-a-poo) to cats and kittens. For when it comes to the pet-shop product, the diseased, the undernourished, and the almost-dead are the rule, not the exception. Which is not surprising considering the filth, the overcrowding, the haphazard feeding, the overbreeding, the ignoring of vaccines, and the substandard housing in which these animals are conceived, whelped, and raised. Unfortunately, few people will ever get to see a puppy mill in person. This is a condition much desired by their operators. Although most keep large, vicious dogs to frighten away the casual, unexpected, or unwanted visitor, some have been known to buttress their "no trespassing" signs with a handy shotgun.

One of the few people who gets inside these puppy mills with any regularity is Robert Nejdl, the Iowa-based chief field inspector for the American Kennel Club. He is the exception, granted entrance only because the operators do not wish to jeopardize their good standing with the AKC. The cachet AKC Registrable makes a pup a valuable commodity in the pet-peddling business. Nejdl is quite candid about the puppy mills, "If people knew what kind of foul holes some of these puppies come from, they'd be out of their minds to buy them."

A tour of such dives would seem to be in order. The first stop, a USDA-licensed kennel, is a converted chicken coop containing 110 dogs. At first glance, the floor appears to be covered with white, fluffy, high-piled wall-to-wall carpeting. Then the carpeting moves. Maggots. Hundreds of thousands of them.

At another Midwestern site, rusting oil tanks—their tops knocked out—are attached to the fronts of some of the homemade wire-mesh crates. This is all the protection pups and their dams will get from snow driven by a relentless prairie wind and summer heat that routinely pushes temperatures up into the nineties.

Many hundreds of miles away from these is an honest-to-goodness kennel complete with cedar posts and chicken-wire-fenced runs. Inside each run, several dogs run back and forth ignoring the carcass on the ground. The owner of this kennel believes in feeding dogs 100 percent meat and meat by-products. A dead calf is thrown into each run and left there until consumed, whether that takes a few days or weeks. In the meantime, the stink of decay mingles with the effluvia of excrement left to stand. The smell is everywhere and remains with you even after you've gotten into your car and driven away.

It is this gagging odor, pungent with urine, cloying with feces, that is the most obvious feature of puppy mills. One can't escape it. As a reporter for *The New York Times* noted, "The stench starts about half-way down the hill. At the bottom there are forty-two wire cages in a row, each roughly the size of a large refrigerator turned on its side, each with a roof of rotting straw, each suspended over a shallow trench." The source of the smell? The shallow trenches Ankeny Kennels in Des Moines, Iowa, uses to hold and dispose of droppings.

At another, even more oppressively odoriferous kennel, the stock is in rows and rows of wire-mesh crates set about six feet off the ground. The droppings fall through the wire and are allowed to build up until they come within inches of the bottom of the crates. At this point, a tractor is hooked up to the whole rack of crates, and the assembly is hauled a few feet away to fresh ground where the process can start all over again. The six-foot piles are ignored, left to provide breeding grounds for maggots, yellow jackets, rats, and the like. Eventually, if they find a buyer for this dog manure, it will be spread upon the fields. And everyone within miles around will know it.

That's why the first thing a person notices on visiting Iowa's largest commercial kennel is the smell. Rather, the lack of it. One visitor noted, "You could eat a picnic in Marguerite Roeglin's kennel. The air is as fresh and sweet inside as out." And no wonder. Mrs. Roeglin is what her fellow, less-concerned breeders call "crazy clean." Which means she cleans the runs daily or more often. She isn't satisfied with simply scooping up the solid wastes; she hoses her runs down. Her barn is well-built, keeping her dogs cool in the summer, warm in the winter. And best of all, it's well-ventilated. Something one appreciates not just for the relief it gives one's nose, but for the fact that this keeps airborne diseases to a minimum—an important as-

*R. Norman Matheny*
Above is a good puppy mill—the dogs have access to a kennel building for protection from the elements, the animals are up on wire for sanitary purposes, and, most important of all, the animals look and act healthy. Below is a bad puppy mill—a barrel is all the shelter this dog has from the Midwest's blizzards and heat waves; the dogs are fed haphazardly and given water so infrequently that this scruffy specimen is half-crazed with thirst.

pect in keeping young puppies healthy. Inside that barn are over 150 dogs, well fed, healthy, and clean. And they number among them many "specials," or official AKC champions, for whom she has willingly paid top dollar. Why? To improve her stock. Those in a position to know will readily admit that Mrs. Roeglin's efforts pay off in terms of the pups she produces. They are top quality, probably the best commercially bred dogs in Iowa, if not in America. And yet Mrs. Roeglin's financial rewards are small—little, if any, more than those achieved by churning out sickly pups under sickeningly filthy conditions. "We clean up all the mess, and the other guy makes all the dough," is the way Marguerite Roeglin puts it in her German-Iowa accent.

Why then does she bother to spend the time and money? Maybe good old-fashioned pride in her work, or the tradition of careful husbanding of stock that has always separated the good farmer from the bad.

Marguerite Roeglin is undoubtedly unique among commercial dog breeders. For one thing, there is the size of her operation. Most puppy mills are much much smaller, having fewer than fifty dogs. And the vast majority aren't even kennels. Instead, they're businesses run by farmwives who have five or more bitches where they used to house a flock of chickens. Instead of gathering the eggs daily, they breed their bitches twice yearly and sell the pups to get the modern-day version of egg money. Many of these women are well-meaning. They spend good money to get their initial stock, they buy good commercial feed, and they order their medicines from the catalogs of top supply houses. Only it's like the proverbial city slicker going into chicken farming—it doesn't work. Dogs aren't chicks, and pups aren't eggs, and the two don't mix.

To understand my point, one would have to watch such an operation over a period of years. Unfortunately, this is easier said than done. Patty Johnson, a German shepherd dog breeder in South Charlestown, Ohio, is one of the few people, to my knowledge, to have had that dubious privilege. And it took a rare combination of events to make it happen. For one thing, one needs an introduction to the puppy miller. In this case, a former roommate and lifelong friend provided it. Second, the puppy miller must be desirous of your help. By a happy accident, this particular one, caught in a cash squeeze after paying through the nose for her first two dogs, desperately needed free advice from Ms. Johnson. The following inside story is the result of their collaboration:

> The breeder under scrutiny turns out white German shepherd dogs. A few years ago she bought her original pair from a *Dog World* ad run by a

Texas breeder of white shepherds, a variant that cannot be shown under AKC rules. Her initial investment: $500. From this start she now has 20 females of breedable age (a first season being considered "breedable"). In addition, she has 3 stud dogs and 8 or 9 half-grown up and coming potential broods. One of her studs is a fence jumper, and when a female comes into season, he jumps the fence and breeds her whether this one is in with a different stud at the time or not. They both get to breed her, and it's anybody's guess who actually sires a given litter.

She keeps no records of when her bitches come into season, or when they are bred. When "Frosty" or "Snowy" is bulging at the sides, her guess is pretty accurate that there will be another batch of puppies soon. She gives no vitamins to a pregnant bitch, no milk, no meat, just commercial dog food. She does not worm her stock prior to mating, though she occasionally uses a mild cat wormer as a general purpose medicant. At whelping time, the animals are on their own. One litter came on a cold, sleet-rainy night— 10 to 11 pups. By the time she realized that there even was another litter, four of the pups had already frozen to death and the others were soaking wet from the rain. She did bring the bitch on her front porch at this point and allowed her to whelp the last pup there. At two weeks, all but one of the puppies had died, the last remaining survivor looked very ill as well. Incidentally, as soon as she had gathered up the freshly born pups, she gave each a distemper shot and an iron shot which she had purchased from a catalog.

Her pens consist of 5-by-15-foot wire. Each has a 3-by-5-foot A-frame dog house, one water pan and one pan for food. There are six to eight half-grown pups in one pen, and as many as three adults in each of the other pens. There are no footers under the pens, and the dogs are constantly digging into each other's pens and fighting, with a lot of resultant broken ears, scars and lameness. Some are permanently crippled from these fights, but a vet is never consulted—only when she needs a health certificate to ship dogs off—which are issued sight unseen. Consequently she proudly claims that she has no vet bills.

Her mortality rate in the summertime is 50 percent, mainly from hookworm and/or coccidiosis. If a dog is badly injured from fighting (which is often), or a puppy dies, she leaves the dead ones lay and the hurt ones bleed until her children—age nine and eleven—come home from school to either separate the fighters or dispose of the dead. It seems she just cannot stand the sight of blood or death.

She also seems to have a problem with feeding, watering, and cleaning, which is left to her youngsters. Dogfood is delivered to her door, but when she runs out, her dogs go hungry until the next delivery date, which may be three to five days hence.

Nonetheless, her buyers are all over the United States, and place their orders mostly in ten-puppy lots—with bigger orders coming in around Christmas. She obtains health certificates from a vet who never sees the pups, and ships them as early as four weeks of age. She even builds her own shipping crates out of plywood. One sheet makes six little crates into which she sticks two to three puppies each.

The payoff? $60 per puppy, with the pet shops paying for the shipping. They can afford to, as they resell the poor things at $150 to $200 each, depending on what traffic will bear in their area. Since the puppies are left to nurse on their dams until three days before shipping, she has very little expense in raising them. She gives them a distemper shot and a worm pill bought from her trusty catalog, and aside from the cost of the plywood . . . she clears most of the $600 she gets for those ten puppies per order.*

Fortunately, this breeder was soon put out of business by a series of natural crises which a larger, better-funded, multibreed puppy miller could have weathered. Spotted all over the Midwest are just such larger kennels, some that even put Marguerite Roeglin's to shame in terms of size. But in size only.

Many of these are run by converted pig farmers who have just transferred their breed 'em—slop 'em—farrow 'em—wean 'em—sell 'em practices from pigs to dogs. If they first bred their young sows at eight months, they breed their bitches just as young. If they used their boars as early as eight months and expected thirty services a season from them, their studs had better do as much. If they expected two large litters a year from each sow, no less is asked of their bitches. And they get away with it. As one of them is quick to admit, "Hell, the day I can't make a buck in dogs, that's when I go back to hogs."

Callous? Yes. Atypical? No. Just another way of stating the farmer's traditional belief that "If something on the place doesn't earn its keep, it goes." It's true of his tractors, his cows, his sheep, his pigs. Why not his dogs?

For example, out in Arkansas there's a USDA-licensed kennel that's run like many of these converted farm operations. The methods used on it were discovered by a young woman who infiltrated a local commercial dog-breeding association. Posing as a widow with a small inheritance who was thinking of going into commercial dog breeding for financial security, she saw, in her own words, "too much." And so, for fear of reprisals, she speaks anonymously:

> The owner is an honest, down-to-earth farmer type who keeps 200-plus brood bitches and studs, and knows each of them by name. Puppies? She never knows how many she has, for she doesn't keep any past eight weeks of age, except to replenish her brood stock with those which do not sell for some reason. This includes genetically defective animals, as she is convinced, like many in her business, that defects "skip a generation"—if they exist at all. So she expects any resultant pups to be just fine.
>
> The kennel is USDA-inspected twice a year unannounced, except for "alarms" sounded by the large, vicious dogs which are kept by this breeder and most others like her. (The dogs patrol the perimeter of the farms and delay unannounced visitors.) In case of complaints, additional inspections may be conducted. But what about the inspection standards? According to the owner, the USDA allows no more than three maggots per whelping box, though the inspectors do not appear to be troubled by the flies and roaches which "visitors" saw crawling over the pups. If drinking water is con-

* Reprinted with permission from *The Midwestern Shepherd.*

taminated, it has to go when it reaches the green algae stage. Puppies—not necessarily from the same litter—are often lumped together in the same cardboard box, awaiting so-called USDA stamps so they can be shipped out. Most of them are about four weeks old (when their teeth come in), none are kept past eight weeks. If pups from the larger breeds do not sell early, the pups are sold to laboratories or destroyed.

At one side of the house, there are post-weaning dams waiting to be put back into breeding pens. For large breeds, these pens are on the ground. For St. Bernards, this breeder has 5- by 7-foot pens which hold one male and three females. There are plywood lean-to shelters containing a bucket of water. During the winter, breeders are supposed to go out and break up the ice, but many don't bother, so the death rate from dehydration in puppy mills is high in winter.

For small breeds, the pens are up on wire, built around an old shed where two to three dogs can get out of the weather by huddling on a platform.

Westie-size dogs and larger are kept up on wire mesh for their entire lives (which last as long as they can produce). Bitches receive pregnant mare serum ($1.95 worth can "do" fifty bitches, depending on size), which brings their cycles down to a more productive and profitable four to five months between litters. Males who are sluggish breeders, or who are constantly used, like this kennel's basenjiis, are given gonadotropins. With difficult whelpers [breeds that have difficulty giving birth] and toy breeds, the kennel uses extra-large and long-bodied bitches, which are bred to small males in order to avoid Caesarians. If a bitch requires a C-section anyhow, she is most likely put down, as the kennel only wants free whelpers. To help things along, this kennel administers "pit" [a pituitary substance that induces uterine contractions] and also does any ear cropping or tail docking on its own.

Pregnant bitches, ready to whelp, are brought into the house and put into chickenwire crates which are stacked to the ceiling. This is where dam and pups spend their next two weeks, after which the pups are removed and put up on wire themselves. If there are ten or more puppies in a litter, some of them are put on another bitch for nursing, with pups as close to the same size and age as possible.

All dams are fed Purina without supplements (if you don't count the hormones as "supplements"!). The pups are taken from their dams as soon as possible, so they will come back into season that much sooner. The puppies are fed Purina Puppy Chow, soaked in warm water. They get DHL-modified live virus shots bought from a local vet who supplies and "educates" the area breeders on stock management techniques, particularly with regard to health problems.*

Shocked? Don't be. Considering the fact that this puppy miller is getting as little as $9 per pup—not profit, total!—she has no choice but to rely on efficient, volume-producing methods. No wonder so many of these puppy millers have to resort to cheap shortcuts, such as buying false health certificates at $1 a book of ten or twenty—each signed (but otherwise blank) by a licensed veterinarian. Not nearly

* Reprinted with permission from Weddle Publications.

so cheap, but still a bargain compared to an office visit, is that same blank paper, presigned by a less accommodating, but more greedy, vet, and priced at $1 each.

Now, don't say that there isn't any justice in this world, because there is. Many of those volume-producing, shortcutting puppy millers are themselves being rooked royally. For example, our good honest farmer type who knows all of her bitches by name; she's being paid less than 20 percent of what her fellow puppy millers are getting from brokers for their product.

Most puppy millers, by the way, do not deal directly with the pet shops. Instead, they operate through brokers. These keep track of local litters, send out "availability lists," and advertise in magazines aimed at the pet-shop industry as well as the public. Once they receive an order—two puppies are generally the minimum, but it depends on the size and price—they go out to the farms on a weekly or biweekly basis and fill it. The broker may pay as little for a pup as the aforementioned $9, but that is rare. More likely, he will pay close to the national average of $40 for a purebred pup. Novelties such as cockapoos and peke-a-poos go for less. Then, according to USDA regulations, the broker or Class B dealer (one-quarter of all those involved in the wholesale end of pets) must keep the pups for one calendar day before shipping them on to their ultimate destination. The broker must then invest about $3 for a plastic crate (even less for a Bruce crate—a modified lettuce crate) in which he can ship two or more pups. He then resells those same pups at an average of $70 plus charges for such extras as docking of ears or tails, shots, or special or under-the-minimum orders.

The pet shop will, in turn, take those same pups and charge an average of $199 apiece. A $129 markup! Almost 200 percent! However, the pet shop takes the most risk. If the pups are sick, it must refund the money or risk facing a law suit. One pet shop willingly refunded a customer's money and then sold the sick animal, untreated, to another customer. One diseased dog I know of was sold to three different customers in all before seeing a vet and being put down.

Then again, if the pups don't sell, it is the pet shop who must feed them while reducing the price until the pups finally sell themselves. Or are disposed of. In the event of the latter, it is the pet-shop owner who takes those pups to a vet and has them put down. That is, if he or she wants to throw good money after bad. Actually, many take their pups to humane societies, declare them lost animals, and let the society use $5 per animal of the taxpayers' money to put the pet shop's excess stock down.

Other pet shops have other ideas. Some wring necks, shoot, bludgeon, or bucket their overage surplus stock; others abandon them near highways. Still others have found a truly carefree way of getting rid of those pups that lose their sales appeal: they put them, live, in a deep freeze. No barks, no howls, no protests—just hours later, frozen carcasses to put out in the trash to be hauled away by the sanitation workers.

But for sheer imagination, the award must go to the pet shop that turned to the trash compactor to solve their problem. Enough said.

Actually, the big outlets and chains seldom have surplus stock to worry about. They are as good at estimating their puppy needs as your butcher is at deciding how much ground beef to grind for any given day. One chain of pet stores sold over 68,000 dogs in one state in one year. Docktors Pet Centers, Inc.,* a chain of more than 100 pet stores, several owned by the company and the balance franchised by independent operators in twenty-three states, has annual sales in excess of $20 million. Overall there are probably 8,500 retail pet stores and 12,000 chain stores that handle live animals. The average one will gross about $85,000 annually, of which 14 percent, or $12,000, will come from the sale of cats and dogs.

However, more and more of the smaller ones are opting for the small animal/fish route and leaving the problems of selling cats and dogs to the bigger operations. One of the major problems they face is simply getting the pups, live and healthy, from the brokers to their pet shops. For example, one Labrador puppy was lost in transit for two weeks. Without food and water, he attempted to eat the sawdust in which he was packed. He finally arrived at his destination. **DOA**. They found him packed, literally, with sawdust. His eyes, his ears, his nose, his mouth, his stomach.

On another occasion, two crates of puppies were shipped into northern New York state, arriving at the local airport on December 17. Somebody goofed, because they were still there ten days later. And for those ten days, they had only an occasional puppy biscuit fed to them by concerned individuals working there. After awhile, the smell was too much even for the animal lovers in the terminal, and the pups had to be moved outside during the day. Out into average December temperatures of 15 degrees, sometimes even as low as zero.

Naturally the pet shop refused shipment. The Christmas rush was over. There was no market for post-Christmas puppies. They should

---

* I knew the two founders from their days of running a pet shop on West Market Street in Philadelphia. One brother sold me my first fish tank and filter; the other, my first fish. All I can say is the tank leaked, the filter didn't work (it was the wrong kind), and the fish soon died.

PET SHOPS 17

go back where they came from. As a sorry postscript to this matter, it should be reported that the airline was busy transporting all their human passengers back and forth during this festive holiday season to see their loved ones. So busy in fact that it could not find space for two small crates of helpless pups. Not before January 6. A full ten days later. To make a long story short, the humane society stepped in and rescued the pups, but not before two had died of exposure.

However, the Air Transport Association claims that according to a survey they made in 1972, of the average 2,000 animal shipments carried daily by the airlines, "less than one-tenth of 1 percent resulted in fatalities." This works out, using the industry minimum shipment of two animals per, to approximately 1,460 deaths per year. But the ATA places the blame for these deaths on what happened before and after the puppies were shipped. Specifically, on "improper packaging, lack of standards for kennels and containers, and delivery to the airlines of sick and/or unhealthy animals through the lack of or through an improperly issued health certificate."

The irony of all this is that none of those fatalities are necessary. The Chihuahua being shipped to the East from the Midwest that died in transit (strangulated, according to the autopsy report, on its own worms) might well have passed a Chihuahua going to the Midwest from the East. The latter was a strange, dabbled color that on

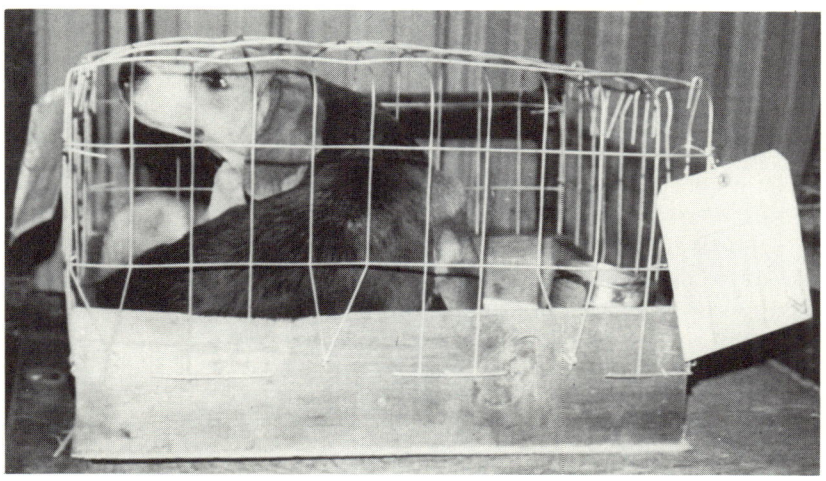

*The Humane Society of the United States*
No room to lie down, no space to turn around, and no escape from sun or rain. God help this poor dog if another crate is piled atop his makeshift, flimsy one.

closer inspection turned out to be a normal chocolate-colored Chihuahua, covered with large patches of fleas. The owner, a breeder in Connecticut, says she uses butter to kill them (from pleasure, maybe?) and treat the coat, too. She also refuses to sell dogs to local buyers. She wants to ship them out of state. That way she doesn't have to worry about their new owners showing up and asking embarrassing questions.

But she is not the only one. Some states document the exits and entries of pets, and they have discovered that *in any given year, as many dogs and cats come into a state for sale in pet shops as go out of the state for sale in pet shops.* Nor do all of those animals come from pet farms or puppy mills. Suffice it to say that many well-known, even famous, kennels have been known to sell their culls or castoffs to out-of-state brokers who, in turn, sell to pet shops. It's a nice profitable way to make money and get rid of potentially embarrassing pups.

But sometimes it backfires. There is, for example, one Midwesterner who has completed his AKC championships on ten dogs purchased from pet shops. The best AKC champion dalmation of all times, in terms of number of dog show wins, was bought as a puppy from a pet shop for $75. One of the most famous Maltese kennels had its origins in a doggy-in-the-window pup bought by a man for a wife with a bad back. The dog was named Lover. His successors were more prestigiously named after Hindu gods. Collectively, they are known as the Aennchen Dancers. Individually, they include Champion Aennchen's Smart Dancer, Ch. Aennchen's Shikar Dancer, Ch. Co-Ca-He's Aennchen Toy Dancer, Ch. Aennchen's Sari Dancer, and Ch. Aennchen's Poona Dancer. Each and every one of them went Best of Breed, the ultimate in achievement among Malteses, at the Westminster Dog Show.

These people were lucky. Or knowledgeable about dogs. Or both. Most buyers of pet-shop pups aren't so fortunate. Why, then, do they buy the sorry specimens that are the pet peddlers' stock-in-trade? Easy credit, for one thing. The customer gets all sorts of plans to make the paying easy. Selection, for another. Nowhere else does one walk in to find as many as two dozen or more different breeds of pups, all the right age, just awaiting your choice.

Sympathy plays a part, too. How can you resist a black Labrador retriever in a cage so low she can barely stand up, yet who, undaunted, tries to play with the only toy available, her tail. Then, in trying to chase it, her nails keep catching in the wire mesh of the floor of her cage, throwing her to the ground. Undismayed, she rises and attempts again to play.

But a good sales spiel is the real secret. The successful pet peddler will talk to, and try to sell to, anyone who enters his store. But he will usually leave a man for a woman customer, an individual for a couple, and a couple for a family. Salesmen know children sell dogs and cats for them.

Nothing works better than a "Sale!" sign. "Put a big red 'For Sale!' or 'Reduced' sign on a cage," says a veteran salesman, "and watch the suckers perk up." However, seldom if ever will those signs show either the original or the newly reduced price. That's because the salesman will adjust those prices after giving his customers a good look-see. The woman with a big diamond ring, the man with a digital watch or Nikon camera, the child with an "alligator" shirt—all these move the price up. Way up. Sometimes above the original price. Of course, if the customer proves reluctant, the price can come down, "because you people look like you could give this lovely pup a good home."

But before they'll reduce the price, they may try other, more diverse tactics. Like high pressure. "Buy now because they may not be around next week," and "Can't guarantee another like this one ever again."

Or snob appeal sometimes works. Especially with the prospect who equates quality with exorbitant price. He'll pay $400 to $500 for a tortie point Siamese kitten because he hasn't seen one before. Or $1,000 for an eight-week-old Afghan that's blue. Or a red elkhound. Or a beige affenpinscher. Or a poodle that's trimmed to look like a bichon frise, the newest craze in dogs. Speaking of poodles, have you heard of the "teacup poodle"? There is no such thing, but they're being advertised and sold all over the country. They're the runts of the litter and are selling for twice the price of their merely miniature brothers.

Exotic or rare breeds sell better than plain old ordinary breeds, as any pet-shop owner knows. So somebody came up with the idea of creating some of their own. Now we have the cockapoo and the peketzu and my favorite, the poohound. It's easy to tell what the rear end is by what it does, but which hound is up front? As one discouraged expert charged, "It is often easier to sell an unusual *worthless* item at a high price than at a low one."

Name-dropping, also known as "testimonials," is a surprisingly effective sales tool. Once President Ford obtained "Liberty," the sale of golden retrievers went up like crazy. Movie personalities also work well; Kim Novak, for example, sold many great Dane pups and Siamese cats for the pet shops. Who can guess how many sales Jacqueline Onassis made for pet shops of English cockers and her other breeds?

Then, too, it pays to boast of a local resident, especially one of some repute, owning a pet from your pet shop. Speaking of which, the last I heard, H & M Pet-A-Rama in Connecticut had some new and exotic Afghan pups in. Their price was $700. But they were on sale. For $275. Only $75 more than for Jay Jay. Why the higher sale price? "A big breeder in Kensington, Connecticut, bought one of our dogs for breeding."

Remember Jay Jay and Joan C. Freda?

## HOW TO TELL WHETHER OR NOT YOU'RE GETTING A HEALTHY PET:

1. *Temperature:* Normal is 101°F. for cats, 102°F. for dogs. A one- or two-degree variation can be caused temporarily by excitement or activity.
2. *Nose:* Wet or cold means little except in cats, where upper respiratory diseases will produce a discharge that keeps the nose wet and cold.
3. *Eyes:* Clear, no discharge, no cloudiness. (Cross-eyes are normal in Siamese cats.) Interior membrane should not show in cats; it is acceptable in dogs.
4. *Ears:* Interior pink, smooth, clean. Beware of gray deposits, chalky appearance, or yellow coloration of skin.
5. *Coat:* Full, not patchy. Not excessively dry. Flaky "dandruff" can indicate poor diet or allergy.
6. *Attitude:* Playful, active. Beware of lethargy. However, do not mistake boredom for disinterest.

## II  KENNEL/CATTERY MAIL ORDER

> Let's face it, there are conscientious breeders and poor breeders. . . . Let's stop hiding our heads in the sand and pretending the only villain is the pet shop.
>
> A SAMOYED BREEDER

America's moving billboards flash by you. Sandwiched in among tattered old signs—"Impeach Nixon," "Hab a Habby Day," "Go, Saints, Go," "Philadelphia '76," "Make Love Not War," and "Hoof-Hearted"—is "Buy from a Breeder!" Tailgate closer and above that command reads, "Protect Purebred Dogs."

And just where do you think the puppy millers got and get their original stock? Jay Jay, the pet shop Afghan, for example, has a pedigree that's simply gorgeous. A six-generation pedigree prepared by Brewster Pedigrees, in Montville, New Jersey, shows 90 official AKC show champions out of 126 listed ancestors. Although his parents were not champions, three of his four grandparents were. People really into Afghans would recognize, back of those, many other names, including those of several international champions and the 1957 Best in Show winner at Westminster, Ch. Shirkhan of Grandeur.

Back in the 1950s things were a lot different on the pet scene than they are today. The vast majority of all pets in this country were of the Heinz 57 variety, even those few found in pet shops. Purebred dogs and cats were, like Cadillacs and Rolls Royces, usually the prerogatives of the rich. Then came more widespread affluence. Pet owners, intent on keeping up with or outdoing the Joneses, discovered what the well-to-do knew all along—that purebred dogs and cats had certain advantages built in or, should I say, bred in. For one thing, their adult size and appearance were predictable. As were certain distinctive personality characteristics that seemed common to all members of their breed. Best of all, when Blacky or Miss Mittens had to be replaced, it was easy to get a close duplicate of that loved one.

It took the American Kennel Club more than three quarters of a century to register their five millionth dog (in 1956). During the next ten years, it registered twice that many. And it is estimated that by the end of our bicentennial year, that figure will have doubled again to twenty million.

What were purebred dog breeders—and cat breeders, since they were also enjoying boom times—doing during all this time? They were rubbing their hands with glee and cashing in for all they were worth. Where before they had to limit their litters during the year to a few because the demand was so slow, now they could breed as much as they liked. It wasn't until the Docktor brothers and other smart merchandisers, the pet-shop people, if you will, got on the gravy train that the breeders felt any great compunction to "protect purebred dogs."

Cats—those independent, buck-the-trend, nonconforming delights—have not relied on human agencies to protect them. Instead, in their purebred strains, they have proven so susceptible to diseases that pet shops have learned to their financial sorrow not to stock them. Instead, when they get an order for a Siamese, Persian, Burmese, or whatever, they do what the general public could do. They contact a breeder. Then they jack up the breeder's price by 50 percent or more "to cover expenses" and make the sale.

When the competition really got rough, when pet shops began outselling the private breeders by better than a three-to-one margin, that's when there was real concern on the part of breeders, dog clubs, associations, and even the American Kennel Club. And well there should have been, since it was these short-sighted groups that had allowed the problem to snowball to its present-day mammoth proportions. But whether parading a slogan around the country on the bumpers of automobiles will solve the problem is another story. If nothing else, it is at least a beginning.

Unfortunately, buying from *some* breeders not only won't protect purebred dogs or cats, it won't protect the purchaser. It is, in fact, worse than buying from a pet shop. At least you can report the pet shop to the Better Business Bureau or sue or picket them. But there is no effective recourse open to you when you get a lemon from a private breeder.

And don't kid yourself, there are plenty of lemons around, starting with the lemon-colored German shorthair pointers; dachshunds whose tongues hang out constantly, permanently, because their lower jaws are more than an inch too short; five- and six-toed poodles; dwarf

Alaskan malemutes; bassetts that are literally "wobblers" because of a deformity of the spine; deaf bull terriers; blind collies; dalmations with patches, not spots (these all carry the gene for heart problems); epileptic bloodhounds; bulldogs that literally can't breathe during hot weather or after the slightest exertion; and Bedlingtons that can't tolerate the smallest amount of anesthesia and have been known to die as the result of such simple surgery as having their teeth cleaned.

One of the prime causes of problems in purebred pets is that there are just too many breeders around with *intriguing* motivations. There is, for example, the totally unmotivated breeder—the *accidental breeder*—who has his status foisted upon him, usually via an open door and a male that's Johnny-on-the-spot. When the male happens to be of the same breed, which happens with great frequency in those neighborhoods where the houses, cars, people, and pets seem all alike, then presto—purebred pups or kits. Sometimes the results are superlative; more often, not. But at least they can be healthy specimens of the breed and make excellent pets provided this amateur, unwilling breeder goes to the trouble of providing the dam and litter with proper care. On the other hand, that's a lot of work and expense, so many won't bother. Moreover, since the breeding was unplanned, almost any genetic problems can pop up in the offspring.

Another common type of breeder is the *educationally oriented breeder,* who does it so "the kids can see the miracle of birth." Admittedly most of these will breed only once, but there are thousands upon thousands of them across the country. Cumulatively, they are responsible for bringing an enormous number of pups and kittens into this world with no idea whatsoever as to what is going to happen to them once born. As one SPCA worker says, "Before they let the little ones see the miracle of birth, let them come around here and see the miracle of death when I have to dispose of those pets they brought into this world."

These breeders do damage to purebred dogs and cats, but unknowingly. Not so the *money-minded breeders.* These know exactly what they're getting into and figure it'll reward them financially. First and foremost of these is the *backyard breeder,* who puts the family pet to work to earn her keep or to help support the family. One woman looked upon her two English springer spaniels as the means of putting her sons through college. But to make backyard breeding pay off, it is essential to cut corners wherever possible. Thus, the closest stud is used, preferably one whose fee will be mere peanuts or a future puppy. The dam and her litter are fed as little as possible. Weaning is delayed until the last possible minute so that inoculations can be avoided. The breeder relies on mother's milk to confer a natural immunity. If worming is done at all, mineral oil or some other ersatz substitute is used. Or some of that cheap, all-purpose worm medicine available at the corner store. If this sounds like a repetition of a puppy miller's methods of operation, you're right. That's exactly what it is, but on a smaller scale. (This breeder deals most frequently in one of the top forty or fifty breeds in popularity, where pups are easiest to place.)

A cut above this breeder, but still profit-oriented, is the *commercial private breeder*. The basic difference between this individual and the backyard breeder is that this person cares. He cares *about* his dogs, he cares *for* them, and he cares *about the homes* they go to. And if you asked him, he would vehemently deny that he was in breeding for the money. Yet press him further and you'll find he really has no other motive in breeding than the selling of dogs. One of the nicest dog people you'd ever want to know admits that the reason she breeds her three Labrador bitches is because there's a market for the puppies or, as she puts it, "because there are people who wish to own *good* Labrador puppies." And she is right on two counts. There are such people, and her puppies are good ones—happy, healthy, people-loving. But are they good *Labrador* puppies?

Those deeply involved with dogs or cats, known respectively as the "dog fancy" and "cat fancy," would—sight unseen—say no. They would say that if you want a good, happy, healthy, people-loving puppy, go to the SPCA. But if you want a good Labrador puppy, go to a serious Labrador breeder, be he at a show or field kennel.

How does one tell a *serious breeder* from a commercial private breeder? According to the fancy, the serious breeder is in dogs or cats as a hobby or for the fun of it, not for money as is the commercial breeder. Making money from breeding dogs or cats, that's bad. Being a serious breeder and losing money, that's good. Accidentally making money, that's acceptable. This may be the only sport, hobby, or business in the world in which you are praised, patted on the back, and admired by your peers because you lost money. In most anything else, of course, you'd be fired, ignored, or boycotted. But not in dogs or cats. Or so the dog and cat fancies would have us believe.

The truth is that the difference between the commercial breeder and the serious breeder, when it comes to money, is nothing. Zero. There isn't a serious breeder in the country giving his studs' services away to improve the breed. Not at all; he charges whatever the market will bear, and he keeps adjusting his prices upward. Try to buy a pup or kitten from one; you'll be charged as much as, or more than, any commercial private breeder charges.

And when it comes time to file state and federal income tax returns

*The Christian Science Monitor/R. Norman Matheny*
Death is this Doberman pinscher's only hope of escape from continuous motherhood and her ramshackle, homemade, backyard kennel.

on April 15, a miracle occurs throughout the length and breadth of this country; by a stroke of a pen, thousands of serious breeders turn their hobbies into businesses to get a deduction for tax purposes.

The basic difference, then, between serious breeders and commercial private breeders is motivation. The commercial private breeder is involved with dogs or cats to supply good pets at a profit. The serious breeder is in it to produce dog- or cat-show winners, field-trial experts, racers, or whatever; the production of profitable pets is simply a by-product. But this is one industry that produces a lot of by-products. A breeder may be lucky to find one show prospect in a litter. Two is a bonanza. Three comes close to a miracle. Over four? That makes the history books.

For example, there was the famous "Opera Litter" of Doberman pinschers born in 1951: Ch. Harding's La Boheme, Ch. Harding's Thais, Ch. Harding's Tosca, Ch. Harding's La Traviata, Ch. Harding's Mignon, Ch. Harding's Rigoletto, Ch. Harding's Oberon, plus Ch. Harding's Faust, who individually achieved seven Best in Show wins, four Best of all Working Dogs (known as Group Firsts), eighty-seven Best of Breeds, and two Best in Specialty Shows (open only to Dobermans). In addition, there was one female that had points toward her championship but was retired to be bred as well as two pups that were never shown at all.

Another litter, this one of golden retrievers, born March 16, 1954, had nine of its thirteen members as champions of record. The other four, although good enough to win, did not, because their owners were not interested in showing and would not exhibit them. So even these two fabulous litters had their share of pet pups.

Thus, the battle lines are drawn. Everyone against the puppy-milling backyard breeder who is selling an inferior product either to pet shops or the public. Commercial private breeders against serious breeders for the good-pet market. The commercial private breeder sees an open market on which he can sell a good, honest product for an honest dollar. The serious breeder, however, wants the market to himself so that he can continue to work to produce better-looking or better-working animals while having someplace to dispose of those who don't measure up. After all, it is the serious breeder who has created the separate breeds, maintained them, and brought them to whatever peak of excellence they may have achieved. Without the serious breeder, the breed would suffer, its standards would fall, and its distinctiveness from the others would blur. Every breed of dogs and cats needs its full quota of serious breeders.

That's a laudable concept about which the general public couldn't care less. Most of them just want a good pet. But 90 percent of all people, in my estimation (and it's probably on the low side), wouldn't know a healthy pet from a sick one, much less a good one from a bad one. They are totally dependent on the seller's expertise to get them their good pet. For those who wish more than a pet—who wish a show cat or a hunting dog—the dependency is even greater. It is essential that they deal with a serious breeder. In fact, if one merely entertains the inkling of an idea of *utilizing* the prospective pet in some way, especially for show, field, or breeding purposes, then the serious breeder should be sought out.

Unfortunately, it is hard to tell the serious breeder from the commercial breeder. In fact, it's almost as difficult to tell the puppy-milling backyard breeder from the others. Especially since the puppy millers have gotten wise and started to improve their front. For example, an organization of out-and-out, grind-'em-out puppy millers could, according to an informed Kansan, "pass for any regular dog club in the country. Even its name, Pet Producers of America, sounds good. Its members have regular 'socials' with respected guest speakers and educational films. In their newsletters, they encourage members to actually show some of their dogs, even if only at matches, so they can advertise them as 'show stock,' [to] get into legitimate kennel clubs and [to] generally assimilate themselves as thoroughly as possible to blur the distinction between commercial [as puppy millers like to call themselves] and private breeders."

This group isn't the only one to hide behind the facade of being a show kennel. As the American Shetland Sheepdog Association warns prospective purchasers, there are "many 'kennels' advertising show-quality puppies for sale that have never bred a champion or even owned a real show-quality dog."

So, *being* a "show" kennel or cattery and *saying* you're one are two different things. Glib expertise is also no indication of real knowledge. Breeders, discussing the issue, echo the refrain over and over again that instant experts are growing up all over the place. "This is one of the biggest problems to a prospective puppy buyer," remarked one breed club official. "People can get stuck with an inferior puppy just by listening to some of our breeders. And we have some bullshit artists, believe me."

Another put it a bit more politely and less pungently but makes the same point. "How can you tell who is reputable and who isn't? The unethical ones usually have a real good selling spiel, and you would think butter would melt in their mouths."

It's true. There is no way for the average person to know who is reputable and who is not. Which is why backyard breeders, commercial private breeders, and serious breeders can coexist within the show community. Coexist? Some of the worst are often officers in the show-giving clubs, even delegates to the AKC or their national cat registry. They wear many different hats, too. Some are community leaders. (One whom I know is an official of the local animal shelter.) Or lawyers or doctors or coupon clippers. When it comes to making money from pets, there is no distinction by social class.

Because this inability to tell the good breeder from the bad is widespread, many systems have grown up to fill the gap. The most popular is writing to the AKC or CFA (The Cat Fanciers' Association) for a list of breeders. What comes back is a list of advertisers of that breed residing in your area. One writes to all of those, and, hopefully, one will get a reply or replies. Many won't answer. They either receive too many requests for information, or they couldn't care less about helping the average person find a pup to his liking. The only way to guarantee a reply is offering to pay any price for their products. Of course, that's an open invitation to pay through the nose.

Another more elaborate but more helpful route is to write the AKC or CFA requesting the name and address of the secretary of the national parent-breed club—the one given the responsibility of determining and of maintaining the breed standard to which everyone else is supposed to adhere. A letter to the club secretary requesting general information and a list of breeders may get results.

When I did just that, contacting more than 140 such clubs and explaining that I was researching this book, only 29 replied. (One of those did so in a column in a national dog magazine, which was nice for my ego, but not exactly where the average letter writer would look for a reply.) Of those 29, one, the American Shetland Sheepdog Association, offered the best booklet I have seen, and it would be worthwhile for any breed, not just sheepdogs. Others sent booklets that dealt exclusively with their breed but did an excellent job of it, especially the Afghan, Belgian sheepdog, boxer, English setter, German shepherd dog, Irish wolfhound, Lakeland terrier, Pembroke Welsh corgi, samoyed, and Welsh terrier clubs. Six others wrote long, personal letters volunteering excellent information: the Briard, golden retriever, white German shepherd dog, lion dog, Norwegian elkhound, and St. Bernard clubs. Eight others also replied in brief, specifically, the borzoi, Boston terrier, German wirehaired pointer, standard schnauzer, Norwich terrier, Yorkshire terrier, Greater Swiss mountain dog, and Portuguese water dog clubs. Two, the miniature schnauzer and Scottish terrier clubs, replied they were forwarding my letter elsewhere, but the forwardees never answered. The twenty-eighth club, that for English cockers, suggested I prove my real interest in their breed by parting with $5 to buy their yearbook. On the other hand, the Rhodesian ridgeback people actually went out and bought a book on their breed to send to me.

As a result of my own experience with these clubs I am forced to the conclusion that the vast majority of the dog and cat breed clubs in this country exist for reasons other than protecting their breed through the dissemination of literature and/or information to newcomers. Thank goodness there are exceptions.

A third method advocated to identify breeders is to buy through ads in national magazines. It is especially believed in by those who place the ads. As one breeder, an old-English-sheepdog woman, put it, "Want to sell your pups fast and at top prices? Put an ad in the national dog magazines the day they are born."

Unfortunately, those on the reading and buying end of the ads are not as thoroughly convinced of their efficacy, primarily because there are three kinds of ads appearing in these magazines (one of which is *Dog World*). The first is that of the legitimate kennel that believes in keeping its name before the dog-buying and breeding public. The second is that of the well-meaning but unknowledgeable person who sincerely believes that his litter is top quality because both the sire and the dam came from well-known kennels. It is the third type of ad that causes the trouble. This is created to deliberately deceive the naive. Seeing a statement in black and white in a national magazine gives it an air of credibility that is terribly convincing. Dog advertisers know that. As one shelty breeder was quick to point out, "people who live in rural areas with a limited market for purebred pets find that they can sell anything by mail if it is called a show prospect."

A fourth method, but one closely related to the ad in the national magazine, is buying through the mail. Either through a catalog (one firm sells more than 15,000 pups this way each year), or through classified ads. These guarantee you a quality dog of your choice of sex, color, age, and so on, shipped directly to you from a "reputable breeder." I know, I was one of the reputable breeders one mail seller contacted. He told me to state my firm price and the cost of replacing the crate that I'd ship the pup in ("Thirty dollars? No problem. Just add it on."). He would then add his percentage on top of all that. His background for selling dogs? He runs a drycleaning establishment, and distributes biblical tracts.

Still a fifth method of finding a breeder is through a local dog club or federation. Of all the ways available, this is the best. Unfortunately, these clubs do not exist in all states nor in all areas of all states; that is, a large state might have one such club located far up in a northwest corner away from 90 percent of the population. However, at the present time, the following states have some form of referral services:

Alabama, California, Connecticut (where the service may be the oldest), Delaware (working on it as of May 1975), Florida, Illinois (very active), Indiana (ditto), Iowa (a dud), Kentucky (actually a kennel club), Maryland, Michigan, Minnesota (very active), Mississippi, Nevada, New Jersey, New York, Ohio (two), Oklahoma (very active), Oregon, Pennsylvania, South Carolina, Virginia, and Washington state.

To the general public, these are free. Each offers an avenue of complaint of which breeders are well aware. If a pup doesn't turn out as promised (or paid for), one can always complain to the referral system, and the chances are that the breeder will not receive many more referrals. These, by the way, are free to the breeder as well, although a donation is requested. In areas where such referral systems are in effect, the dog situation is much better. Unfortunately, at this time, none has expanded to include cats. Nor can they expand in dogs beyond what they are already doing. The advantage of staying so small is that nine out of ten times the referral system will actually know the breeder being named—they may even have checked up on him. This is not true of the AKC, the parent clubs, or the dog magazines.

Generally speaking, it is logical to assume that the person out to "Buy from a Breeder" is as much at the breeder's mercy as is the impulse-buyer at the pet shop. Although certain breed clubs have attempted to institute a code of ethics, what is going to stop a disreputable person from signing it? The parent club? They're powerless. The AKC? They couldn't care less. Thus, other than in those states where there is a nonprofit referral service to screen out the bad eggs, the prospective pet owner is on his own.

There *are* ways, however, of telling a serious breeder from a commercial private breeder, and a commercial private breeder from a backyard breeder. For example, the serious breeder knows the virtues and faults of most, if not all, of the ancestors of his litter—not just one generation or two generations back, but three or four. Because he breeds for a purpose other than money, he usually keeps at least one or two pups from each litter. He studies that litter carefully to make sure he gets the best. In effect, he grades it. He takes into consideration conformation, or the physical ability to do a job; intelligence, the mental ability to do a job, including coping with people; beauty, the frosting on the cake that enables each to closely approximate the breed standard; and finally, personality, for every pup or kit is an individual. There is the roughhouser that will take a firm hand but will never do for the aged or nonactive. The gregarious one that thinks he's people and can't get enough contact with them. The quiet one who will idolize the one master he prefers. Then, there are al-

## KENNEL/CATTERY MAIL ORDER   31

ways the negatives—the one with a screw loose or the potential fear-biter. One of these may not pop up in a hundred litters; but if one does, it must be culled and discarded, not sold.

When each pup or kitten has been assessed and compared with its littermates, the serious breeder ranks them from the most desirable to the least—knowing full well as he does that the least desirable to him might be just exactly the perfect one for a particular home or family. Once he has ranked them, he prices them accordingly. And he says as much.

He has a price list and it doesn't change. It doesn't go up because a buyer looks prosperous. It doesn't go down because a customer can't afford the buying price. The serious breeder who is concerned for his litter knows that if someone can't afford the purchase price, they probably can't afford the upkeep either.

Not only will he not lower his price, he will also charge as much as the market will bear. This for several reasons. For one thing, he undoubtedly has more invested in each of the animals he produces than do other breeders—in terms of time, expenses, and extras—for each littermate is treated as if it were the one he is going to keep. (And only the best is good enough for the one he chooses.) Then, too, he knows that anything bought cheaply is considered cheap. Nobody cares for inexpensive, throwaway stuff like jelly glasses and plastic cups. It's the cut glass and silver, the diamonds, and furs—and the expensive cats and dogs—that are appreciated and cared for.

But the serious breeder makes the price worth every cent by doing what no pet shop, backyard breeder, or accidental breeder can do. He is a matchmaker par excellence. He knows how to match people and pets. And he will not sell a mismatch.

Although many commercial private breeders care for their pups, it is in the area of refusing to sell that they come a cropper. They can't turn down a sale, not if money is their motivation. Of course, once it isn't, they have made the first step toward becoming serious breeders.

There is only one major problem with serious breeders: They are difficult to find, sometimes almost impossible. This is especially true of cat breeders. Unless one knows the registries or that the April issues of the cat magazines are the directory issues, one has a devil of a time simply tracking down a cattery—good or bad.

Since serious breeders are so rare, it becomes necessary to deal with what's left, the commercial private breeder and the backyard breeder. There are certain tip-offs to a backyard breeder. One is, obviously, the condition of the backyard. There is nothing wrong with being small; many serious breeders are, out of choice. But cleanliness is imperative no matter what the size of the operation.

Next is the matter of price. Many backyard breeders, like their pet-shop counterparts, price their puppies and kittens by the year and make of the car in which a prospect arrives. Still others seem to have a jeweler's loupe in their eye when introducing themselves, so intent are they on checking out a woman's jewelry. Others can, in their knowledge of cameras, put a pawn-shop owner to shame. There's another device used: the you-pay-your-money-and-take-your-pick game. You get what you pay for, which certainly isn't any expertise or knowledge on the breeder's part.

Can you get a good pet from a backyard breeder? Certainly. Just as easily as you can get a good one from a pet shop.

Obviously, the serious breeder or concerned commercial private breeder is a better bet. Just as obviously, many prospective pet owners won't be willing to go to the bother of tracking down the right breeder or winnowing out the bad ones. Like their hamburgers and their french fries, they want to get a pet when they want one. Without long lines or long waits. Why else would pet shops, puppy mills, backyard breeders, and the rest of their ilk exist? Buying fast foods is fine. Buying pets fast is fun. But the fun can be over fast, too.

## DO-IT-YOURSELF TEST OF A PRIVATE BREEDER'S LITTER:

1. *Heartbeat test:* Expect a fast heartbeat when the pet is first picked up, but it should calm down rapidly. If not, be concerned.
2. *Chin-licker test:* Hold puppy to face. The alert, well-adjusted pup will attempt to lick the natural deposit of facial oils from the chin area. No makeup, please. For kittens, a comparable reaction would be to rub noses.
3. *Prefers people test:* Leaves the rest to seek out your attention, even when food is put down. Beware the hesitant, cautious or ultra-shy, especially if you have young children.
4. *Playful test:* The emotionally secure pup or kitten is hypercurious. He is interested in scratching fingers, dangling shoelaces, balls, but especially people.

# III ADOPTION AGENCIES/ CHARITIES

> Joxer, bouncing harlequin,
> All ingratiating grin,
> Which begat thee, jolly Joxer?
> Airedale, poodle, beagle, boxer?
> Scottie braw or Irish terrier?
> Never mind, the more the merrier;
> A pedigree so heterodox
> Perks up thy personality, Jox,
> For thou, rambunctious residual,
> Wert whelped unique and individual
>
> FROM "TO A FOOLISH DOG,"
> copyright © 1970 by Ogden Nash
>
> Reprinted from *The Old Dog Barks Backward,* by Ogden Nash, by permission of Little, Brown and Co.

> He was the classic example of a pound dog, thin to the point of literally looking like a rack of bones with some skin pulled over them. When I first saw him, I could actually place a thumb deep between his ribs.
>
> A DOG OWNER

Today the average humane society is glutted with dogs and cats, many of which must, inevitably, be purebred. During 1975, an estimated 17 million animals passed through the doors of shelters and pounds; at least 80 percent of them were euthanised. When turning thumbs up or down on each entrant, shelter officials will frequently save the purebred, simply because a purebred animal is considered more prestigious by the general public than the lowly melange and, therefore, easier to place with a new owner.

34    THE PET PROFITEERS

There is no breed that does not find its way to the local shelter. For example, one shelter says they are *never* without several Siamese cats and German shepherd dogs. Speaking of which, Margaret M. Megahan, a German shepherd breed columnist, has written, "I knew a person who was showing a beautiful shepherd bitch between two and three years old. She always came into the ring in excellent condition with her coat clean and shining; she finished her title in about a year [that's faster than usual]. Less than a year ago, when she was about ten years old, what was left of her was taken to an SPCA—thin,

*The New York Times*
Crawling with cats, humane societies have been forced to take a tip from the pet shops and put their merchandise on display in hopes that a kitten at play will prove irresistible to a passer-by.

dirty, unkempt. The owners explained that they got tired of taking care of her. When they left, she pulled to go with them! She whined, and cried, and refused food, and finally had to be put to sleep."

Only because she was purebred and a champion was this ten-year-old even given a chance to find another home. The average dog is considered too old to be adoptable once he reaches the grand old age of two. Even when young, he'd better be housebroken, obedient, and a nonchewer. Otherwise, off with his head, for he's lost his only advantages over the cuter, cuddlier, softer, more appealing puppy. The kitten always wins over the full-grown cat, unless the latter happens to be purebred, fixed, or uncommonly pretty. This is one beauty contest that is truly a matter of life or death.

So common are purebreds in shelters that the animal-welfare people have become just as adept at stocking their shelters with the right animals as have pet-shop owners. Shelters even use a sliding price scale, just as the pet shop does, for their adoptable purebreds—$15 to $50, depending on breed, without pedigree and/or registration papers. They know certain breeds are always in demand. These are—what a sad commentary on the quality of life in America—the guard dogs, such as Doberman pinschers, German shepherd dogs, and Rottweilers, and the ferocious-looking ones, such as bulldogs, boxers, and bullmastiffs. These are saved and priced high.

In times when the nation is enjoying great prosperity, expensive-to-feed breeds, such as the great Dane, the St. Bernard, and the Russian wolfhound (now known as the borzoi), are in demand, as are the expensive-to-groom breeds, such as the miniature and toy French poodle, the lhasa apso, and the cocker. Especially in demand are those dogs that are both expensive to feed and to groom, such as the Afghan, the old English sheepdog, and the standard French poodle.

During bad times, the smaller the appetite and the shorter the hair, the easier to get the animal adopted. Ironically, it is at this very time that the owners of the expensive-to-feed-and/or-groom breeds are turning them over in droves to the local shelters because they can't afford to care for them. One shelter operator claims that he can predict upturns and downturns in the economy from checking the breeds being surrendered at his shelter.

The economy also influences the population makeup at the local shelter in another way. In our upwardly mobile society, moving up the economic ladder often means moving physically as well, and of all the reasons given for surrendering pets at the shelter, moving is the most common. The next most common is allergies, followed by, as one shelter operator put it, "Novelty of pet ownership wears off. Children for whom a pet was acquired are not interested. The mother is unwilling to do the necessary work involved." Another operator said it more succinctly, "I think when the puppy stage and kitten stage are over, owners tire of them." This would seem to bear out research that shows that the average duration of pet ownership is four and a half months; that is, by the time the average pet reaches adult size, his owners will be ready to give him up.

Among other reasons quoted in a report, entitled "Unwanted Pets and the Animal Shelter," prepared by Argus Archives, a New York foundation, were:

> Nasty . . . sick . . . pregnant . . . injured . . . destructive . . . unmanageable . . . barks too much . . . doesn't bark . . . chases cows . . . not housebroken . . . old (There are persons who will tell you they never keep a pet after a certain age) . . . and They neglect or can't afford to have their pet spayed so they give up the puppies or kittens, as the case may be. Sometimes they will keep one puppy or kitten out of the litter and give up the mother and the rest of the litter.

If the last seems callous to you, it at least gives the rest of that litter a chance to be adopted. Not a good one, mind you, but 100 percent better than those of a pet labeled "nasty . . . sick . . . destructive." After all, who wants somebody else's troubles? As Eloise G. Danenhower, director of public relations of the Pennsylvania SPCA, notes, the very reasons given for surrendering an animal are exactly those reasons that would make that animal unadoptable. Which is why fewer than 20 percent of all animals brought to a shelter are considered eligible for adoption. When you realize that the vast majority of that 20 percent are kittens or pups, you can understand that taking a full-grown pet to a shelter in hopes of finding a good home for it is wishful thinking. Doing so amounts virtually to sentencing that pet to death—and under strange and terrifying circumstances. If one truly loves that pet, as harsh as these words sound, it is far better to have him put down at the vet's—in a place he knows, by a person he knows, and with the person he loves.

But that is wishful thinking on my part. The fact is that it is so much easier on one's conscience and pocketbook to deposit a pet at a shelter, to pay a small donation—$2 or $3, generally tax deductible—and to walk away secure in the knowledge that those humanitarians will find him a good home. As they say, ignorance is bliss.

Of course, many such pet owners are wise in the ways of shelters. They know a way to save a few more bucks. They simply say the animal is a stray to avoid paying any donation whatsoever. It is penny pinchers like these that explain why the average person's chances of getting a healthy pet from an adoption agency are no better than the average pet's of being adopted—less than one in five.

Penny pinchers feel, as far as a litter of pups or kittens is concerned, the less expense the better. And, if one doesn't bother to have the female spayed to begin with, one is not going to give the animal the inoculations, vitamin supplements, and high-protein foods required to bring those puppies up properly. The most expensive animal in the world to keep is a lactating mother. If she isn't fed properly, her young and her own body will suffer from it, and the cat or dog off to an unthrifty start is apt to have expensive medical problems the rest of his life.

Shelter pets have other health problems. For one thing, most young ones have been weaned too early to be fully protected against most viruses. For another, the shelter itself is a sure place to get a disease, since so many of the animals brought in are already sick. Yes, of course, a vet *usually* checks all those animals being put up for adoption, but the incubation period for many viruses—especially of cats—is as much as three to seven times longer than the average adoptee's allotted three to five days in the shelter. Thus the animal may not show that it is infected during the examination. Only when some poor, unsuspecting soul takes it home. Then, that soul had better not be so poor. For that cheap adoption can become a veterinarian's dream and a pet owner's nightmare. Many pet owners find, to their surprise, that after they've dosed, treated, hand-fed, and tenderly cared for that young adoptee, they have more money invested in that pet than does one who goes to the fanciest kennel or cattery and buys the healthiest, most expensive young one there.

The owner may also find that that little puppy has giant ancestors and an enormous appetite. When fully grown, he's not the cute, hoped-for lap dog, but a monster that takes up most of the bed. With mixed breeds, there is no sure way to determine size in advance. For example, the size of the paws does not tell you the eventual size of the adult. Some big breeds have small cat's paws, some small breeds have large paws. Poor nourishment may have made that puppy small for its age. Once properly fed, its genetic makeup will assert itself, and the pup will grow and grow and grow—almost, it may seem, as quickly as Jack's beanstalk. Of course, if you were looking for a big dog, the opposite is just as likely to happen. The animal will remain a big-footed midget.

It is not true that the average, or even above-average, vet can determine what breeds are behind a pup just from looking at it. Many pups, for example, have soft, fluffy coats that will grow into wirey, easily tangled bundles of hairy trouble standing out in a doggy version of an Afro haircut. Just as many others will lose that fluff and develop short coats that seem to have a barb at the end of each hair designed expressly for the purpose of getting on your dark clothes and staying there permanently. Even the washing machine has been known to fail at dislodging them.

It is also a fallacy common to those who get their pets at adoption agencies that a mixed-breed is healthier than a purebred by virtue of hybrid vigor, or heterosis. The assumption here is that man is inbreeding dogs (mother to son, father to daughter, brother to sister) as geneticists East and Jones inbred plants as a first step toward creating the first hybrid corn. Choosing two excellent, but different, strains of corn, East and Jones forced each of twelve generations to self-fertilize, the closest type of inbreeding. During each successive generation, some weird, wild-looking plants would appear. Any plants displaying these undesirable, or recessive, characteristics were eliminated from the program. Only when all quirks of nature stopped appearing did East and Jones decide to breed these two totally unrelated strains together. The resulting outcrossed, or hybrid, corn was not only superior to its parents, but vastly better than the corn they started with, because of hybrid vigor.

Man—coward and financial realist that he is—does not inbreed like this because he can't or won't weed out the bad traits that appear in each generation. With an acre of corn to work with, one can afford to eliminate 75 percent. With four puppies to work with, eliminating three is financial disaster, even though one knows that the fourth puppy is noticeably superior to his littermates or his parents.

So while it is true that vigor lost by inbreeding can be restored by outcrossing, that assumes that purebred dogs are being inbred like crazy. But they aren't. Moreover, the vigor restored is only relative to the degree of *harmful* inbreeding that has occurred. Actually, as we have seen, it is inbreeding that reveals genetic problems so that they can be bred out. Outcrossing only hides them until a future generation, when out they may pop again. There is a maxim among dog breeders that goes something like this: Breed the best to the best regardless of relationship to get the best, provided you are willing to accept the worst. For inbreeding doubles everything. The good and the bad. Don't rely on hybrid vigor to solve health problems.

If one wants a guarantee of size, appearance, and health, one is much better off getting an *older* pet from a shelter. However, here one can encounter personality problems that may be impossible to overcome since, it is generally acknowledged, a pet's personality is set by the time it reaches six months of age. Of course, one always faces the problem that the true story of why its owner gave it up will not be known until it bites a neighbor or chews its way through the dining-room table's leg.

There is another problem in adopting pets, a psychological one that has nothing to do with the individual animal per se. That is the fact that the animal is under a death sentence. Shelter operators who are concerned with keeping their adoption ratio high use this knowledge to blackmail—there's no other way to put it—a prospective adopter into taking a pet. Perhaps it's the wrong pet for him. If so, the pet adopted out of pity faces a rougher time than he would have if he'd gone right into the decompression chamber after his allotted time. Only love of a pet and love from a pet makes all the work and money and trouble involved in owning a pet worthwhile. If one can hardly bring one's self to clean the litter pan for a beloved pet, just how long is the owner of an unwanted and unloved pet going to do it? Which means the pet comes back to the shelter, either by way of his new owner or by being picked up as a stray after his abandonment. Either way, a returnee, or "repeater" as they are sometimes called, has even less of a chance of escaping the death chamber than does the first-time "offender."

Because abandonment and the returnee problem have become acute, more and more shelters are concerning themselves with lowering their return ratio rather than upping their adoption ratio. They recognize that a high adoption ratio usually leads to a high return ratio unless drastic measures are imposed. Thus, at most shelters, free adoptions are a thing of the past. In fact, humane-society officials are the first to condemn those societies that have either no or low fees, noting that "they are nothing better than cut-rate pet shops."

Indeed, it is frequently easier to buy a pet at a pet shop than to get one from a humane society, not because society officials don't wish to find homes for as many pets as possible, but because they are determined that those homes be *good* homes. They are instituting stiff screening procedures and raising their fees to put economic pressure on prospective owners. As one shelter official put it, "nobody puts much value on something that's free. But when you've paid a stiff price for it, you take care of it."

The prognosis of future easing of adoption procedures is not good. If anything, they should become even more rigid. For example, the Humane Society of the United States, Washington, D.C. 20036, working from the experiences of hundreds of local humane societies, compiled the following:

SUGGESTED STANDARDS FOR ADOPTION OF PETS
FROM HUMANE SOCIETY AND PUBLIC
ANIMAL SHELTERS

1. No animal will be released for adoption except as a household pet. (No cat will be placed as a "mouser"; no dog as an outside watchdog, etc.)
2. Animals adopted remain the legal property of the humane society; the

adopter must sign a contract establishing that fact. No animal that is property of the society may be sold or given away by the adopter and the contract shall establish the legal right of the society to sue for damages if the animal is illegally disposed of or harmed by negligence or mistreatment, including lack of needed veterinary care, or if the animal is endangered by failure to observe all locally effective animal control and anti-cruelty laws.
3. Regardless of local laws, in urban and suburban communities no dogs will be released for adoption unless the adopter provides an adequately fenced area for the dog or unless it is certain that through other arrangements the dog will be provided with a humane opportunity for adequate exercise under control. (An outside "dog house" with chain is not adequate.)
4. Besides any legally required license and vaccination tags, the adopter must agree to keep on the adopted dog or cat a collar (in case of cats an elastic collar) bearing the name, address, and telephone number of the adopter.
5. No unspayed female dog or cat will be released for adoption except that puppies or kittens too young for spaying, or animals that for medical reasons should not be immediately spayed, may be released if the fee for spaying is first deposited with the humane society and the adopter contracts either to return the animal to the humane society or take it to a veterinarian of his own choice for spaying before the first period of heat. (Failure by the adopter to execute this agreement will be cause for the humane society to repossess the animal and the deposit for spaying shall not be refunded.)

As a general policy although not an absolute rule, the humane society will not release small kittens and puppies for adoption in homes having children under six years old, will not place animals in homes where no adults are present during the day, and will require that applications for adoption be signed by both husband and wife.

Furthermore, at the National Conference on the Ecology of the Surplus Dog and Cat Problem, held in Chicago in May 1974, one hundred participants conferred about the problem of easy adoptions. They agreed that when prospective owners are not adequately screened, many of these adoptees will be found later in the community as free-roaming animals, either abandoned or improperly tended. To solve this problem, the conferees agreed that so long as the numbers of dogs and cats exceed the supply of adequate homes, "only those animals best suited for adoption should be placed, and then only with responsible owners in accordance with definite screening standards."

If America continues to tolerate the spawning of animals by puppy mills, backyard breeders, and commercial private breeders, there is little that the local animal welfare society can do about it—except euthanise the inferior results of those breeding programs. However, most humane societies and animal-adoption agencies are determined to stop the pet population explosion, one way or another.

## DO'S AND DON'T'S OF GETTING A PET FROM AN ADOPTION AGENCY:

1. *Do* consider the older, more mature animal rather than the young pup or kit. Many of the problems and much of the training is out of the way. And one avoids "surprises" in terms of eventual size, looks, and personality.
2. *Don't* expect the older dog to be as outgoing and rambunctious as a puppy. Wouldn't you be a bit cautious about pouring out your love when you'd just been rejected by the ones you'd loved?
3. *Do* spend enough time with the pet before making up your mind. You won't have days—only hours, maybe minutes. But a returnee is a sure candidate for death.
4. *Don't* fall for the pretty animal over the more commonplace. A valuable purebred isn't turned in unless there is a very good reason, whereas very few people even try to sell a mongrel before turning to the SPCA.

*Animal Shelters*

The most common and most controversial adoption agencies, the ones we all know well—maybe our last pet came from one—are the local animal shelters. "Are Animal Welfare Societies a Rip-Off?" asks the headline on the front page of the December 1974 *Report to Humanitarians,* a quarterly newspaper published by Human Information Services, Inc., an organization founded in 1965 because of the belief that too many welfare societies were not doing their job. "Some of these seemed to exist more for the benefit of their officers and staff than for that of the animals," states founder Dr. Frederick L. Thomsen. "Their principal aim appeared to be maintaining or increasing their memberships and contributions. Some had accumulated very large endowments, representing bequests received over the years. This insured enough annual income to pay very good salaries and expenses to a select few, provided nothing was done to rock the boat and raise any questions about the society's activities. So they tended to do nothing significant, especially if it involved anything controversial. They got fat and lazy."

Dr. Thomsen isn't the only one who feels that way. "The whole scene for helping animals in the USA smells. I and many others," says another concerned individual, "are convinced the societies are just fronts for keeping humans employed with pay—and pretty good pay at that."

"Pretty good" may be the understatement of the year. The head of a local animal-welfare shelter occasionally makes more than the head of a local welfare agency for people; the president of one society makes more than the governor of his state. Fringe benefits often make a seemingly modest salary a lucrative recompense. One society—New York's ASPCA—paid its president's $750-a-year membership fee for a private club—which had a separate ladies' entrance, of course—provided him with a chauffeured limousine, and paid for all his haircuts and manicures. Board members who found out about this and felt they were not the only ones being trimmed have filed a lawsuit against their fellow members charging them with, among other things, a waste of public funds.

Others suggest that it is necessary to pay a top salary to get a good administrator for any charitable endeavor, especially that of heading the local animal death factory. Which is what running a shelter boils down to, today, in most cases.

Of the 450 animal shelters operated by animal-welfare organizations and the 900 or more shelters operated by municipalities, "No more than 12 or 15," according to Guy Hodge, director of research and data services for the Humane Society of the United States, "operate under policies dictating that animals can't be destroyed." However, there are many privately funded societies that are against euthanasia. The most famous of these is probably New York's Bide-A-Wee.

According to their annual report, during the fiscal year ending August 31, 1974, Bide-A-Wee accepted 12,554 pets for adoption and adopted out 1,195 more than they brought in. The cost of adopting out those 13,749 animals (less than .001 percent of the total number available for adoption in this country) works out to $99.46 apiece, for a total expenditure of $1,367,519. At that rate it would cost us $1,292,980,000 to place all the unwanted pets in this country—each year. This is more than the total annual budget of many countries in the world, and many states in the union.

The North Shore Animal League of Long Island may be familiar to you because of the ads they write. The ones that appeared in 28,000 mail boxes on a September day in 1969 were signed by Perry Como and asked, "Would you give a dollar—just $1—TO SAVE THEIR LIVES?" The lives in question were those of a puppy and a kitten pictured together. Those letters brought in a total of 3,100 contributions, totaling $11,000.

It is more than seven years since that first mailing, and like the Cutty Sark ads of old, the pitch remains essentially the same; only the photos of the puppy and kitten change. (The names are hauntingly, romantically, appealingly alike—those of famous lovers. One time, Romeo and Juliet; the next, "We call this button-nosed pup Samson, and the other bundle of fur is Delilah.") The annual contributors now number over 100,000. The advertising budget for 1974 came to $50,000, or $13.51 per animal adopted. For their money, those 100,000 contributors managed to save only 3,700 lives in 1974, perhaps as many as 4,800 in 1975.

One of the reasons that more were not saved is that the society's adoption standards are rigorous. For example, the league turns down three out of every ten potential adopters, for cause. Age, marital status, place of employment, type of residence, and pet-ownership history are just some of the items covered in the preadoption interview. A bad mark in any of these could have you turned down. Especially frowned upon are single people who work all day. However, being small, the league can be flexible. As it was in the case of Herman, a Weimaraner most memorable for his voracious appetite.

Herman was first brought in by his original family, who claimed that he was eating them out of house and home. Although he was good in every other way, including being an excellent watchdog, they

This clever poster is just one example of the sophisticated advertising devices used effectively by humane societies to find homes for animals or raise monies to run their shelters.

just couldn't afford to feed him. Quickly, Herman was accepted; almost as quickly, adopted; even more quickly, returned, having overeaten his welcome. At about that time, two young working women came in and chose Herman. Ordinarily, according to the general manager, they wouldn't even have been considered. However, they had one thing in their favor: They owned a restaurant-supply business, and Herman would be in doggy heaven forever.

Not many shelters would have persevered so long with Herman, but then not many shelters are headed by a man like Alexander Lewyt. Lewyt, the inventor of the vacuum cleaner of the same name and former head of the Lewyt Air Conditioner Corporation, is one of "America's Twelve Master Salesmen," according to a book by that title. And it takes a master salesman to get someone to adopt a cat with a hairless tail and a generally scruffy, woebegone look. Or a deaf one that is difficult to housebreak. Or Ahab, the three-legged cat that wasn't adopted until the following newspaper ad was written, according to *The Wall Street Journal:* "Big beautiful gentle American short-hair grey & white cat with a head like a lion. But Ahab has only three paws. You wouldn't notice it unless we told you. He gets around fine." (In short order, Ahab found a home.)

Societies that don't have a master salesman find other solutions. One shelter, which boasts that "it never puts down an animal," adds one small, quiet afterthought: "unless incurably ill." When pressed for a definition of that, a top official not only said that it included all dogs mentally unfit, but he also admitted that "an animal deteriorates so rapidly in a kennel environment, personality-wise, that the great majority go off their rockers."

"Does this mean that they're put down?" I asked. He hemmed and hawed but eventually did concede that at times some animals just couldn't make the adjustment and had to be put down. "How many do they total?" I asked. Well, he didn't know exactly, but believed it was "very, very few, less than 1 or 2 percent."

A former employee there contradicted this. He maintained that lots and lots were put down, although he couldn't give exact figures. He also maintained that there was one floor of the building on which visitors were not allowed. On my tour, that was the floor I was not allowed on. "That's for the new pets that are still making the adjustment and we'd just disturb them unnecessarily if we went in," explained my guide.

Does this no-kill shelter kill? I don't know. I do know that I have never heard so many euphemisms for incurably ill, that is, mentally unfit, in any one conversation: wacky, crazy, psyched out, freaked out, gone bananas, maladjusted.

Is killing any worse than what does go on in these shelters? Gretchen Wyler, who heads up a small shelter in Warwick, New York, says, "I have seen more cruelty in animal shelters than I have in pet shops or anywhere else. I got a court order against a so-called humane society in Westchester . . . to go in with a vet and destroy the suffering animals. They don't believe in euthanasia, and, as a result, they had about 300 where they should have had 60. Dogs tied to trees. Cats with their eyes shut with mucus. Seven dogs that couldn't bear weight on one or more legs. That sort of thing. It's disgusting what these humane societies do."

When questioned about the Bide-A-Wee approach to nonkilling, Miss Wyler replied, "It's unrealistic. They asked me to be on their board. But I said, 'You must cling to that philosophy because it brings you lots of money, because killing is so repellent to society.' It's a very sophisticated subject, killing. But I run my own shelter, and I would rather never turn an animal away. To me that's a luxury. Their luxury is never killing. So, as a result, they turn them away by the droves."

Owners of pets who have been refused acceptance have been known to turn their backs calmly on the pet and walk out the shelter door; go outside and tie the animal to a lamppost and leave; or, and this is most common of all, get in their car, drive a short distance, open the car door, and let the animal out to fend for itself as best it can. Of those abandoned pets few can fend for themselves. They will die the slowest death of all, from starvation; or the most cruel and agonizing, from disease; or the most common, from automobiles.

"If nobody wants the animal," continues Miss Wyler, "I would rather put it to sleep and go on to the next. It takes a lot of strength, but that is absolutely the only way. I think the other things are totally unrealistic, and as a result, they—number one—turn away, or—number two—crowd and make an inhumane shelter. So, you cannot have that luxury. There were 13 million destroyed in shelters last year. If they hadn't been destroyed, where would they be?"

Good question. The number destroyed in our shelters is as great as the population of Tokyo, or about the size of the total combined populations of Paris, Leningrad, and San Francisco. Every hour, in the United States alone, an estimated 2,000 to 3,000 dogs and cats are born. In order to maintain the current pet population, some 60,000 cats and dogs must die or be killed each day, a total of 21,900,000 each year. That job has, by default, fallen to the "regular" humane-society shelter or the public pound, where there are new homes for only a small fraction of the unwanted pets we discard each year.

Some shelters brag about their adoption ratio. These are the ones that other shelters describe derogatorily but accurately as "cut-rate pet shops." In order to get as many animals adopted out as possible, they don't investigate prospective adoptors, nor do they demand that the animals be neutered, nor do they charge a fee high enough to guarantee that the animal will be kept or returned to them. Instead, a donation is asked. As little as fifty cents, in one case, for a cat. These are the shelters where dogfighters find their training "tools." These are the ones that laboratories like to frequent; it is much cheaper than buying a healthy beagle bred and fed for laboratory research.

Obviously, not all pet societies are alike. Nor are all SPCAs. They are not even related. Instead, each operates separately, merely paying a license fee to the ASPCA in New York, which owns the title. Some SPCAs, as Eloise G. Danenhower of the Pennsylvania SPCA points out, are run by dedicated volunteers; others are run by people who must cut corners in order to continue to work at the low salaries paid; still others are run by professionals who accept killing as only part of their job but believe that the major portion of their work must be devoted to the living.

Not to be confused with SPCAs, local nonprofit animal shelters, or privately funded ones, are the municipal pounds. There are at least 900 of these—probably a great many more, but they differ from all the other animal-welfare organizations in that they do not need to wonder when or from where the next dollar will be coming. That's because they are supported by you and me, the local taxpayer. Not only are they supported by tax revenues, but the employees are frequently political-patronage appointees who wouldn't know a great Dane from a Chihuahua.

I want to focus on one municipal pound in Mississippi for the moment, not because it's necessarily typical, but because even one like this is an outrage. The following report is from Stephen Boyd, former member of the Board of Directors of his state's animal-rescue league, after he inspected the municipal pound:

> The first thing in the morning the attendant in charge of the animals washed out all cages with a high pressure water hose. The animals were not removed from the cages during this cleaning process. This meant that most of the animals were thoroughly wet when the attendant was finished. Puppies remained wet most of the day, encouraging the development of disease, not to mention being a source of great discomfort for the animals. Young kittens and puppies have drowned in the back of the cages during this cleaning. After the animals were fed in the afternoon, the cages were again washed down.
> 
> Each afternoon an attendant went to the city jail with a garbage can to get the "food" left over by the prisoners from their lunch. These leftovers consisted of rice, beans, peas, potato peels, lemon rinds, spinach, chicken

bones, etc. When the league's [animal-rescue league] representative first went to the pound, the animals were being fed nothing but this slop, while there was stored in the storage room hundreds of pounds of commercial dog food.

Six cages were specified as the sick ward. These cages were not isolated from the other cages. Many sick dogs came up for adoption, some with contagious disease. Animals were destroyed only on Tuesday mornings. This meant that if an animal which was very sick or badly injured came in on Tuesday afternoon, it was made to wait until the next Tuesday to be put out of its misery (if it lived). These sick and injured animals included dogs which were paralyzed, orphan animals which were unable to eat, dogs and cats with distemper, animals with broken bones, animals in convulsions, etc.

On Tuesday mornings each animal to be destroyed was taken from his cage by means of a noose around his neck, the noose being attached to a pole. The animal was held up by his neck, often with all four legs in the air. His front legs were spread apart, and the needle stabbed in the chest. The needle would frequently miss the heart often hitting the rib bones and also often injecting into the lungs. The animals when not injected properly into the heart would scream in pain and sometimes go into convulsions, retching, clawing, and exhibiting many signs of distress.

While still fully conscious, in many instances, the animals were then thrown into the back of a truck. The men assisting were afraid to hold the animal after it was injected for fear they would absorb the solution through their skin and die also. If the animal crawled off of the pile, he was kicked back onto the pile, often several times. Many times young puppies had to be injected two or three times before losing consciousness.

On Wednesday mornings a truck would back up to the door, and all dogs over fifteen pounds on the east side were loaded into the truck and taken to the University Medical Center. This included taking mother dogs away from their newborn puppies (leaving her puppies to starve and her to grieve). On one occasion a dog was observed being taken to the Medical Center while in labor. Sick animals were also taken (including dogs and cats with distemper; one cat observed was in convulsions).

If, when animals were sick or frightened, they didn't respond the way the attendant wished, they were kicked, or hit over the head or back with a steel pipe. This steel pipe has a loop on the end which is used to catch the animals.

About once a week (usually Tuesday or Wednesday) the animals were moved from their cages, and their cages were steam cleaned. Occasionally, an animal was left in a cage when it was cleaned.

The employees at the pound frequently were observed giving erroneous information to the public. They told the people coming to the pound or calling in that they don't usually have to put any animals to sleep. They said they find homes for nearly all the animals, when actually only a small percent were adopted.

When dogs with collars and tags came into the pound, the driver would take the information from the tags and turn it in to the office. No apparent attempt was made to call the owners, although the public was told that they did. We know this as fact, because the league representative has taken this information from the tags and called the owners to see if they had been contacted by the pound.

Very poor records were kept. Often the office had no idea how long the dogs had been there. Frequently the attendant would tell a prospective customer that a dog had been there only a couple of days and then tell another customer a different story about the same dog.

The drivers sat around in the office a large part of the day. Dead dogs were picked up and hauled in the same truck with healthy dogs. Dead dogs full of maggots were carried in the same truck with healthy dogs. Most of the drivers' time was spent picking up dead dogs instead of picking up strays. This information was obtained from reports turned in by the drivers themselves.*

If there is one area of animal abuse that could be corrected, and corrected quickly, it is our country's municipal pounds.

There are all kinds of charities organized for the benefit of people. And there are almost as many devoted to animal welfare. In both areas, one finds good ones and bad ones. However, there is one basic difference between the charities for people and those for animals: The human recipient's of America's good works can speak up, protest, even refuse such efforts. The animals are truly helpless. Totally at the mercy of man, and dependent upon the charitable contributions of humanitarians.

One can't be an animal lover for any length of time without having one's heart pulled by some appeal to our humanity. The trouble is that there are so many appeals, so many humanitarian agencies. It is difficult to choose among them, especially because it takes so long to establish if they are effective.

For instance, there is the Orthopedic Foundation of America, Inc., about which a book could be written. Except that its founder got there first, scared the bejesus out of the dog fancy with tales of the crippling effects of hip dysplasia, and cashed in. After more years than one cares to remember and all the money spent (much of it that of John Olin, owner of Cannonade, the famous Kentucky Derby winner, as well as many field trial dogs), hip dysplasia has hardly been licked.

On the other hand, it was the Morris Animal Foundation, which Mr. Olin also supports and of which he is a trustee, that paid for the research done by Dr. George Cardinet III at Kansas State University that proved that surgery on the pectineus muscle was not the answer to hip dysplasia. Other projects of this organization include finding ways of prolonging the shelf life of canine blood needed for blood transfusions. In the past, unlike human blood, canine blood could be stored for no longer than three weeks. Many vets refused to use it if it was more than two weeks old. Still others insisted on direct animal-to-animal transfusions. Without a donor at hand, surgery was not only

---

* Reprinted with permission from *Report to Humanitarians*, Humane Information Services, St. Petersburg, Florida.

dangerous, but often not done at all because of the risk factor. Thanks to the Morris Animal Foundation, canine blood can now safely be stored and used for periods up to three months.

If there is one organization that the average pet owner has reason to support it is this one. On the very mundane but practical level, whenever any of its research proves to have direct practical application or interest to the average pet owner, the foundation sends out mailings, which alert the contributor as to how his money is being spent. On a higher level, we can thank this once private, now public, foundation for the great strides that have been made in attempting to bring man's scientific knowledge of human medicine to the animal world. Since its founding in 1948, it has been responsible for opening up approximately 160 new areas of veterinary medicine and creating specialties within them.

Through the foundation's grants of aid to veterinary colleges, brain surgery on animals has become a reality, bone grafts are now an answer to fractures, and kidney disease, the greatest killer of dogs, is being brought under control. Bloat, mange, heartworm, collie-eye syndrome, excessive tearing, epilepsy, pancreatic disfunction, even a one-shot, single-injection hormonal form of birth control—research into all these has been and continues to be funded by this organization.

It should be pointed out that while the Morris Animal Foundation can proudly boast of its many *specific* projects to better the lives of our pets, other organizations, although equally dedicated, do not have this advantage. For example, Friends of Animals, which has created a model national spay program, cannot come forth with impressive statistics. Nor can WARDS, which is very deeply involved with those animals being shipped from puppy mills or for research. The Anti-Vivisectionists have not, for all their years of effort, made inhumane scientific research with animals a thing of the past, although they did just recently stop the use of beagles in some gas research. But it was not only money contributed to them that did it; it was also a national outpouring of letters to Congress.

## HOW TO DETERMINE IF YOUR LOCAL ANIMAL SHELTER/SPCA/POUND IS UP TO SNUFF:

1. Does it maintain 24-hour ambulance service to come to the rescue of the sick, the needy, the abandoned?

2. Does it investigate cases of abuse and prosecute the same?
3. Does it accept *any* animal, as it must if a public shelter, as it should if a private one?
4. Does it check each animal surrendered for possible tattoos that would help return it to its owner, or determine the person to be prosecuted?
5. Does it read all lost-and-found ads to help find owners of lost pets?
6. Does it take advantage of free and/or reduced rates for newspaper classified ads—or feature photographs—pertaining to dogs they have found, and if such rates are not available, does it advertise anyway?
7. Does it investigate all prospective owners, require a reasonable or, as some put it, an unreasonable fee to guarantee that the owner doesn't abandon the pet later?
8. Does it make spaying and neutering a requirement?
9. Does it check up on the pets adopted out, and not just by postcard?
10. Does it keep a list of vets or have staff veterinarians who will do altering at reasonable prices?
11. Does it hold obedience classes to keep owners happy with their pets?
12. Does it work to educate the public on the responsibilities of pet ownership?
13. Does it do all this in spite of a measly, meager budget?

# IV  VETS

> Being admitted to the profession of veterinary medicine, I solemnly swear to use my scientific knowledge and skills for the benefit of society through the protection of animal health, the relief of animal suffering, the conservation of livestock resources, the promotion of public health, and the advancement of medical knowledge.
> I will practice my profession conscientiously, with dignity, and in keeping with the principles of veterinary medical ethics.
> I accept as a lifelong obligation the continual improvement of my professional knowledge and competence.
>
> THE VETERINARY VERSION OF THE HIPPOCRATIC OATH, adopted by the American Veterinary Medical Association, House of Delegates, July 1969

There are good vets and there are bad vets, but there are few poor vets. In recent years, the pet population explosion combined with the health problems created by puppy mills has made treating animals one of the most lucrative professions in the nation. Whereas once upon a time a kid who couldn't make the grade in medical school could always fall back on veterinary medicine, today the vet schools wouldn't take him either. They're crammed full of applicants. And why not? A new vet still wet behind the ears can earn $25,000 to $30,000 the first year in his own practice. As one vet groused, "The demand for them's so great, they ask the sun and the moon and $16,000 minimum and you better damn well have the newest, fanciest equipment or they won't even consider working with you."

The American Veterinary Medical Association (AVMA) estimates that the average vet in practice for himself will clear 39 percent of his yearly gross. A figure that is probably on the low side since it is

*The New York Times/Ernie Sisto*
Patience is a necessity when visiting a vet, especially if the doctor doesn't believe in making individual appointments.

based on *reported* gross income, while some vets deal mostly in cash, which they fail to record and for which they give no receipts.

Considering the dearth of veterinarians in this country, those figures aren't startling; they might even seem low. The AVMA estimates that there are between 29,000 and 30,000 vets in the United States. Of the 27,568 listed in their 1974 directory, only 31 percent (8,630) were engaged strictly in small-animal practice; another 33 percent combined small- and large-animal practice, for a total of 17,714, which sounds like a lot, but isn't. Not when you consider that better than 6,000 of those vets are in five states: California, Texas, New York, Illinois, and Ohio. Leaving about 271 vets a state for the other forty-five. Which isn't enough, as anyone living in those states will testify. Which is why knowledgeable people will drive miles for the services of a good vet without giving it a second thought. Breeders will even relocate their kennels to be close to the vet of their choice (I know—we did it). Others will spend hours in the waiting room of a vet who works on a first-come-first-served basis, and then brag about it.

Would you believe, today, some twenty-five years later, one former New Yorker still recounts with glee and nostalgia his experiences back in the 1950s playing the who-gets-to-the-vet's-office-first game. "On the day I decided to play this game," he says, "I arose at five in the morning and proceeded to arrive at Dr. K——'s office by six.

Usually there was someone ahead of me. If one was among the first six, you could usually plan to be back home, with your dogs, by one in the afternoon."

I know of a similar case involving a vet who had evening hours. First you had to arrange for a baby-sitter who could stay past midnight during the week, just in case. Then, the workers in the family had to leave the office early because the ideal time to arrive at the vet's was during the dinner hour when, if you were lucky, everybody else was occupied. Naturally, a picnic lunch was in order or a quick stop at Gino's for food to be consumed in the waiting room. If you were early enough, there would even be chairs to sit on while you ate. By the middle of the evening, the place looked like Woodstock the day after and smelled of french fries and onions.

Here, you waited. And waited some more. For this was a vet that really preferred to work with horses and even kept a shortwave radio in his car just in case some horse owner called. If a horse within twenty miles was down with the trots, the dog and cat people were out of luck. I have left that vet's office as late as one in the morning, and there were still determined squatters patiently waiting their turn. Once, faced with going home late and coming back at the crack of dawn, we stayed the night, finally arriving home at 11:00 A.M.

Since veterinary medicine is quite obviously one of the busiest professions around, I am continually amazed to discover the number of vets who are greedy to the point of creating business. Consider the case of the vet who treated a cocker spaniel for months on end with expensive cortisone shots for its arthritis. That episode ended only when a boarding-kennel operator discovered that the dog was limping only because its toenails were so long, they'd become ingrown.

Or the vet in New York City with the two brownstones on the east side who is referred to, not so affectionately, by many of his clients as "the robber baron." When one pet-shop Persian cat was purchased complete with ear mites, she was taken promptly to this vet for attention. "I was given a clear glass bottle containing an oily solution which was to be administered three times daily and told to return every other day for check-ups," the owner of the Persian told me. "The whole episode cost a fortune, as each visit was $6 and I went back for three solid weeks. Guess what? The mites didn't go away even though the poor cat looked like a drowned rat around the head because of the oil that matted in her fur." Eventually, out of desperation, the owner called the breeder, who told her how to cure the ear mites using mineral oil and boric acid powder.

The practice of scheduling unnecessary visits is not uncommon. Far from it. In fact, even more common are the dedicated checkers who insist an animal be brought in faithfully every three months to be checked for roundworms, at a cost of $7 to $10 per visit. (The good vet would just as soon you send or drop off at his office a small—one-half teaspoon, not one-half cup—sample of stool for examination at his convenience, at a cost of $1 to $3.) I know of a vet who suggested a series of abortive drugs for a bitch who may or may not have been bred, and this without making a vaginal smear to determine if sperm were present. Or the vet who, examining a new puppy, ignored the inoculations given by the breeder and instead prescribed his own, which included three (or more) temporary shots, followed by two or more permanent shots.

Or how about this: On October 16, 1973, the Keystone Veterinary Association went on record as saying that no vet in Pennsylvania could afford to spay a dog for less than $28. At the time, Dr. Lillian Giuliani, former president of the William Penn Poodle Club, estimated spaying charges were averaging between $50 and $60. A Pennsylvania Department of Agriculture survey showed that actual charges by vets for spaying operations ran as high as $125. Yet with all that camouflage, at the very same time the Pennsylvania SPCA maintained a list of vets, with more names being added to it constantly, who were willing to spay a dog for $15 or a cat for $10. That list and those prices were still in effect in late 1975.

Or how about the poodle owner who found her dog having difficulty breathing. Unable to reach her regular vet, she called the emergency number and went to the address given. There she was told it would cost $6 for the office call and $10 for the doctor's trip and that he would be there in about fifteen minutes. In the meantime, the clerk demanded the dog's life history and the owner's driver's license. When the doctor finally arrived, he took the dog's temperature, gave it a drop of digitalis, administered three shots, filled out the charge form, and left. That added $12 more to the bill. Before they got as far as the car, the dog stiffened suddenly. Just as quickly it went limp, urinated, and defecated as its muscles relaxed and it lost control of its body functions as is usual just before death. They rushed back in and were told by the clerk that now they would have to go to the doctor's hospital "as the dog needed a muscle relaxant." The dog was already in a coma; his eyes glazed, his heart gave a few more beats—and a great little dog was gone.

Of course, there is another side of the story. For example, a veterinarian reported some interesting statistics regarding his emergency calls. About 75 percent were from people he had never seen before. About 35 percent were from people who had never seen any vet before. Only about 60 percent of the calls were ever paid for. According to another vet, Paul Berg, a speaker at a University of Pennsylvania Veterinary School symposium, "fully 90 percent of the emergency calls I receive could have been handled at home."

The good vet, obviously, does not want or need unnecessary visits from his clients; he has his hands full with the ones who really need help. The bad vet? The greedy vet? He'll take whatever goodies come his way. If pet owners want to make something terrible out of nothing, vets will gladly make a buck out of it, too.

There isn't a vet around who doesn't have his share of stories about "emergency calls" that really weren't. For example, the average vet gets more calls about lack of appetite than anything else. Says one vet, "They buy a German shepherd pup, get it home, and expect it to eat everything in sight with the postman for dessert." Another vet told me he wished he owned stock in a liverwurst company "since there must be thousands of us recommending it daily for picky eaters." (Actually, as any responsible breeder knows, the change of environment will throw off a young animal's appetite. Even worse is a change of diet, which is why many of us give the new owner a generous sample of the food we use to help tide the animal over during the transition period.) And then, when the owners get the animal to eat—sometimes by hand or even force-feeding—spit-ups occur. Another call to the vet. Dr. Berg suggests a rather radical solution for this: "Feed yogurt for two days. If the dog or cat eats it, that's fine. If they don't, that's fine, too, since it lets the stomach relax."

To many animal owners, just as important as what goes in and what comes up is what comes out. They keep track of that stool, noting the color, size, and firmness with such interest one might be tempted to call them fecalphiles. One can imagine with what rapidity they get on the phone to the vet when they discover that their pet is showing just as much interest in the subject. Eating it up in fact. Literally. Coprophagy is rare in cats but not in dogs. Some authorities believe it is caused by a dietary deficiency. Others feel it is the result of boredom. Nobody knows for sure. However, it is a frequent enough problem that someone has come out with a product to stop it. It's called "Forbid." (Adolph's Meat Tenderizer works about as well but costs less, unless you find that out from a vet, in which case it'll cost you a fiver for advice.)

Cats have their own favorite dietary vice: wool. They chew on it. And if it isn't available, they'll suck on any foreign object, including their own paws, skin, or tail. Again, there are commercial preparations like Bitter Apple available to prevent wool chewing. They are about as effective as those sold to stop thumb-sucking in children.

Take this free advice (the best I've heard yet) from another vet: "Tell buyers to find vets who are familiar with the breed of dog they own. I have had more trouble with other vets who do not recognize signs which may be characteristic of the breed. For instance, in great Dane pups, at age eight to twelve weeks, they often get a staph infection on their muzzles. It looks terrible and spreads fast, but is harmless and usually goes away by itself if the owner will wash the pup's muzzle after each meal with soap and water and then alcohol. Stubborn cases respond to penicillin. One vet in a prominent clinic [in the New York City area] had never seen a Dane puppy, thought they were warts and was going to surgically remove the pimples, permanently disfiguring the dog."

Being a vet has certain fringe benefits, besides the money, especially for the vet with a keen sense of humor. As, when sex rears its head. Dr. Priscilla Stockner for example, likes to tell the story about the senior citizen with the obese cat that was doing strange things. It was urgent that Dr. Stockner make a house call as soon as possible to see for herself. The appointment was made for that very afternoon. Reports Dr. Stockner, "I sat down and said, 'Your cat is going to have kittens, and very soon.' The owner was aghast, 'That can't be. She has never left this apartment, and if she had slipped out, we're four flights up.' I said again, 'Well, I don't know what we'll call it, but she is going to have kittens.' At that moment, from behind the divan on which I sat came a beautifully endowed tom cat. I smiled as he sauntered across the floor, 'What about him?' 'Oh, no,' she wailed, 'he's her brother'!"

It's not quite so funny when the joke's on you. As, for example, when I thought our first male dog—he was only a pup—had developed two tumors of the penis. I, too, called the vet. "Emergency. Can I see you immediately?" I rushed the dog to his office, he led us in, put the dog on the table, looked at the dog, looked at me, walked over and shut the door. Then he told me about the birds and the bees and the workings of a dog's penis. Red in the face, I couldn't wait to get out of there, but the vet was enjoying every moment of my embarrassment too much to let me escape fast. When I finally escaped, it was only momentary. I was quickly called back to pay for the office call.

Most male-dog owners will never go through such an experience, but many are the female-dog owners who have called their vet about finding blood in the urine or drops of blood about the house. They, too, may end up paying for the privilege of learning all the external signs of a bitch's first estrus.

But for every dog owner who comes face-to-face with the sex life of his or her pet, there are ten cat owners who will have the experience. You ain't seen nothing 'til you've seen a female cat in the mating mood. She rolls, she runs around in circles. She cries as if in agony. And then she begins her rutting strut. Standing in place, she marks time with her rear legs while keeping the hindquarters provocatively, enticingly elevated. If that doesn't disturb a new owner, there's only one thing else that will: catching two cats in the act. My first time, I thought I'd come upon a catfight and rushed out to separate the two. I don't know which was madder, the male or the female, but I'm inclined to think it was the latter. Bordellos didn't get the nickname "cat houses" for nothing.

If one is going to own a whole, rather than a desexed, pet, one can expect such potentially awkward visits to a vet. Under those circumstances, it's nice to have an understanding vet. Under any circumstances, it's important to have a good one. Unfortunately, every profession has its problem children. Those vets up to their necks in the puppy-mill business are no credit to mankind much less medicine. But they are the exception. What's more, the average pet owner will never cross their path.

What they will come up against are vets who not only don't like animals, but who are scared to death of them. And when that adrenaline starts flowing, the pets know it, too, making for truly ugly scenes. In too many cases the vet will avoid doing things like cutting toenails for fear he'll cut too short and the dog will let him know it.

Very common are those vets who like to squeeze in the greatest number of patients each day. Rather than risk having an empty space on their appointment schedule, they use the butcher's take-a-number system. Bad cases don't get to jump to the front, especially if they're messy or look like they'll take time. These may, in fact, be kept waiting until last so as not to encourage any other client to get up and leave early.

Other vets are like new-car addicts—they can't resist buying all the new, shiny surgical or diagnostic apparatus that instrument makers turn out with as much frequency and regularity as Detroit introduces new models. The equipment may be impressive, but somebody's fees are paying for it. Then, too, like new toys, they must be played with. Guess whose pet is going to play doctor, only for real?

Then there are vets who are test-happy. One presumes, and other vets concur, that such vets have gone the way of the human medical profession, preferring the diagnosis of a machine to their own judgment. Be that as it may, they take their extra X rays, urine samples, and blood tests. Especially blood tests. No one doubts for a minute the importance of blood testing for heartworms in those states where they are a problem. But testing the aged family pet to determine the level of immunity, or titer, in his bloodstream against distemper and other diseases—that borders on the ridiculous.

These blood-tapping testers and others of their ilk are continually being aided, abetted, and egged on by the drug companies who, with profit, not healing, as the motive, never cease looking for (and taking seemingly positive delight in finding) new diseases that lend themselves to testing and/or vaccinating. The latest of these is canine brucellosis.

Actually, the disease has been known to occur in dogs since 1931, but it was considered a medical rarity, an oddity. Then, in 1966, there was a widespread outbreak of canine abortions caused by it. Although first recognized in a single beagle kennel, within eighteen months it had appeared in other beagle kennels across the country. One might, in view of the surplus pet situation, suppose that such abortions would be welcomed, but they were not. In fact, they were considered a calamity, since these kennels were and are the prime source of dogs used for research.

The disease is, as a form of undulant fever, communicable to man. For dogs infected, there is no cure. For the puppy miller and serious breeder alike, it has dire long-range financial and genetic implications. The disease is hard to spot, since 99 percent of the carriers, or affected dogs, appear healthy. The female, for example, may conceive and appear perfectly normal. Then, on the forty-fifth to fifty-fifth day of her pregnancy, she will walk across the room, stop momentarily to abort, and continue on as if nothing had happened.

But more than one drug company saw in this disaster a potential bonanza. Herein might be another canine disease requiring periodic inoculations, as do distemper, hepatitis, leptospirosis, and rabies—those canine Four Horsemen of the Apocalypse and best friends of the drug companies.

One of the men approached about developing a vaccine was George E. Lewis, Jr., D.V.M., who did extensive research on canine brucellosis at the Walter Reed Army Institute of Research, Division of Veterinary Medicine, and who is recognized as one of the two experts on the subject. Feeling that the money would be better spent getting owners of animals to have them immunized against rabies (fatality rate among humans is close to 100 percent), he declined.

The drug companies were not discouraged. In the mid-1970s, Pitman-Moore, Inc., introduced a diagnostic test for canine brucellosis. With a claimed accuracy rate in the upper ninetieth percentile, the kits cost a mere $25 apiece. Not much when you consider that each kit can be used to test better than a dozen dogs at a charge of $7 to $10 each. And that such testing could be a part of every routine checkup for, say, heartworms, that involved taking a sample of blood.

Pitman-Moore put together a sizable advertising and public-relations program to convince veterinarians. Part of that program was aimed not at the vets, but at their clients. (After all, how long could any vet resist if pressured by both his supplier and his clients?) Most vets succumbed. Some immediately, others later. And wouldn't you, if you read or your clients started parroting these statements Pitman-Moore was making? Judge for yourself:

> Every positive result . . . is a warning signal to the veterinarian and his assistant—and to all other pet-care personnel who might have had contact with such infected dogs—to watch for telltale symptoms of human brucellosis *among themselves* [my italics].
>
> "There's no question, the disease is communicable to humans," says Dr. P. R. Glick, Vice President of Marketing for Pitman-Moore.
>
> Undoubtedly people are going to their family physicians complaining of the disease symptoms, but physicians are still too unfamiliar with the disease to consider it as a possible cause.
>
> "If the test is positive, the dog should be isolated and treated. The veterinarian and his personnel should be alert to symptoms among themselves and certainly the family doctor of the pet owners should be notified," Dr. Glick cautions.
>
> As a precaution, Pitman-Moore, Inc., urges all dog-owners to have their pets tested for brucellosis.

In advertising circles there's a phrase that describes the above: scare tactics. They are very effective. I know whereof I speak: our kennel was checked for brucellosis even though we had never had a case of spontaneous abortion in our thirteen-year kennel history.

I must confess my experiences with this rapid diagnostic test were educational. The first dogs at our kennel to be tested were a pair of matrons. One had not conceived in her last three seasons; the other had just had a lovely large litter some months before. Both tested positive. In remembrance of that "communicable to humans" line, they were both immediately put down. Then the rest of the kennel was tested. Sixty percent tested positive, including our first homebred male champion.

That's when I started doing some investigating. I learned that according to the Center for Disease Control, Brucellosis Surveillance report, issued March 1975, up through 1973 there had been only a *dozen* known canine brucellosis infections in man. "Six of the twelve cases resulted from accidental exposure of laboratory workers, four from exposure to infected dogs, and two from exposure to an undetermined source."

I learned that the vaunted 90 percent-plus accuracy of the diagnostic test pertains only to screening out those that do *not* have it. We will never know whether those two fine bitches had it or not. We do know that *all* of those others who tested positive did *not* have it. We know because we had the University of Pennsylvania College of Veterinary Medicine test them. We know because we sent blood samples to Washington's Crossing, New Jersey, where the people who did the final testing were researchers at Pitman-Moore.

Admittedly, I am biased and bitter about the canine-brucellosis scare. I can't help but concur with Dr. Lewis that mankind and dogdom would have fared much better if all the money and research so far devoted to *Brucella canis* had been spent to control and irradicate hydrophobia.

Two questions are foremost: (1) Will responsible vets realize in time (before thousands of misdiagnosed pets are unnecessarily killed) that painstaking multiple testing is in order before sounding the death knell? (2) How long will pharmaceutical firms persist in putting marketing goals above humane values?

## HOW TO FIND A GOOD VETERINARIAN FOR YOUR PET AND YOUR PEACE OF MIND:

1. Look for one who combines his office and his home. You can always get him that way in an emergency (as we proved one Palm Sunday morning when instead of hearing a sermon, he performed a Caesarian).
2. Look for one who works by appointment yet can still squeeze in an emergency.
3. Look for one who specializes in small animals. Cows, horses, and sheep often get preference to cats and dogs in direct proportion to the size difference.
4. Look for one who is recommended and used by area breeders. *They* know.
5. Look for one who willingly cuts pets' toenails, expresses anal glands, and performs other distasteful but necessary functions.
6. Look for one who not only will listen to your problems on the phone but is willing to give advice by phone.

# V  FOOD

> More money is spent each year on pet food research than is spent on cancer research.
>
> JAY SIMMONS, V. M. D.

Of the estimated $7 billion spent in America each year on pets, more than $2 billion goes for pet foods bought at U.S. food stores, according to the Pet Food Institute. Today there are somewhere between 1,500 and 3,000 pet-food manufacturers (depending on which authority you use) selling some 10,000 to 15,000 brands of pet foods, mostly through grocery stores and supermarkets.

Perhaps a dozen or so of these are large, well-known food companies with nationwide distribution: Ralston-Purina (Dog and Cat Chow, etc.), Liggett and Myers (Alpo), General Foods (Gaines), Carnation (Friskies and Mighty Dog), H. J. Heinz (9-Lives), Quaker Oats (Ken-L Ration and Puss 'n Boots), Mars (Kal Kan), Allied Mills (Wayne and Solo), Standard Brands (Burgerbits), Campbell Soup (Champion Valley Farms Recipe), Agway (Respond and Big-Red), National (Skippy), Nabisco (Milk-Bones), Thomas Lipton (Tabby Canned), and so on.

Pet foods rank in sales with the leading-selling items in supermarkets—canned milk, bread, coffee, and salad dressings—and outsell baby foods four to one. They are now the largest-selling dry-food category in the grocery market.

I know of at least fifteen different combinations of flavors in one canned-cat-food line alone. Flavors such as kidney and cream gravy, liver ditto, liver and eggs, chicken parts and liver, savory stew, chopped platter, mackerel, seafood platter, and tuna and chicken parts. These took up eighteen feet of shelf space at one particular supermarket, leaving only about thirty-five or forty feet for all the other makes of canned cat foods.

## 62 THE PET PROFITEERS

To fully appreciate how this industry has grown in recent years, one simply has to look at the figures, again supplied by the Pet Food Institute. In 1969, dry-dog-food sales were at the $259-million mark. In 1974, they topped $675 million. Canned-dog-food sales went from $385 million to $565 million. Semimoist from $108 million to $265 million. Dry-cat-food retail sales of $61 million in 1969 came close to tripling by 1974 to $160 million. Canned cat foods came up from $237 million to hit the $400-million mark, while semimoist, introduced in 1970 and doing less than $1 million the first year, soared to a nice juicy $70 million.

All told, dog- and cat-food sales more than doubled in just six years, increasing 103 percent, from $1,050,000,000 to $2,135,000,000. At the same time, for you and me and the pet owners down the street the average per-pound price went up from 19.8 cents to 29.2 cents. Over the possible life-span of a cat, which is about 15 years, it would cost $1,475 to feed it just one can of a popular cat food per day. This works out to about $100 a year, or about the same amount it costs us to feed a kennel dog.

Remember, as you read those fantastic sales figures, that the pet-food industry is still relatively young. It started some fifty years ago when a maker of canned horsemeat for human consumption here and abroad

*The New York Times/Gary Settle*
No, this isn't the Manned Flight Control Center in Houston. It's an electronic monitoring facility in Topeka, Kansas, where General Foods makes pet food.

conceived the idea of canning some of the less edible—and less desirable to humans—parts of the carcass. It then sold these as pet foods for dogs (and eventually cats). The breakfast-cereal manufacturers saw the success of these canned pet foods and, not to be outdone, came up with the idea of using some of *their* by-products to produce dry meals for pets.

The industry may be young, but it learned fast. According to *Pet Mass Marketing*, a trade magazine, "the manufacturing of pet foods today is a science. Pet food manufacturers are not the ghouls\* skulking around stockyards at night picking up carcass remnants and stuffing them into cans that some would like us to believe. On the other hand, their manufacturing facilities, quality control, and testing rival or surpass food canned for human consumption."

Not only did these manufacturers learn how to make the food, they also learned how to market and sell it. The research and development done by Campbell Soup before they brought out the Champion Valley Farms Recipe canned dog food illustrates what is needed to put a new pet food on the market. Interviewers went to people's homes and organized consumer panels. They gathered information such as:

— Kids feed dogs at first, but because the kids don't like the bad smell of some of the foods, the mother takes over the job eventually. With that knowledge Campbell made sure Recipe had a smell attractive to humans.
— People do not like to use their silverware to dig the food out of the can. Recipe comes out of the can without prodding.
— If the food was homogenized, people had doubts about the identity of the ingredients. So, Recipe is full of distinguishable pieces, not an unrecognizable mass.

Rival Pet Foods also pays a great deal of attention to the consumer. Believing a home-housed pet is in a different psychological state from that of a kennel-housed dog, they ask pet owners to test-feed the food and advise them of the dog's reactions.

Every major pet-food manufacturer has its own research and development facilities in one way, shape, or form. Ralston-Purina, perhaps, has the largest single research kennel facility in the industry; over 650 dogs (all supposedly purebred) and an equal number of cats enjoy a cozy life where food and shelter are never a problem. The only other research facilities to compare with Purina in size are those of Gaines, in Kankakee, Illinois. However, Alpo's new and sophisticated test center in Allentown, Pennsylvania, has a multithousand-dollar blood analyzer that is found in only a few large hospitals in the country, like the Mayo Clinic.

---

\* This is open to debate, as you'll find out in the final chapter.

So the pet-food industry has learned a basic lesson of marketing and selling a product: Find out not who uses it, but who buys it. And the "buy-word" with pet food is people: Pets don't buy cat and dog food, people do. Their marketing lessons learned, the food producers have catered to the owners' practice of attributing human tastes to their animals. Stews, for example, appeal to us, not to dogs, which can't digest the vegetables in them. The so-called gravy dog foods—add warm water and the dog will have a gravy-flavored dinner—again appeal to the buyer's own taste. To make it appeal to dogs, caramel flavoring—which is sweet—is often substituted for gravy.

How far will a manufacturer go to cash in on a pet owner's desire to treat his pet like people? You be the judge. One manufacturer seriously considered producing an extruded product, much like Korn Kurls, that would contain so much air that an owner could safely feed her pet three meals a day, as the marketing experts say she wants to do. The plan was reluctantly abandoned when it was pointed out that the owner of a large dog, such as a great Dane, would have to resurrect the coal bin in her basement for the storage of one week's supply.

There is also the matter of salt. Everybody knows that every animal needs and likes salt. Right? Wrong. Dr. Donald Collins, author of *The Collins Guide to Dog Nutrition* (Howell Book House), conducted some tests to find out. "We discovered that, given the same food, with and without salt, dogs preferred the saltless food almost two to one."

Anybody who has watched a dog eat must begin to question whether it even tastes its food. Simply terrible table manners to bolt food down that way. Now cats, they're a different story. Very dainty. Very picky. Which is borne out in a study conducted by Dr. Alan D. Walker, an authority on animal nutrition. He found that cats do not like sweets; but dogs love them, as we've already noted in regard to those caramel-flavored "gravy dinners." While cats demand fresh food, dogs have a fondness for "gamey and well-matured" meat. His study bears out what many of us already knew: liver is the favorite taste of both cats and dogs, followed closely, as far as dogs are concerned, by anything fatty. But Dr. Walker discovered that, contrary to my and other pet owners' beliefs, sheep is the favorite meat of both dogs and cats, followed by ox and horse. Beef is not even a close fourth in the flavor-rating race, but it rates higher than pig, while chicken comes in a cowardly last. Although there is some variation among cats, the vast majority do not give fish a favorable rating and, in fact, put it near the bottom of the scale.

Regardless of the ingredients, pet food itself can be divided into four basic kinds: canned, semimoist, dry, and snacks.

*Canned Regular*

In return for buying a convenient, relatively safe, certainly unbreakable package, which does not require refrigeration until opened, and is subject to little or no spoilage or infestation, the buyer of canned dog food spends three-fourths of his money for water. On a caloric basis, it takes four fifteen-ounce cans to give a pet the same amount of usable food contained in two cups of dry solids. Translated into dollars and cents, it would cost approximately $1.32 for four cans of a good grade of pet food as compared to twenty-two cents for a dry food. Or six times more for canned food than for dry food that would do the same job. Suppose one bought a cheaper canned food? In 1975 the cheapest sixteen-ounce can of dog food in the supermarket cost about fifteen cents.

To produce that can, it cost the manufacturer no less than seven cents a can for certain irreducible fixed costs: the tin plate, solder, food processing, loading, sealing, sterilizing, labeling, shipping carton, labor, overhead (factory heat, light, power, depreciation of machines and equipment), plus administration. There are also the flexible costs, which can vary from factory to factory, company to company, and year to year. These would include advertising and sales promotion, commissions, transportation, manufacturer's profit, store markup, and the cost of the can's ingredients themselves, which can vary from less than one cent to more than eight cents a can. These flexible costs run from about five cents a can to twenty-three cents. If we use the five-cent figure, adding this to the roughly seven cents of fixed costs would give a minimum price for a can of dog food of about twelve cents, with less than one cent of that going for the food. How much nourishment will one cent buy?

If one's goal is to feed a pet as cheaply but as nutritionally as possible, then dry food is the answer. If one insists on feeding canned food while still saving money, then Dr. Collins has a suggestion: save even more by just not feeding the dog at all, accomplishing the same end (death by starvation), only more quickly.

The marketing of cheap dog foods does not have the health of the animal uppermost in mind, just the manufacturers' own pockets. Many "chunk style" canned dog foods on supermarket shelves contain textured vegetable proteins that look like chunks of meat. Many is the breeder and even veterinarian who thinks they are chunks of real meat. Even when the chunk *is* real meat, don't expect to see hunks of meat or even a meaty texture when you cut it open. The chunk is not meat alone, but a mixture of ingredients deliberately macerated so one can't see the individual ingredients. You and I wouldn't like what we'd see: pieces of trachea, blood vessels, lungs. Of course, one would never guess that from the titles on the cans: "Chunky Beef," "Chunky Liver," "Beef Chunks Dinner" or "Chunky Beef By-Products Dinner." Note the use of the word *dinner*. It's deliberate; now our pet has "din-din" the same as his owners. How perfectly human.

*Semimoist*

For people who'd like to buy canned food but know it's too expensive, yet can't bring themselves to feed plain, dry foods—*voila!* A la MacDonald's, the pet-food industry's answer to the problem: ersatz hamburger. Also known as Gainesburgers and Ken-L Burgers, as well as any other variation on burgers that one can think of. The ad men have even gone so far as to show a pound of this stuff and a pound of the real thing and challenge the reader to choose the real one. The thinking here is that if it looks like hamburger to us, it will taste like hamburger to a dog or cat. For this dubious benefit, we pay a surcharge of anywhere from 17 percent to 30 percent, 25 percent average, just for water. In addition, to avoid spoilage, the foods are treated by lacing them with salt, sugar, or other binding agents to prevent bacterial action.

The cat-food manufacturers are relatively new to this area of food making, but they've managed to come up with a wrinkle or two. Their products are not hamburger-wrapped as the dog foods are; instead they come in a bag like packets of dried mashed potatoes. Each packet is good for half a meal for an average-size cat. Figure it out. The average cat is going to go through two or more of these per day, depending on size and any mouse-hunting on the side. One hundred dollars a year wouldn't go far if one feeds these semimoist products. Of course, they don't require mixing, wetting, stirring, or even smelling. For rich, fastidious people, they're perfect.

*Dry*

Dry pet foods contain about 5 to 10 percent water (average, 6 percent). Any foods with less than 10 percent water will not spoil even though not refrigerated. Which should make these the perfect pet food, except for one thing. They are subject to the law of supply and demand. Most of the large dry-food manufacturers allow themselves a large leeway in their formulations to permit their products to remain competitive when the costs or availability of the usual ingredients in the foods fluctuate. Thus, one batch may have corn as the main source of carbohydrates, and another batch wheat, barley, or rice.

With the aid of their computer, producers can usually supply an adequately nourishing, well-balanced food that will meet the guaranteed analysis on the label. But it makes a joke out of the list of ingredients. As one expert admits, simply listing the ingredients is no guarantee they are in the food. What's more, he says, "It is virtually impossible to determine the presence or absence of a particular ingredient in a processed product. This is particularly true of dry, expanded dog foods."

One of the benefits of such "open-end" formulas is that they may make supplementing the diet a thing of the past. For the economy-minded, truly caring pet owner, it should be fairly obvious that supplementation is not only a waste of time and money, but a risky proposition. After all, how can you possibly know what or how much to add when you don't know what it is that you are supplementing?

*Snacks*

Remember animal crackers? Now pets have people crackers. And Milk Bones, whose name I never could figure out. And Treats, and dozens of other similar products. The pet shops love them and use a great deal of ingenuity in displaying them. You'll find them in cracker boxes, produce baskets, abandoned aquariums, wicker baskets, old-fashioned candy jars, wicker pet beds, bicycle baskets, macrame-hung jars, you name it. The name of the game is money. The rules, according to *Pets/Supplies/Marketing,* a trade magazine, are simple: "Treats are impulse items; display them as such."

Snacks are totally nonessential to the nutrition and health of a dog (those "bones" won't make a dent in any real amount of tartar), but absolutely essential to the beginner who is attempting to train a dog in the "reward them for what they do right, ignore what they do wrong" school of training. Of which I am a charter member. Nothing I like better than feeding a "postman" to a dog that's done something, anything, resembling what I've been trying to teach it. At least snacks give you a good training aid for your money, which is not the case with the newest food gimmick.

*Doggy Vitamins/Cat Salad Greens*

Actually, by the time you read this or sometime shortly afterward, that heading will probably read Doggy and Kitty Vitamins/Cat and Dog Salad Greens. Makes no difference. If you are feeding your pet a well-balanced diet, these are unnecessary. In fact, excessive amounts of Vitamins A and/or D can be fatal.

Faced with this myriad of products, one tries to buy with the help of ads. That causes some problems. General Foods Corporation, for instance, pioneer in semimoist dog foods with their Gainesburgers, has been prevented by the Federal Trade Commission (FTC) from using deception in their advertising of that particular product. The deception consisted of using such typical advertising claims as: "Gainesburgers . . . a tasty combination of meat by-products and meat plus all the vitamins, minerals, vegetables, and *milk protein* your dog needs" or "Gainesburgers have all the milk protein he needs."

In truth, according to the FTC, dogs do not have a special need for milk or milk protein, and Gainesburgers do not contain a nutritionally significant amount of milk protein. As a matter of fact, if dogs are not kept on a small amount of milk continuously after weaning, they will, in about six weeks, no longer manufacture in their systems the enzymes needed to digest milk. After that, milk just gives them diarrhea, which makes sense because it's a bit difficult for a dog in the wild to milk a cow.

The FTC also has prohibited General Foods from: (1) representing that Gainesburgers contain any nutrient unless the ingredient is present in a nutritionally significant amount; (2) representing that pets have a need for a nutrient that they do not in fact need; and (3) making any representation concerning nutritional value of pet food unless it has a reasonable basis to support the claim.

While manufacturers may stretch the truth a bit and skimp on the quality of their food a lot, they still put up a good front to the public. A very good one, in fact, since many of them spend millions of dollars on ads aimed at the public. In 1973, for example, Ralston-Purina was the champ with an ad budget of $22,749,000. Alpo knocked cereal for dogs to the tune of $9,049,000. Maybe if General Foods hadn't backed its Gaines products so vigorously ($7,487,000), the FTC wouldn't have heard about it. Campbell Soup ladled out $5,402,000 for its Recipe. (I wonder how much Lassie got for eating it. In fact, I wonder if Lassie really does eat it? I asked Campbell Soup, but they aren't talking.) Between them, the next four largest advertisers—Carnation for Friskies and Mighty Dog; H. J. Heinz for 9-Lives; Quaker Oats for Ken-L Ration and Puss 'n Boots; and Mars for Kal Kan—spent less than Ralston-Purina, or a mere $17,146,000. The combined total of $61,833,000 spent by these advertisers paid for a lot of admen's three-martini lunches.

Occasionally, ads even helped the American consumer to buy intelligently. Unfortunately, the most noteworthy of these ads ran back in 1972 and hasn't been seen since. The ad in question was run by Purina. Like the famous Ford Motor Company ad that told one to "Look at all three," this suggested you read the labels on canned cat food before buying. Not only that, it proceeded to show those labels and interpret what each means. Because those labels are still with us, because the comments are still pertinent, and because Purina isn't running the ad any more, here is my candidate for the consumer-oriented cat-food ad of all time:

The ad shows a stack of cans. The uppermost has a label reading, "Kidney Flavor Feast." Next to it, Purina comments, "Any cat food that says 'kidney flavor' needs only enough kidney or kidney flavoring to be detected by the pet or by a recognized test method. But the label doesn't tell us how much." The next label reads, "Kidney Dinner." Purina's comment, "Any cat food called 'kidney dinner' needs only 25 percent kidney to meet regulations for use of the word dinner. It may contain more, but the label doesn't tell us so." The next label reads, "Kidney in Creamed Gravy." Purina comments, "This product contains kidney 'in gravy.' How much kidney we don't know. The label says the gravy includes beef fat, non-fat milk blend, wheat flour, etc." The final label reads, "Purina Variety Menu—Kidney." Purina notes that this has to be at least 95 percent kidney, because no other word appears with "Kidney."

With thanks to Purina for this public-service ad, let us let them make their whole sales pitch: "It could be 100 percent kidney, except it is better for your cat to get 5 percent added vitamins, minerals, and other nutrients. Each one of Purina's sixteen varieties assures you of 95 percent of whatever it says on the label. No cereal fillers. No gravy fillers. Just 95 percent, plus 5 percent vitamins, minerals, and other nutrients."

Rarely does an ad find a way to do a favor for the consumer while patting itself on the back. Usually, they resort to puffery—also known as blowing their own horns—or taking pokes at their competition. For example, Gaines ran an ad saying, "Your dog doesn't eat cans. So why pay for them?" Make sense? Not, apparently, to Gaines, which test-marketed in 1973 and 1974 a new product, Gaines "Supreme," a canned combination of beef by-products and beef in gravy. In five flavors, yet.

Then there was Alpo's "Your Dog Needs Meat" (which they were forced to change to "Not a Speck of Cereal") campaign. Purina, stung by Alpo's jabs at them on TV ("Cereal is for cows"), responded in ads that said Purina provided twice the protein of Alpo at half the price. Purina should have known that all of this was in good clean fun, that Alpo didn't really mean to knock cereal. How could they when they've been market-testing "Alamo" brand dry food with meat and bone meal, as well as a dry product with "25 percent real beef" (it's called Beefbites Dinner, but it carries no other brand identication). The war in the industry between the canned and dry types seems to be degenerating into a skirmish, and détente is obviously on the way now that most of the leaders produce both types.

You may not be able to believe the ads, but then again, you may not be able to trust the labeling either. The Purina ad proves that. There are just too many nuances involved; the simple juxtaposition of words has too serious and great an import; the terminology itself doesn't seem to mean what one expects certain words to mean. The whole thing is just too confusing.

Of course, there is one term we all know that appears on labels: Government Inspected. The breakfast-food company that bought the canner of horsemeat which invented commercial dog foods states in recent advertisements that it sells "the only leading brand of canned dog food government inspected for wholesomeness." Their cans have a seal saying "packed under continuous inspection of U.S. Dept. of Agriculture."

Big deal. All dog foods intended for canning, after being sealed in the cans, go through a sterilization process to prevent spoilage. The can and its contents are heated to at least 250 degrees F. for at least three minutes, with the atmospheric pressure increased to at least fifteen or more pounds per square inch. Those cans that have not undergone proper sterilization become obvious mighty quickly. As the unkilled bacteria grow, they produce gases that, unable to escape because of the seal, build up pressure inside the can. When the pressure gets great enough, the gases usually burst through at places of least resistance—usually lids or side seams. Boom!

The point is that, because of this sterilization process, canned dog foods are basically germfree and sanitary whether U.S. government-inspected or not. As a kicker, the Pet Foods Institute, in its *Fact Sheet 1974*, states, "At the Federal level, pet food labeling and advertising claims are regulated by the FDA, FTC and USDA. *All pet food plants are subject to FDA inspection and FDA's low-acid canned food regulations apply to pet foods just as they do to canned foods processed for human use.*" It goes on to say "Most of the fifty states require, under state animal feed laws and regulations, that pet food labels be registered and approved . . . [these labels] are required to:

1. Conspicuously identify the product as a dog or cat food.
2. Select a brand name which is not misleading as to content or nutritional properties."

So "government inspected" is virtually meaningless. What about the one thing that appears on every can and every bag and every package: the guaranteed chemical analysis? Requirements for it are generally set by the food-control officials in each state. The list usually includes a guarantee of the lowest (minimum) percentages of crude protein and crude fat and the maximum percentages of moisture, crude fiber, and ash. Certain other key ingredients, such as the percentages of calcium and phosphorus, may also be guaranteed and if so should also be included on the guaranteed-analysis panel.

What actually happens is that the food's less-costly ingredients, such as water, fiber, and ash, will approach the maximums guaranteed. But the food's more costly items, such as various proteins and fats, will be close to the minimums guaranteed. This is dictated by simple economics and keen competition among the commercial pet-food manufacturers.

The guaranteed chemical analysis does not guarantee good pet nutrition. In fact, for dog owners, it's meaningless. Not so for cat owners. The statement of ash content can be very valuable. For example, cat experts will tell you to stay away from canned foods with more than 4 percent ash, dry foods with more than 12 percent.

Labeling can be helpful to cat owners in other ways, too. For example, in determining those manufacturers trying to cash in on our mistaken idea that fish is the ideal cat food. Remember Dr. Walker's findings? They were elaborated on by Dr. Patricia Scott for a presentation at Gaines Dog Research Center's 1971 Small Animal Nutrition Workshop. She pointed out that the specialized and unique nutritional requirements of felines come first from the fact that the cat is a desert-type animal, having originated in subtropical areas. Second, that under natural conditions, it is a true and complete carnivore. Cats *do* need meat—what else would they find in the desert? Certainly not fish! She also noted that as a hunter, the cat is used to being an occasional, not a continuous, feeder. No matter how loudly Squeaky cries, be assured that she can easily wait another minute or two to have her din-din.

If a manufacturer is capitalizing on the fish idea, he may have put it in everything he makes for cats. Unfortunately, as Anna P. Gilbride, D.V.M., confirms, these manufacturers are suspect for their quality standards. "The fish may be covering up an impalatable, low grade, offensive base." Besides, fish protein is not as high quality as meat.

Dr. Gilbride goes even further, suggesting that people judge cat food by odor and texture. Canned liver, for example, should be recognizable by odor, however cooked or processed. Texture is important. A tacky food is unpleasant and difficult for a cat to eat, and it is usually made of poor-quality filler products. She also recommends that one stay away from mixtures and concentrate on buying straight liver, kidney, heart, and so on. That way one can judge by odor and appearance whether or not the can contains what the label says. She believes that, as with dog foods, the analyses printed on the labels have only comparative value.

In that regard, it should be pointed out that one manufacturer determined that a combination of desirable caloric values for a pet could be legally and scientifically produced from a mixture of old boots, coal, sump oil, and water. Don't laugh; your pet may be eating it soon.

Starving dogs and cats there certainly are, but we in America are also experiencing the reverse as well: the fat pet. As Dr. Collins bluntly puts it, "Encouraged by his own impulsiveness to overfeed his dog, and supported by some equally guilty pet-food manufacturers, America's modern dog feeder robbed the dog of his built-in protection against obesity."

In these days when some people are forced to eat dog food for economic reasons—as documented at hearings held by the Senate's Select Committee on Nutrition and Human Needs in 1974—others have over-pampered their dogs to the point of feeding them *people* food, in fancy restaurants, yet.

There is, in mid-Manhattan, a gourmet restaurant for pets set up by two enterprising partners. The caliber of meat or fish used in cooking meals for clients' pets is said to match that of some of the best restaurants feeding humans. Lunch or dinner for a small or medium-size dog runs about $1 to $2. (A can of a premium commercial dog food in a supermarket would run only about thirty-five cents.) This restaurant is in a fashionable neighborhood, is colorfully decorated (cats and dogs are color-blind, by the way), and is kept impeccably clean. The pets' owners can choose from a menu that lists a fine assortment of meals, adapted from recipes for humans. For example, boeuf à la bourguignon, steak and kidney ragout, shrimp cocktail, chicken chow mein, braised chicken livers, chicken supreme, braised fish fillet, liver paté, and Swedish meatballs. They serve some three hundred or more meals a week in a special dining area with four "booths" where cleanliness and an environment free from offensive odors is provided. Since the pet owner is the real customer, no effort is spared to encourage that customer from watching the animals eat. The partners' own dogs are fed in a display window, advertising the services available inside.

Giving birthday parties for pets is encouraged. Friends of the pet are invited (the restaurant sells invitations, too), an attractive centerpiece is set up, and a birthday cake is provided, combining dog meal and liver and covered with whipped skim-milk powder and cream.

The partners keep their restaurant well stocked with a wide range of private-label and national-brand pet foods, available as a supplement to the pet's gourmet diet (which is not usually a balanced diet and does not offer complete nutrition). Only the highest quality is offered on these shelves. Canned foods cost about twice as much there as they do at a supermarket.

If you don't have one of these shops in your neighborhood, just wait. It's coming. Next door to the franchised fast-food eatery for people may soon be a franchised restaurant for their pets. If you find that hard to believe, remember what Alice in Wonderland said to the Queen: "There's no use trying," she said, "one can't believe impossible things."

Like pet cookbooks. Ellen Graham has written one, *The Growling Gourmet* (Simon & Schuster), which gives recipes for such goodies as Shih Tsu Stew and Finian Bake (a Gaelic pudding for Yorkshire terriers). Martin Gardner has written a cookbook for dogs as well as *The Secret of Cooking for Cats* (Doubleday). His recipes include "The Cat's Whiskers," a concoction for senior felines calling for beef heart, margarine, and cottage cheese. Another, "Chicken Lickin' "—a recipe

*The New York Times/Joyce Dopkeen*
A birthday party given for Fellow, a black schipperke, by his owner at a dog delicatessen in New York City called the Animal Gourmet. It supplies everything from invitations to party favors.

that includes not just leftover chicken but one-half small onion, one-half carrot, and one teaspoon mayonnaise—is actually misnamed; it should be called "Chicken Pickin,' " because that's what most cats do with it—pick out the chicken and leave the rest. Still a third, "Summer Cheese," calls for an ingredient I can't get: "Chunks of your cat's favorite fresh fruit." My cats consider fruit for the birds, and birds for cats.

I am quite sure I shall live to see the day when a canine version of *Calories Don't Count* will hit the best-seller list.

TIPS ON FEEDING YOUR PETS:

1. Feed the food the breeder or pet shop did, at least at first; make any changes gradually.
2. Once a pet stops eating, don't coax him to continue. Decide in advance to leave food in a pan for only fifteen minutes or so, then pick it up. No snacks, no nothing, until next meal.
3. Do not feed supplements to commercial dog or cat food. Since you can't tell what's in them, there's no way to tell what's left out of them, and you can then create nutrient-balance problems.
4. If you have but one pet and that pet has constant access to a toilet area, either via a kitty litter pan or a pet-door in the house, try self-feeding. With this, food is kept available constantly and the pet learns to eat only as much as it needs. At the beginning it is, to say the least, *messy*.
5. Keep water available at all times, and keep it fresh. A dog or cat can go for weeks without food, only a short time without water.

# VI  ACCESSORIES

> This year, Americans will spend more than $1.3 billion for accessories to clothe, feed, protect, pamper, and play with their cats and dogs.
>
> *The New York Post Daily Magazine*

In California, there is a veddy, veddy exclusive furrier. Caters only to the carriage trade. You know the type of place. Soft lights, plush carpets, and those skinny mirrors that can make a fat woman look thin. Well, that plush carpet has seen its share of wet spots, because *Monsieur* not only includes many a *madame* and *mademoiselle* among his clientele, but also more than one *le chien*. Creating matching mink or sable coats for two- and four-legged clotheshorses is nothing new to him.

On the other side of the continent, in New York, there is a tailor who is supposed to have been hired, at an exorbitant fee, to fly out to the Midwest to fit an industrialist's pet poodle with a fur coat. Not feeling quite so flush? Then Du-Say's, pet dressers since 1928, in New Orleans, has a mock sheepskin at $14.98 that will keep your pet just as warm.

And in Pennsylvania's anthracite region, two of the sweetest little old ladies you'd ever want to know are devoting their lives to the designing, manufacturing, and selling of coats, snow-mobile suits, and outfits at prices anyone can afford. Their Double S line of fashions for Fido and Fifi recently included a Santa Claus suit at $3.95, quilt pajamas for $15, and dresses with pockets for $9. They're even into the jeans thing with a denim-look casual work outfit for $8. One of their specialties, sanitary britches at $7.50 per set, comes complete with a matching collar cover. The pet sanitary pads are extra. Don't laugh. If Mimsi doesn't mind wearing them, they can save their owner a bundle on board bills. Owners of big dogs, however, are out of luck. They come in many styles but only one size: petite.

One needn't go that far from home. There isn't a modern, money-minded department store worthy of the name that is ignoring the profit potential in pet accessories. One that's nationally known and has branches all over the place even has its own line of exclusive, made-just-for-them, fashions. Like suede coats at $50. Snow suits at $40. Tennis outfits at $20.

And every supermarket has its mini-department. The concentration there is more on squeaky toys and fake bones and collars and leashes. But there, too, one will find one of the greatest boons to mankind since "Quick, Henry, the Flit." I speak of the flea and tick collars, first brought out by Sargeant's and now made by practically everybody.

If you have ever sat spraddle-legged on the floor with fifty pounds of dog draped over your lap while you wielded a pair of tweezers and dropped ticks into a jar of kerosene, you, too, would appreciate the ingenuity and beauty of these collars. Even worse than de-ticking a dog is de-fleaing a cat. It makes me itch just to remember sitting there running that fine-toothed flea comb through her hair then through the flame of a candle to burn the buggers. And that was one job you didn't neglect. Because a house infested with ticks is crawling, but one taken over with cat fleas is unbearable, and means a sure visit from the exterminator before those things eat you—I mean it—alive. (We once had too many cats and not enough exterminator money, so we resorted to burning sulphur candles instead. It's cheaper, but one has to close the house up for at least twenty-four hours for them to work. Then it takes a superlative act of courage to rush in, throw them out, open the doors and windows—all without being fatally gassed.)

Some smart people tried to get around both the exterminator and the sulphur fumes. They began wearing the collars themselves. If you've ever seen the nasty sores allergic dogs get from these collars, you can imagine what happened to some of their human counterparts. I understand, too, that wearing such a collar can interfere with one's kidney functions, which is why strips hung from the ceiling are not recommended for use in the bedroom.

While Sargeant's and Shell and the others have made millions from the killing off of parasites, that will seem piddling compared to the bundles someone else is going to make—the developer of the perfect pet contraceptive. With so much money at stake, you can bet there are several entries in this research-and-development derby. One is experimenting with a pet "pill." Another is going the chemically treated canned food route. Still a third entrant has been working with a "morning-after" oral agent that prevents implantations of the fertilized eggs. A fourth has created a canine IUD. Present plans call for a product that would cost about $11 including the cost of having it fitted by a vet. (Sorry, cat owners. No such device is in the cards for your pet.) And almost all of these are ready to go. They await only government approval, which may take months on top of the years already invested in research. One major drug company has been at work on pet contraception for ten years. I'm rooting for them—all of them. May their products work and their profits be enormous, just so long as they solve the pet population problem.

There's another major problem that needs to be solved, as any city dweller will tell you. And that's the use of our sidewalks and parks as toilets for dogs. So vehement have the complaints become that legislation has been proposed in New York and other cities that would impose fines on dog owners who did not clean up after their pets. In Reykjavik, Iceland, the elimination problem became so acute, they finally eliminated the source. All dogs are now banned from the city.

To avoid fines and the banning of dogs, it is suggested that city dwellers do clean-up duty after their dogs. Suggested procedures include, the carry-a-piece-of-newspaper-and-shove-it-under-the-behind-at-just-the-right-time technique. This, however, involves agility that many of us don't have. Besides, those contrary creatures, canines, are apt to take alarm and move off as they have their movement. The resulting leap-frogging down the street is apt to attract more than a little attention and a great deal of kindly but embarrassing advice.

Most people prefer the after-the-fact method. One of these involves cutting a paper plate into halves and using the two as scoops. Hopefully, there will be a litter basket nearby. Otherwise one is left with one's hands full.

Preferable to that is the "Baggies" method. This involves choosing a Baggie of the proper graduated size to hold the dog's excrement. Then put your hand inside like a glove, pick up the fecal matter, turn the bag inside out. Presto! Instant sanitation. Since many people do not like to be seen carrying a see-through bag containing stool, they double-bag it. Using a plain ordinary brown bag on the outside for cosmetic purposes. This, in turn, can lead to some strange happenings. Like the time the little old lady walking her peke fell victim to a purse snatcher. He not only grabbed her bag but also the brown sack she was carrying. Imagine his face when he saw his booty.

Those lucky people with yards and children also have a clean-up problem. For them, the "super dooper pooper scooper" has been money well spent. (My father pays my six-year-old a penny a pile to be his backyard pooper scout.) But one needn't be confined to one model. There are scoops with a hinged, clamshell-like type of operation. Others have lids, much like a silent butler. Some are all metal. Others metal and wood. But not all are very practical. It is suggested that one, if not easily embarrassed, try out one's choice in the store—in pantomime, of course. Just as satisfactory is the use of a child's toy rake in one hand and toy shovel in the other. However, it is recommended that one have one set for the poop and another for the child. And don't get them mixed up.

Since outdoor training has its onerous and odorous side, more and more pet-owners are being enticed to buy the newest version of sheets of newspaper: "Puppy Piddle Pads" or "Train-O-Mat" or "Poluto Mats"—all attempts to fool the pet into thinking he's on grass. Either my pets are smarter than most, or the grass is too gross. Besides, they are only effective with pups and females. Once a male starts lifting his leg, you have to rig up aluminum foil wall-protectors around two sides of the mat. Then you buy a fake fire hydrant or other device for the dog to decorate. Add it all up and the Sunday *New York Times* that lasts a week still comes out cheaper.

Of more promise is the "Tidypet Indoor Dog Toilet." This is the brainchild of Heather Latimer, who is deeply concerned with the dog-litter problem. So much so that she has become known as an authority on community dog-litter control. As she puts it, "a strange distinction, but there it is." The Tidypet is a boxlike device not unlike a Parisian *pissoir*. The high sides, besides concealing the occupant, also keep the circling dog confined so he'll hit the right spot (which is a problem with newspapers). At the present time, the Tidypet is made of paper, but there's a plastic version in its future. Which will, of course, up the price. However, I sincerely suggest that you great Dane owners keep walking, since the giant-sized Tidypet that you'd need would fill a garage and cost a fortune.

However, price is no object to many pet owners. They gladly spend their money on such paraphernalia as canine sunglasses, rain umbrellas and sun parasols, Wellington boots, swimming vests, wigs of real hair (canine, I hope), and bejeweled collars—the real thing, putting most diamond wedding bands to shame. There are those things designed to make Poopsie more comfortable: modernistic cat tree houses of carpeting guaranteed to dominate any room they're in, portable swimming pools, a kitty gym exercisor for the shut-ins, canopied beds for pets whose owners are inconsiderate enough to read in bed, and hand-carved beds that, inch for inch, make an antique four-poster look cheap, since these retail from $1,000 to $1,800. Of course, the mattress is included.

## ACCESSORIES 79

You've heard of being born with a silver spoon in your mouth? The pet world's version must be a sterling-silver food dish, appropriately engraved, for only $105. If you want to be a piker but do your long-eared dog a favor, save $101 of that money and instead invest $4 in a veterinary-designed eating dish for dogs. Essentially round at the base, this dish has a narrow, rectangular feeding area that forces the dog to eat only from each end. That way his ears hang clear of the bowl. Clever fellow, that veterinarian; or maybe he was just tired of cleaning glop from dogs' ears. In any case, this dish, from Illinois, or the swivel-topped one from California, does a much better job than all the plastic ear mittens, ear clips, socks, muffs, and whatever previously available. (We cut the tops off old nylon stockings and put them over the dog's head like a turtleneck, being careful not to free the

*The New York Times/ Edward Hausner*
Some dogs will put up with anything, including wearing an umbrella hooked onto their collar. But in this case although the idea is right, the dog is shaped wrong—there's no way that umbrella is going to keep both ends dry.

ears. With the advent of panty hose, we've experienced something of a shortage of hosiery tops.)

Another accessory many pet owners swear by is the crate, or pet carrier. It certainly makes toilet training a dog a cinch. And it comes in handy when traveling, especially if you're not fond of sharing the driver's seat with your pet. I understand that one new carrier can make traveling easier another way. The advertisement for the new lightweight Louis Vuitton cat/small dog carrier boasts that it "tells bellhops the world over how important you are." Or stupid, as the case may be, since the 18-inch size retails for $185 plus tax.

The bewildering array of fashions, furnishings, and fun things for the pet seems endless. An impression confirmed when one visits one of the many "Pet Industry Expositions," unfortunately open only to the trade.

The selection is staggering. Some items seem sensible. Some even essential. Still others absolutely crazy and worthless. And many are not designed to be used by the pet at all; instead, they're solely for the amusement and pleasure of the pet owner:

*Pet sculptures,* either typical of your breed, or specifically sculpted to look like your particular pet. An 8-inch long statuette will cost you at least $75.

*Custom head plaque* on walnut base, $9.75.

*Lithographic prints* in limited editions of 500, signed and numbered by the artist, only $5 per.

*Photo address labels,* a real steal at $2.95 for 500.

*Photographic blowups,* just like the people ones, for $3.50. Or $5 if all you have is a slide or negative. Or $7 if you want rush service.

*Cat-lover's calendar,* about $1, but often available as a premium item with cat products.

*Pet stamps.* A starter collection of genuine postage stamps depicting pets is available for all you philatelists who just happen to have a pet. $1 for the set.

*Silk-screened cat tile* in ceramic, only $2.50.

*Dog-head mugs,* six different ones, about $1 apiece.

*Kitten prayer pendant,* by mail order for $3.50.

*Poems for pets.* Believe it or not, a man who bills himself as "the pet bard" will write a poem to "preserve the memory of your pet" for only $5.

*Kitten kitchen towels* of imported linen, three for $4.95.

*Dogluxe wristwatch* with your pet's photo on the dial. Swiss movement. Guaranteed 2 years. Only $19.

*Kitten cutting board,* for wall decoration and countertop cutting. Imagine cutting through that lovely kitten design each time you slice bread or cut a roast. Only $3.95.

*Dog antiques.* A California couple specializes in selling antique figurines, paintings, prints, glassware, jewelry, and books on pets at anything but antique prices.

*Coat of arms,* plus a history of your breed, is available by mail order for $6.95 to $11.95.

*Pet oil portraits* from $49.95. The ads for this service ask you to compare these to other "fine quality portraits that sell from $150 to $750." Pet or human, I wonder?

*Cat posters.* One on the market includes an impassioned plea for spaying and neutering of pets. It's put out by the Humane Society of the United States for $1.

*Dog crime-watch decal.* For $1.25 each, you can buy stickers for your door or windows warning of your ferocious watchdog.

*Needlepoint kits,* costing from $7.50 to $50 and more, depending on whether the wool is supplied or not. They can keep one busy for hours. And hours. And hours.

What's more, these things sell and sell and sell. The funny thing is that many of them aren't even good representations of the breeds they're supposed to be. For example, there's a porcelain figurine that sells for $750 (it's life-size; at that price, it ought to be ) that's supposed to be an English springer spaniel. Well, it has the head of an English cocker, the feathering of an American cocker, and the spots of an English setter. Only the tail could be springer; but that's hard to tell, since the figurine is sitting on it.

Another example, the aforementioned needlepoint kits. The boxer isn't! It's a great Dane. What the schnauzer really is is anybody's guess. And the Siamese cat has black points and round pupils. But that's not the point. Anything that vaguely resembles what it is supposed to be will find its way into some pet owner's home.

Needless to say, the variety and ingenuity shown by the creators of all these things simply boggles the mind. And this list merely scratches the surface. There are t-shirts, photo buttons, auto decals, bumper stickers, jewelry, even a Dog Lovers International Club membership. Not to mention one of the biggest categories of accessories of all:

books, books, and more books. There are so many books about dogs that it takes a whole book just to list them. E. Gwynne Jones' *Bibliography of the Dog: Books Published in the English Language from 1570 to 1965* (Gale Tower), has 3,986 entries on 431 pages, 132 of which are simply the index.

Just as dog and cat people are not alike, one would think the books aimed at each would be as different as, well, as cats and dogs. But they're not. A rather natural consequence of having the same publisher putting out books for both. The self-styled largest publisher of pet literature, for example, has, in addition to books on tropical fish, birds, small animals, reptiles, and other pets, some 15 cat books and 187 dog books. The vast majority of these are what is known as "breed books," or books devoted each to a single breed of dog or cat. It is the very rare breed in this country that does not have at least one or as many as one-half-dozen books devoted solely to it.

All breed books, however, fall into one of four general categories. The first and most common is, as one reviewer put it, the "fairly typical breed book, neither thorough nor well-written." Frequently, these are banged out by a professional or semiprofessional writer (but you'd never guess it from the writing) who knows little or nothing about the subject. Fortunately, many of these are worth their price in the photographs alone. And even better yet, many of these are the cheapies you find in the racks at pet stores.

The second type, which can be hard to come by, is the book sponsored, written, and published by the national parent club for that breed. It has the disadvantage that it is written by committee, so it tends to be less than controversial; but it has the advantage of containing slews of material that would not have been available to an individual writer. Somebody really interested in a breed, especially in pedigrees and history, will find this type of breed book right up his tree. That is, if he can find such a book. Normally, it is sold by the breed club itself, not distributed through regular publishing channels. To track it down, one has to contact the AKC for the name and address of the parent club's secretary. Contact him, and hope for the best.

The third type of breed book is the one that covers all the topics a neophyte needs and wants to know about a breed: picking a puppy, grooming, training, breeding, and so on. Sometimes the book is written by an expert in the breed who has a lot to say and knows whereof he speaks. Other times, the book is done by someone whose heart is in the right place, but whose track record is nil and his knowledge skin-deep. What he has to say wouldn't fill a book of matches. This did not discourage one intrepid publisher, who came up with a way of padding out the thinnest material. At first, he divided the contents of the book in half, the first part being specific to one breed, the second pertinent to any breed. Then, he came up with a new twist on this. Now, he takes those same general chapters and intersperses them among specific material. Watch out for repetitious chapters. Example: one chapter on grooming the particular breed, another chapter on grooming and general coat care. In every one of this publisher's books, you'll find the same, not particularly informative, chapters on nutrition, maintaining the dog's health, housing, history of the genus *Canis,* manners for the family dog, bench shows, obedience competition, genetics, and breeding and whelping. In short, ten out of twenty-one chapters are so general and vague they can apply to any breed. Save your money.

The fourth type of breed book is written by a fantastically successful breeder—the one at whose feet the whole show-dog fancy sits, just waiting for those words of wisdom garnered over the years. This is the person whose knowledge of genetics, breeding, evaluating pups, training, and grooming is infinitely valuable. For this type of information, no book could be priced too high. And what does one get more often than not? Lists. Lists of winners, lists of kennels, lists of top-producing dams and sires (most of which, not surprisingly, come from the breeder's own kennel).

This type of book could have been written by a computer. Maybe even better. The computer would take the pedigrees of all the winning dogs over any given period of time and—transistors flashing—moments later give us a readout of the dams and sires that appeared most frequently in all the pedigrees, or in only the specialty-show winning dogs' pedigrees, or in the Best in Show winners' pedigrees. Or, it could do all of that. The major advantage of such a computerized book would be its complete objectivity. A rare attribute in a list-happy breed book.

Instead of getting a book devoted to just one breed, many readers prefer something more inclusive. These people may still be shopping around for a breed or interested in several breeds or really into the dog-show scene. For any of these reasons and others, the year in, year out, best-selling dog book in print is the *AKC Complete Dog Book*—the official publication of the American Kennel Club, now in its fourteenth edition. Part of it, about 20 percent, is devoted to a simplified description of buying and caring for a dog. The balance of the book contains a photograph, brief history, and the official "standard" for each breed.

A breed standard, by the way, is a verbal blueprint of the way a dog of that breed should look; it also includes his demeanor, manners, and general appearance when in a show ring. It is important to note that faults, disqualifications, and the like contained in the standard pertain only to dogs being considered for shows, not to the dog itself as criteria for determining whether it is purebred or even AKC registrable. The dog most often victimized by the false conception of what the standard signifies is the white German shepherd dog. He is indeed purebred and AKC registrable even if not eligible to be shown at an AKC-licensed show. The same pertains to white boxers and keeshonden.

Since the dog fancy has, over the years, created a peculiar vocabulary all its own (as my editor can testify), those verbal blueprints are often interpreted differently by different people. Thus, many decades ago, George Foley came up with the idea of doing a *Visualization of the Standard,* a picture book illustrating the verbal descriptions. Using a photograph of what was generally recognized (if not universally admired—dog people are too catty for that) as a top show specimen of each breed, he could graphically show what each point of the standard meant. So revolutionary was the idea that it caught on immediately. So great was the honor to be selected as the dog pictured in any breed that its owner paid gladly and *handsomely* for the privilege. (It is interesting to compare one of these visualizations from years ago with a current one. Even where the standard has changed not at all or practically imperceptibly, the change in the dogs themselves is radical.)

George Foley is gone now, but his idea continues on. It has, however, undergone a change or two or three—some of which I think would have George Foley, the grand old man of show dogs, turning over in his grave. The whole thing started simply enough.

In the early 1970s, thousands of dog owners opened their mail to discover an invitation to participate in the first annual edition of *The American Blue Book of Dog Breeders.* The purpose of the book, as stated in the invitation, was threefold: to inform the dog-buying public that well-bred dogs often cost less than the puppy-mill variety, to sell well-bred dogs to good homes, and to expose those who peddled poorly bred dogs to the American dog-buying public. This was to be the first national step toward putting the puppy mills, disreputable pet shops, and pet farms out of business forever.

But they offered still more: a Blue Book Information Center, with a registry for lost or stolen dogs, credit information on national credit-card holders, travel information, and more. Readers who bought dogs from the listed breeders would be eligible for the lost-pet registry, discounts on purchases of certain goods, and even free samples. In addition, they'd get articles on how to buy a pup, care of their pup, showing, breeding, veterinarians, and product advertising.

The cost? Just $25 for a "handsomely bound National Edition," plus listing the breeder's name and address in the book right next to his breed. As to the descriptions of the breeds themselves, they, too, would be handled uniquely: "with details of personality, physical characteristics as well as the special traits of each type *as opposed to the Show Standard which the novice may not understand*" (my italics).

In all, 838 breeders/groomers/breed clubs bought the idea. So did 23 people who took expensive display ads. And 52 more who paid extra to be "patrons." We're listed on page 271 of the first edition.

When the book finally arrived, several years later, the handsomely bound edition turned out to be paperback. There was, indeed, a listing of breeders—but in the back and nowhere near the descriptions of the breeds. Where were they? Up front. Remember that "show standard which the novice may not understand"? It's there. Along with a visualization, in black and white, of the standard. But wait one minute. Something new has happened. The dogs are anonymous; how come? According to Matt Stander, speaking as editor, they weren't identified because "they weren't paid for, besides many are dead." Instead, facing every standard—well almost every one, actually only eighty-four in all—are full-color, full-page ads of current winning show dogs. For which each owner paid a mere $400: $275 to buy the page, $125 for production costs to reproduce the color photos.

In all, according to my calculations, dog people paid more than $50,000 to be included in this book, which is now called *Popular Dogs Dog Lovers Complete Guide*. For which the public is charged $19.95.

Is the public getting its money's worth? Judge for yourself. Besides all the paid advertising (which, of course, is not so labeled), this complete guide includes one article about puppies—eight pages long—by a former pet-shop owner. A three-page article on traveling in Europe with your dog by a dog trainer. A page on grooming a fox terrier; a one-page "explanation" (reads more like fiction) on how the toy breeds developed; four pages of anatomical drawings. And then, two one-pagers by columnists, both of which had appeared in a national dog magazine before publication in this book.

The irony of all this is that it is being perpetrated by the people at *Popular Dogs* magazine, a magazine that had been published by George Foley's Foley Organization all the years of his life.

Now if one wants to get his money's worth of dog pictures, *The Encyclopedia of Dogs*, published by J. M. Crowell, will provide it. It includes pictures of 308 internationally recognized breeds. But its real appeal is to the true dog nut. The average person, who has difficulty identifying the five different dogs he sees on his daily walk, is not likely to appreciate it. This person might enjoy *The International Encyclopedia of Dogs* (Howell Book House). This is a smorgasbord of dog information, with some of the best photographs I have ever seen.

Unfortunately, like a list of appetizers at a fancy restaurant, it whets the appetite, but never satisfies. Not even the photographs; they're so good it makes one jealous that his breed doesn't rate more than the single one he's given.

As for cats, there are many, many picture books about them (why are cats so photogenic when dogs are not?). The real masterpiece of pet literature may be one on cats: *The Tiger in the House,* by Carl Van Vechten (Knopf). A book to enjoy and to buy.

It is not often that one has the chance to go literally from the sublime to the ridiculous, so I leap at the chance to go from a hep cat to a real dog, *Our Puppy's Baby Book.* In blue or pink, yet. And it sells by the thousands, making Mr. Van Vechten's royalty checks look like pittances.

Books or whatever, there is no need to pay full retail price on many of the items you need to properly care for your pet. Hundreds of items are sold by discount mail-order firms such as Animal Specialties in Camden, New Jersey. The catalogs are explicit, the merchandise is generally of good quality, and the service tends to be very prompt. Ask a breed club or local breeder how to get on the mailing list of one of these discount houses, or borrow the catalog for a few days and make your selections.

For clothing and many other items, one can shop through Du-Say's catalog (P.O. Box 22407, New Orleans, La.). Not only are they cheaper than many, if not most, of their competitors; they guarantee in their annual catalog that the prices will not be raised. In effect, you have one of the few hedges against inflation in the whole of petdom.

For books, get on one of the "remainder house" direct-mail lists. Marboro (205 Moonachie Rd., Moonachie, N.J. 07074) holds periodic sales. Publishers Central Bureau (33-20 Hunters Point Ave., Long Island City, N.Y. 11101), on the other hand, will inundate you with catalogs. But the nice thing is that dog and cat books never go out of date, they go on forever.

There is still another way to save money, and that's simply not to buy—but I don't need to tell you that.

## TIPS ON ACCESSORIZING YOUR PET:

1. Don't expect your pet to appreciate the difference between a diamond-studded collar and a good cheap one. However, round

collars are best for long-haired cats and dogs, and flat collars are best for short hairs.
2. Sharp teeth and plastic don't mix, especially when it comes to feed bowls.
3. A dog grows the most comfortable, warmest coat himself—better than any mink. So save money: don't trim, don't buy him a coat. A dog shaved of his coat is at the complete mercy of the elements. For this dog, a coat isn't a luxury, it's a necessity.

# VII GROOMING

> Grooming services income increased 7.1 percent with sales of $241,000,000 in 1974.
>
> *Pets/Supplies/Marketing*
> May 1975

In Manhattan Beach, California, there's a grooming parlor with some 1,500 square feet of well-lighted, immaculate space; eleven wielders of scissors and clippers; and a high noise level, thanks to the dozens of dogs waiting their turns, the many clippers buzzing simultaneously, and the insidious whine of hair dryers. Presiding over this organized bedlam is a proprietor with many years of experience—she judged the first National Dog Groomers of America Association (NDGAA) grooming contest—plus a wry sense of humor, reflected in her choice of a name for her shop: The Clip Joint.

Compare, if you will, Barbara Baillargeon's legitimate Clip Joint with other kinds of clip joints. One is run by George (not his real name). He gets most of his business by way of classified ads similar to this:

> GROOMING À LA GEORGE
> Any Breed   $8
> FREE pickup and delivery
> call

Sounds rather classy, doesn't it, with that "à la" business? Besides, he's dirt cheap, at least a third less than any of his competitors. You can imagine why George gets a lot of calls. His sales pitch includes a description of all the fancy trims he does, the choice of ribbons for the hair, the woodsy, fruity, or floral fragrances you might wish. And there's no waiting. An appointment is almost immediately available.

*Times Wide World Photos*
Pricing by size is the rule when it comes to grooming dogs—and always has been.

And don't forget that wonderful door-to-door pickup and delivery. Don't want it? Oh, but you have to, or George won't take you.

As a groomer, George doesn't do a bad job. But your dog seems rather groggy when returned home. George explains that away easily enough: The dog became carsick on the way to the shop, so he tranquilized it to prevent a repetition on the return trip. It certainly sounds plausible enough, even if the dog hasn't been carsick since he was an eight-week-old puppy.

Actually what happened is that George made his life easier and his trimming job speedier by tranquilizing the dog. That "carsick" business is a bunch of hooey. All of George's trim jobs get a downer as well.

Now Gregory—George's first cousin—also insists on pickup and he returns a dog that's alert enough. He's just shaking like crazy. Naturally, the ride in the van with all those other dogs had him upset; "maybe he thought he had been caught by the dog catcher, ha, ha, that would make me shake, too." Gregory thinks a little joke strengthens his arguments. Gregory doesn't go the tranquilizing route, where one has to wait awhile for the stuff to work. Instead, he's a great believer in the "man has to be boss" theory of dog-people relations. So, he just manhandles his clients into obedience.

Sound far-fetched? It isn't. For example, one version of this pickup and delivery trim job involved a traveling dog groomer who did his work in a van outside each owner's home. A Fort Lauderdale, Florida, dog owner contended that her poodle had been frightened out of its playful personality, had suffered mental trauma, and had been cut as the result of its clipping. The cut was covered up instead of treated, and the dog acted like a mentally disturbed child. The upshot of this matter was a $9,000 jury award to the owner—$1,500 in compensatory damages and $7,500 in punitive damages. As a result, practically every groomer in the country now carries malpractice insurance.

A pet shop may also offer a grooming service on the side (or in the basement, as the case may be). These are usually found through the Yellow Pages, and it doesn't make much difference where one looks —Pet Shops, Pet Washing and Grooming, Pet Supplies and Foods, Pet Training (yes, it's there, too), Pet Services—the aggressive pet shop makes itself known.

One such, and it's typical of too many, looks more like a supermarket than a pet shop. It has a canned-goods department, frozen-foods and meat departments, dry foods in small bins much like a normal produce department, a book-and-magazine rack, and a wall full of pharmacopoeia that would make a drugstore envious. Plus the hundreds of leashes, collars, toys, and other small accessories. Not to mention doghouses, cat beds, dog beds, kitty-litter pans—you name it, this shop has it. But nowhere conspicuous is a beauty department.

Before the bemused customer in a shop like this has a chance to ask, he's double-teamed. The proprietor gets him from one side, "need to fill out your lovely dog's record card," while from the other, an assistant grabs the dog. Before one knows what's happening, the dog is gone. Whisked out of sight through a door, to be groomed elsewhere. In the meantime, the customer is not just welcome to wait, it is virtually a condition. There may even be a free coffee machine on hand. Because a pet owner must have a soul of steel, a backbone of iron, and an absolutely barren wallet to stay in a pet shop for thirty minutes without finding at least one, two, or a dozen things to buy. And if nothing attracts him immediately, the proprietor will pull out the newest goodies he's got and push them. If the customer resists, he's a better man than I and a Superman among men.

If our heroic pet owner also had Superman's x-ray vision, he could see for himself the terrible conditions under which his dog is being trimmed. Although there is an occasional pet shop with a garage in the rear that can act as a grooming parlor, 99 percent of them make room in the basement for the groomer to work. There, surrounded by packing boxes, bags of food, and piles of merchandise, the groomer's got himself some sort of grooming table. Frequently, he's asked to use a packing crate with a nonslip mat stapled on top. Instead of a grooming post (looks like a hangman's tree), he has to use an old leather leash and hang it from one of the pipes overhead.

A portable laundry tub or a kitchen sink from the Salvation Army must do for the bathing of every size breed. The first is too deep, the second too shallow, and both are terribly inadequate. As for the lighting, a couple of bare 100-watt bulbs with pull-chains are good enough for the owner to find the merchandise he needs, so they ought to be good enough for the groomer. After all, on a dog there's nothing to read.

"It was awful," said one groomer who worked at such a place. "The place smelled of mildew and wet dog hair. I couldn't take it. I quit after two days."

And what groomer worth the title wouldn't? So, one can imagine what type of expertise that assistant has who is currently working under those same conditions on our man's dog. Is it surprising that what comes out of that door, some thirty minutes later, is not exactly what the pet owner might have expected?

I was once confronted with a four-legged, hairy-headed sausage. It's true. I swear it. And the only reason they left the hair on his head was King's temper. He must have put up a fuss when they came near his head. Something else he had that I didn't know about: modesty. When I got him home, he spent the next three months hiding under sofas and tables waiting for the hair to grow out. Unfortunately, it itched. He scratched. Result—more than one vet bill. And we learned something else from this trimming—dogs get sunburned. Even poodles who are used to being shaved down to the skin should be kept out of the sun for any long period of time.

Another type of groomer is also an enterprising individual, only she hasn't gone after the work. It's come to her, and she's glad to accept it. This type of groomer is found through the well-meaning efforts of a friend who heard about her from a friend. This is because the individual doesn't advertise. She can't. She's working out of her house and doesn't want to get into trouble with the authorities. Zoning, you know. Besides there's the small matter of not having a mercantile license. Or what about Uncle Sam? Maybe she isn't reporting her income to him. After all, "it's only a hobby, to help pay for the dog food and cover the real estate taxes."

Anyway, in the morning, every morning of the week, there arrives a small but steady stream of poodles. Mostly miniatures and toys, "the standards take too much work." And occasionally one will see a bichon, a cocker, a bedlington, or a terrier. In the evening, every evening of the week, there leaves another steady stream of the cleanest, sweetest-smelling, most adorable poodles you've ever seen. But this is never the case with a bichon, cocker, or terrier. The Bedlington, for example, looks like a lamb, with its sparse but cute topknot. He should. He's been given a poodle lamb-cut. Just as all the other dogs have been given a poodle cut of some type or description. That's because the only book on grooming this small-scale groomer has is the one she needs most, a book on poodles.

Actually, all these examples are rather innocuous compared to the things that have happened to dogs in the hands of inept groomers. Some of whom have, for example, been known to cut off the tip of a dog's tongue (another did the whole job). Still another turned out a dog with one pointed ear and one half ear. Hanging a dog? That doesn't take much doing. Just fasten the noose around his neck and turn your back. Before you can shout "Down," you have one dog dangling. Turn around fast enough and no real damage is done. Not so with the groomer who did the incomplete castration of one of his clients' animals. It took a vet to finish the job.

Of course, accidents will happen; for one thing, dogs don't like clippers—they tickle. What dogs don't like, they have a tendency to bite. Nipso fasto, one cut tongue (that's why you'll find sugar in many a grooming establishment; old-timers swear it clots the blood faster than anything else). As for toenails cut too short, that can happen at any time, especially on dogs with black nails where it's hard to see the beginning of the quick.

Clipper burns are another story. They, too, happen with great frequency, but the cause is the groomer's carelessness in using the clipper for too long without allowing it to cool off now and then. A clipper

GROOMING 93

burn, with its redness, should not be confused with a clipper rash of pimples; the latter is caused by sensitive skin, not an insensitive groomer.

Although carelessness is certainly one cause of these accidents,

*The New York Times/Neal Boenzi*
This poodle, and 2½ million of his fellows, needs trimming about eight times a year at a minimum of $12 each trip, which doesn't include such extras as ribbons or choice of nail polish.

hastiness is still another. In grooming, time is money. The more dogs done in a day, the more money made. Which is why very few groomers will do anything but a pet trim. A show trim requires a great deal of time-consuming handwork and combing. A pet trim goes zip, zip, with the clippers buzzing all but the final few minutes.

But more accidents can be attributed to inexperience than anything. Inexperience in terms of knowing dogs and how to handle them and of knowing step one about how to trim. All it takes to become a trimmer, after all, is a pair of scissors and a set of clippers—both of which can be purchased cheaply through the discount animal-supply houses previously mentioned. Unlike hairdressers, pet groomers are not licensed by any state in the country. However, dog-grooming professional organizations in Pennsylvania, California, Illinois, and other states have tried and are trying to get such licensing legislation passed. Most bills have been laughed off the legislative floor.

Not only do they not need to be licensed or go through union-type apprentice systems, a groomer doesn't even have to take a single lesson in grooming to become one. And the vast majority never have. What many have done is to take a correspondence course. Would you want the graduate of a correspondence course to give you a perm, frost your hair, or even cut it? Neither would I. And I certainly don't like the idea of one of them practicing on my pet either. Besides, although I've investigated many of these courses, I have as yet to find one that sounds worth taking. In fact, as far as I can determine, it's the schools that do the taking and the students who get took. One school, for example, advertises that you can "Learn dog grooming at home in five days for $30." The course includes three long-playing records, a picture album, and a "Business Opportunity Section with an A to Z explanation of the dog-grooming business."

Another school proudly boasts that the owner "Founded the first home-study school of dog grooming in the country." Here's how his plan worked. In return for $195, you got a book and a price list for buying his equipment. If you were smart enough not to pay $195 for a book, you'd get a follow-up letter offering you the same course plus "a Free Offer of a Pet Grooming Kit (a $23.95 value) . . . for the novice." Note the "novice." It's your tip-off. This kit is of no use to a professional groomer and would have to be replaced almost immediately by anyone taking the course. Now, if the free offer didn't get you, there would be this follow-up offer: "After consulting with the printers, we have worked out a plan which we hope will bring our course within the reach of everyone. We have slashed the tuition from $195 to $95, a saving of $100." In addition, the free offer of the novice's useless grooming kit would still be honored. And still another incentive is offered: If you pay cash for that book and the price list, they'll knock another $20 off the tuition, bringing it down to $75 (subtract from that the kit's value, of course), or $50 all told.

Obviously, the cash plan was a good idea from their point of view, since most people don't cotton lightly to paying $95 for a book—a skimpy one at that—dealing only with poodles. Too many, upon receiving the book, decide not to pay the rest of the installments on the plan. (The newer, more sophisticated home-study courses allow you to use Mastercharge or BankAmericard—another way to be sure they're paid before they send out the "materials.")

It is interesting to note that the founder of the first home-study school of dog grooming decided about five years ago to notify potential applicants that "We have come to the conclusion, after long experience, that this art and craft cannot be taught through correspondence. There is nothing that can take the place of a live dog for the purposes same individual heads a school that offers a "home study (Poodle same individual now heads a school that offers a "home study (Poodle Grooming) course." Ah, yes, history doth repeat itself when the profit potential is there.

As to on-the-spot residential courses, these include the Michigan Grooming School's $295-course that guarantees "in five days you can trim professionally, providing you are ambitious to earn an excellent income." These people are evidently disciples or former pupils of the founder of the home-study school, because they, too, state: "We believe that the art of Dog Grooming cannot be taught successfully by correspondence. There is nothing that can take the place of a live dog for purposes of instruction, correction, and practice while under the constant supervision of an instructor."

Another school, the Western Vocational School of Dog Grooming, offers a 12-week resident course for $200 but states that $750 is the actual cost of training to them. The difference is paid for by the owners of dogs groomed by the students during their training. Since each student can be expected to groom over 125 dogs during the course, the dog owners should be getting this service for $4.40 each, which is quite a bargain when you consider that the national average is $12 per grooming. Another way of looking at this is that the dog-grooming school is getting the services of a free groomer for every 125 dogs they do (in fact, the student is paying for the privilege of working for free).

Back on the East Coast, another resident course costs $725 for four weeks, $1,250 for eight weeks, and $1,850 for 12 weeks. All this to learn pet grooming—not show grooming. The first courses prepare a student only for poodles and terriers; the second course, which is the basic course plus 150 more hours of instruction, gets into other long-haired breeds; the third, which includes the basic and intermediate course, spends an additional 150 hours on retail management. The school, which at this writing is the only one accredited by the National Association of Trade and Technical Schools, is one of the few to actually break down its course into number of hours spent per subject. To the dedicated breeder, it is probably disheartening to discover that out of the 450 hours in the complete course, only one hour is spent on the poodle breed standard, while seven hours are available for learning how to make bows for poodles and long-haired dogs. The owner of the school explains the apparent discrepancy by noting that the seven hours are actually quite elastic (no pun intended) and designed to enable the instructors to devote extra time to teaching and reteaching skills in which the student has not proved proficient. You must remember that unlike other schools, these do not try to weed the bad students from the good—their aim is to graduate everybody.

Even so, the number of school graduates (whether correspondence or resident) in the total pet-grooming profession is minimal. The New York School of Dog Grooming estimates that in its fourteen-year history, it has graduated fewer than 3,000 students—not enough to cover the normal annual attrition within the profession.

No one knows for sure how many groomers there are actually at work these days. Tommy Barnes of the NDGAA thinks 25,000 to 30,000 would be accurate. Sam Kohl of the New York School of Dog Grooming estimates 20,000 to 25,000 would be tops. In any case *Pets/Supplies/Marketing*, in a recent issue, reported sales of $225,000,000 for grooming services in 1973 from *retail* outlets alone (there are between 10,000 and 20,000 grooming parlors or retail outlets in the U.S.).

All of which adds up to the fact that the groomers of America have us by the proverbial short hairs. We need them more than they need us. Or, rather, our pets do. Consider poodles, the love of the grooming profession (but only in the small and medium sizes; the large ones take too much work). There are, in this country, conservatively speaking, more than 2½ million poodles who will need trimming every six to eight weeks, or approximately eight times a year. Since the average groomer's top capability is eight dogs a day, it would take the services of 8,654 groomers working full-time at top speed to trim only the poodles.

But poodles are only one of the 104 most common breeds of dog that need grooming; 38 of these need the services of a professional, and I don't mean a correspondence-school graduate, much less a dropout. I mean someone who doesn't simply snip with his scissors and zip with his clippers. Ever see a yellow Irish setter? You will when a rank amateur groomer gets through with him. (Only the top coat's red—underneath, the coat is yellow. Trim the top too closely, and you expose the bottom.)

Not only that, different breeds need different treatment. For example, the Boston terrier and Pekingese both must be handled gently around the head, and the skin there must never be stretched; otherwise, their eyes pop out. The Italian greyhound, which is a love, must be watched like a hawk and held as carefully but completely as a chick. Otherwise, if it jumps to the floor, it could break every bone in its body. If the mats on a Maltese are pulled out instead of combed out, inches of skin will come with them.

In order to get some breeds groomed at all, their owners will have little choice in groomers and pay through the nose to boot. The Afghan, for instance, has a skin like a chicken, tears easily, and needs to be groomed at home, not in the shop. The Irish wolfhound takes two people to help it into the tub (and then only if it cooperates) as do the mastiff and the St. Bernard. You have to wash the komondor and corded puli like you wash a sweater, squeezing the cords to get the water and soap to penetrate, then repeating and repeating to get the soap out. (Fortunately, the cords are self-styled and need no combing and braiding.) The giant schnauzer is a "giant-sized problem that no groomer in his right mind needs," says one grooming authority who is admittedly prejudiced about the dogs she grooms. Pomeranians, she says, are "smart, but feisty little bastards." And as for the lhasa apso, "they're nasty bastards, mean as sin and as quick to bite."

But of them all, the owners of one breed have the most problems—and those are the proud, proud owners of the bobtail, or old English sheepdog. If one of these gets out in the rain or is thrown in a pool, it can take a full day to comb it out. And those that aren't touched between visits to the groomers can cost their owners a bundle, since sometimes it will take two full days to get those dogs back into condition. A sampling of the charges: $150 by a woman in the Bronx, $200 by a groomer in New Jersey, $300 in Connecticut.

The old English sheepdog owner's search for a groomer, though, is nothing compared to that of the owner of a cat—even one who simply wants her pet bathed. And no wonder: it takes two people suitably dressed, preferably in armor plate, to do it. Cats damn well better keep themselves clean because groomers aren't about to do it. Nor do they take kindly to simply combing the cats out, which I find surprising because every one of mine goes absolutely limp as a rag at the sight of a comb or brush. Be that as it may, most groomers do not like to do cats. About the only way one may be able to get a cat groomed is to go out and buy a dog that will require frequent groomings, such as the Skye terrier, which needs one monthly. When faced with the prospect of that revenue, the groomer may reluctantly allow the cat to piggyback in. But don't count on it. Not unless you're willing to pay twice what you would for a dog.

Speaking of prices, the shop of the good old grooming à la George that charges one price for all breeds is a good deal for someone with a hard-to-groom breed such as a poodle or Maltese. But not necessarily for a breed like a Japanese toy spaniel or beagle, which requires little or no work. The idea here is that the groomer, in attempting to be competitive, undercharges for the time-taking breeds and overcharges for the easy ones. Although everything evens out for him, the poodle owner is getting a break while others are getting taken.

Prices are highest in New York—$25 and up for a pet trim—and near metropolitan areas. The further you go into the suburbs and rural areas, the lower the prices, with $12 a national average. The exception to this rule is the state of California, where prices are lower than would be expected. Why? No one seems to know for sure. Maybe it's weather, or population, or the Hollywood influence.

But not all prices include the same things. For example, some groomers with makeshift facilities (or the in-home ones with inadequate ones) have a "you bathe, I'll groom" policy, perhaps taking a dollar off their price. Which sounds fine except that knowledgeable groomers will insist that the dog be combed and dematted *before* bathing and trimming. And this combing and dematting is the time-consuming drudgery that every groomer would like to avoid. With other groomers, the price doesn't include what they deem hazardous-duty pay. Translated into dollars and sense and everyday language, this frequently works out to $5 per bite and $2 per scratch extra. Of course, there is no discount if they cut your dog—or. bite it, for that matter. Then there's the matter of hours. In order to get your dog trimmed, you may have to patronize a boarding kennel with evening hours. You bring the dog in one night, pick him up the next, and pay a two-day boarding bill on top of everything else.

You can imagine why working people treasure such customer-oriented shops as Poodle Perfect in Arcadia, California, and Sharon's Poodle Shoppe in Tulsa, Oklahoma, which don't stick to the traditional nine-to-five day. Robin Meason of Poodle Perfect has been known to start as early at 6:00 A.M., while the Glendenings, who own the Poodle Shoppe, have a regular opening hour of 7:00 A.M.

Not all of us can get to Arcadia or Tulsa regularly, but these shops can serve as models in our search for the right grooming establishment for our dogs. For one thing, they welcome a visit in person from a prospective client. However, they prefer you to call first and make an appointment. Although an impromptu caller won't be turned away, he may get short shrift if it's just his luck that that's the day when the groomer or shop is overworked or undermanned. In any event, the conversation won't be long since the groomer's time is money. If he spends forty-five minutes with a prospect, he's lost the money he could have made doing a pet miniature poodle. However, visitors are free to look around for themselves.

What to look for? That's easy. Begin with the pets. Are they standing there dejected and droopy looking? Maybe they're tranquilized. Are they shaking with fear? Then they've had a bad grooming experience somewhere, maybe here. Are they pulled up high by a noose around the neck? They shouldn't be—the noose is to prevent the animal from jumping down, not from moving around at all. Are the dogs muzzled? Then don't bring your dog here. Are the cats purring, the dogs alert looking, even wagging their tails? They should be—the vast majority of pets love to be groomed. It's a sensuous experience for them.

If the groomer prefers not to tie the dog to the grooming post as a precaution against the dog hanging himself, then other precautions have to be taken to insure that the dog can't jump down and slip through an outside door when another customer enters. The usual solution? A safety gate between the grooming area and the outside door. Is the place clean? Of course there may be hair on the floor; expect it, but check to see if the coat colors match the dogs being groomed. If not, then this place's housekeeping is off.

What of the equipment? Is it professional and adequate. The clippers should be heavy-duty dog clippers, not home-barbering ones. There should be thinning shears and curved-end trimming shears (for use on the face) as well as the regular pointed ones. At least two combs should be in evidence—one medium, the other fine-toothed—and the same number of brushes, one a pin brush, the other a slicker brush. A look at the dryer can tell you much about the operation. The use of cage dryers exclusively tells you that your dog won't be fluff-dried; however, the use of a free-standing heavy-duty dryer tells you that this groomer has invested money in getting the right tools. (Such a dryer costs $225 or more.) Although fluff-drying, like blow-drying of your own hair, is preferable, it's time consuming, and many shops or one-man establishments just can't do it. In which case some arrangement must be made in the crates to prevent the dog from lying in pools of water after having been bathed. Some crates have made-to-measure slatted wooden bottoms. Others rely on towels. Speaking of crates, are they flimsy? Or do they have doohickey locks that might not catch properly or be forced open? If you've ever had your dog force his way out a door when you were trying to hold him in, you know how important proper locks can be to his safety.

Finally, look around for some charts. Although a groomer with many years of experience won't need such charts to do the work, he should have something available to check against in case the customer wants some esoteric clip that he might not know about. (For example, the Standard Poodle Clips chart, compiled by the National Dog Groomers Association of America and prepared courtesy of Hills Division, Riviana Foods, shows fifteen different poodle clips that together bear forty-nine names.) There is another reason for having these charts on hand; they are valuable for the owner of a new dog, who has no idea of what the dog will look like once he's trimmed.

Many people, faced with the ineptness, scarcity, and expense of groomers, choose to do their own thing. Why should you be any worse than the individual who's listened to three records and then gone into business? Even that $23.95 home-barbering kit will do just fine when it's called upon to do its job just every other month or so. Actually, if you'll just brush and comb your pet with some regularity, you could —with the exception of poodles—get away without trimming your pet more than two or three times a year: in the spring, when he blows (another doggerism), or sheds, his winter coat; in the fall, when he blows his summer coat and begins to grow in his heavier winter coat; and before the winter holidays, so he'll look nice for company.

If groomed frequently, poodles can go much longer between clippings. It should be pointed out that trimming is not a substitute for grooming. All the dead hair and mats that can be taken out at home with a little perseverance must otherwise be taken out at the grooming parlor. Trimming is the shaping of the coat by hand (known as stripping) with scissors and/or electric clippers. Grooming is the combing and brushing and bathing of the coat. Granted, it takes some training, or some trial-and-error, to do trimming, but grooming is another story. If you can take care of your own hair, you can adequately groom your pet's.

## DO-IT-YOURSELF GROOMING TIPS:

1. *Equipment:* Buy a grooming table or make one of plywood atop folding metal legs. Get a brush appropriate for your breed; avoid awkward-to-use two-sided ones. A hound glove or regular scrub

brush is fine for short-coated animals. Get two combs, a fine- and a medium-toothed one, but not a combination of both. Invest in nail scissors for cats and small dogs, nail clippers for large; but cut only after bathing, when the nails have softened. Rounded-end scissors are safest for cutting whiskers. Tangle-splitters are lifesavers for owners of long-haired dogs and cats, but they should be handled carefully.
2. *Technique:* Brush, then comb with medium comb, then fine comb. Do any dematting necessary. Then bathe. Put a gob of steel wool in the bathtub or sink drain to catch dead hairs. Use a rubber shower mat to prevent slipping. A drop of mineral oil in each eye prevents soap irritation. Towel dry. Or use a hair dryer. Clip nails, scissor whiskers, comb out. Keep the animal indoors and out of drafts until completely dry.

# VIII  BOARDING

> A deluxe suite with balcony, circular stairway, chandelier,
> and photos on the wall
>
> Description of cat accommodations in Dallas, Texas

That deluxe suite with the chandelier goes for $25 per day, single occupancy. The canine version of a "poochie penthouse," complete with fake fireplace, four-poster bed, and a lead-us-into-temptation old shoe, also brings in $25 a day to the owner who invested $300,000 in his boarding facility. That's nothing compared to the former industrial engineer for General Motors who built himself a $900,000 pet motel that grosses more than $350,000 a year, 95 percent from boarding, the rest from grooming and sales. There is no animal that he can't accommodate. Included within the complex is a kennel, cattery, aquarium, aviary, serpentarium, simian salon, stable, and an "exotic empery," a fancy name for a catch-all that takes whatever doesn't fit anywhere else. And that's not all, this man hasn't missed a trick; he offers dog owners a senior-citizens' home, a day-care center, a summer-camp program, and a maternity ward. People should have it so good.

Of course, the prototype for this and all other "pet motels" is Aranwood, in Mahwah, New Jersey. Started by Arthur and Ann Sachs, who had never found a boarding facility that they would choose to leave their own dogs in, this kennel was, according to the owner, "created to duplicate as nearly as possible the home situation." To accomplish this, "each room has been designed in an esthetic color scheme, with appointments to match, including a full floor carpet and separate cathedral, sky-lighted ceiling." Moreover, the attendants wear Spanish-gold uniforms, embellished with Aranwood's motto: "Singulare Ministerium." Although the owners acknowledge that all this color is wasted on the canine guests, who are born color-blind, it makes a

Large, spacious outdoor runs with resting platforms and overhead protection from sun and rain are part of the service at Aranwood, a deluxe boarding kennel in Mahwah, New Jersey.

fantastic impression on visitors. Especially when, at registration time, over coffee, tea, or sherry, they must choose between two plans.

The all-inclusive Personal Services Plan costs $8.50 to $21.50 a day, depending on choice of room. For this, the dog is fed whatever he eats at home—even if it's table scraps, which Aranwood cooks up specially for him—and whenever he would normally eat, whether that be once, twice, or thrice a day. He is also groomed. His room is carpeted, and his bed has a 3-inch thick mattress. And once a day, he has the exclusive use of a one-acre fenced-in paddock for running, frolicking, and exercising. However, with only four such paddocks available for forty-eight guests, his paddock time is obviously limited. The Economy Plan, at $1.50 less per day, cuts out all the grooming, outdoor exercising, and choice of menu. Not surprisingly, less than 1 percent of the clientele opt for the economy rate.

In spite of these rates, Aranwood's forty-eight rooms (two more are kept as isolation wards in case of illness) are usually booked eighteen months in advance, with clients coming from Europe, South America,

Canada, Sweden, and the Far East. The cat owner has a better chance of getting to use Aranwood's Catarama without a lengthy stay on the waiting list. This is because cats are not confined to cages but are allowed to run loose in a large enclosed indoor area. Thus, there is more flexibility in the number that Aranwood can take; but there is no flexibility at all when it comes to sex. Only she's and it's allowed; no he's admitted.

Recognizing a profitable thing when they see one (the Sachses refuse to give out any income figures other than to say, "Yes, boarding is profitable, *very* profitable"), many entrepreneurs have approached Aranwood about franchising the operation. Unfortunately for them—fortunately for dogs—the Sachses refuse on the grounds that there is no way to duplicate the personal approach that has brought Aranwood worldwide publicity in magazines, newspapers, and television.

When it comes to making money, though, some people just won't take no for an answer. Thus, they, too, have taken tips from the people-accommodation people and opened their own versions of Aranwood. All of these have much in common. For example, they don't call themselves boarding kennels, they're "pet motels" or "pet hotels." Their business is "animal hostelry" or "the hospitality end of the pet industry." And they prefer hotel terminology as euphemisms for their pens, cages, and runs. A 20-square-foot enclosure (4 by 5) is a "room," "efficiency apartment," or "suite." Slightly larger enclosures are known as "family quarters," "deluxe suites," or "family suites"; in the more expensive places, each suite is given its own name.

The outdoor runs are "exercise areas," "private 'gymnasiums," or "recreation facilities." If they are communal or larger than the usual rectangular chain-link-fencing-enclosed area, they are known as "dog parks" or "paddocks." Now if the owner has decided to double his capacity by stacking his pens in two tiers, one above the other, the runs are also stacked. The upper one, which extends only a few feet into and over the lower one, is known as a "porch," "balcony," or "patio," depending on the whims of the owner and the price charged. The lower one also benefits prestige-wise from this arrangement, because now it is a "canopied terrace."

Rates are based on many variables, beginning with the accommodations chosen. But even for the same 20-square-foot bread-and-butter basic suite, the rate can vary as much as $3 a day, depending on the dog. Large dogs that eat more are charged more; old dogs that carry potential medical risks carry a higher fee, too; ferocious-looking dogs that scare personnel get the more ferocious rate.

On top of the different base charges, there are the various options. First, and foremost, the service plans. These differ greatly, especially in name. One kennel operator's regular plan is another's deluxe plan and another's economy package. The cost? Anywhere from $1 to $3 a day extra. The more enterprising and profit-seeking of these kennel operators prefer to go the a la carte route. Here, one is given the choice of a great many options and pays extra for *each*. Some kennel operators conveniently forget to inform their clients these are extras. So clients check off the features they'd like, naturally assuming they're included in the regular fee.

Pickup day becomes the day of reckoning, with bills running into the hundreds just for extras. And no payee, no doggie. (Some kennel operators charge the basic rate in advance to ensure payment of those extras later on.) Here are a few of those extras found on final bills throughout the country:

- playing ball with a person, daily/weekly
- playing Frisbee with a person (takes more space than ball playing, so costs accordingly more), daily/weekly
- being given medications
- liver sausage used in administering medications
- flea collars
- flea dips upon entering and leaving
- baths, weekly/occasional
- brushing, daily/weekly
- being allowed to use his own bedding
- being allowed to continue his regular diet
- being fed regular food supplied by you
- special diet because "dog wouldn't eat, was starving to death"
- feeding twice a day
- feeding more than twice a day
- feeding snacks
- feeding snacks supplied by you
- feeding teeth-cleaning snacks and/or bones
- being allowed to receive mail
- having mail read to the pet
- extra cleanup required
- housebreaking
- odedience training
- disobedient pet
- sickness (This includes veterinary charges, charges for transportation to and from vet, medication charges, plus giving of medications.)
- funeral charges (Not charged as such. Bill will read "autopsy," "death certificate," "crematory charges," "medical expenses," as above. The owner will also be expected to pay the board bill. Naturally, if the death was not the result of natural causes, there will be no autopsy, no death certificate, only the crematory expense—if that. In any event, the kennel still expects to be paid the boarding charges.)

There are also charges for the special diets, baths, and walks the dog never had. Including a charge for private accommodations when the dog may actually have shared his pen with as many as five others. This is a common practice in the large kennels accommodating 350 to 500 dogs; they have to board three to six dogs a pen. One kennel operator, a very successful one, boards up to 150 dogs with only twenty-five available pens. A variation on this is the "boarder" who advertises facilities for 120 dogs. He has a basement full of crates and twenty runs. He rotates the dogs. Once a week, each gets a chance to sit in the sun, maybe.

All these kennels operate at full capacity because there is such a shortage of any kind of boarding space—regardless of whether it's good, bad, or indifferent—thanks to local zoning boards, who know there is nothing more nerve-racking than a barking dog unless it's a howling dog. Multiply that howler by a kennel-full, all off-key and out of sync, naturally, and you have din designed to drive the most dedicated dog lover—much less next-door neighbor—up a bedroom wall. And what neighbors don't like, zoning boards don't allow and community officials ban. When something becomes scarce, the prices go up, profit seekers move in, and the average pet owner is glad to pay Aranwood's admittedly high fees for a decent place for his dog to stay.

Or, for that matter, to leave their animals with one of the imitators. Although in business to make a buck, Aranwood's competitors have invested great sums of money to make their places as clean, sanitary, and comfortable as economically feasible. So what if the care of the dogs is entrusted to teen-agers or minimum-wage earners? So what if the owner needs a computer readout to tell him what dogs are on the premises? So what if this kennel is being used to teach kennel management to a bunch of franchisers? What other choices does a pet owner have?

Plenty, not all of which are as good or as bad as the above. There is in-home boarding for the dog, the advantages of which are readily apparent, the disadvantages less so. For example, there is no way of knowing how the dogs are treated. Since doing such boarding is illegal in most communities, the dogs may never go out of the house. In fact, they may not even have the run of the house but instead be confined to crates in the basement.

This is because the maximum number of strange dogs that can be allowed the freedom of the house without totally destroying themselves, much less the house, is five. Five dogs per day at $5 a day yields $9,000 a year. However, it doesn't take a genius to realize that increasing the number of dogs will proportionately increase the income. The obvious solution to the destruction problem is, of course, confinement, i.e., crates. The obvious place for the crates, the basement. Especially when one accumulates ten, twenty, thirty, or more of them. Which is easy to do when it becomes apparent that there's no trouble filling them. A two-line classified ad in any metropolitan newspaper—even 100 miles or more away—will keep the phone ringing all day. Often as a result you'll meet the little old lady with the one-bedroom bungalow who offers in-home boarding complete with home cooking for toy dogs at $3 to $5 a day. She's doing it, or so the story goes, to supplement her social security check; and yes, what she's doing is illegal, but without her "little visitors," she might be eating dog food instead of her own home cooking. Very convincing.

Unlike those fence-enclosed pet hotels with the institutionalized atmosphere you are trying to avoid, the average home offers dozens of opportunities and as many escape routes to a determined dog, which is the one characteristic that most boarders have in common. So, in this case, crating with in-home boarding is a damned-if-you-do, damned-if-you-don't situation. With crates, the dog doesn't escape, but then he isn't getting in-home boarding either.

Diametrically opposed to the homelike atmosphere of the in-home boarding establishment is the "country kennel." Taking advantage of the facts of life—that boarding kennels have to locate where the zoning is lax or nil and that means out in the boondocks—their operators tout the advantages of getting away from it all in the country. One brochure for a country kennel extolls the room service, "outdoor nature walks, a howling good nightlife, daily mail delivery as well as a happy hour at night." The capacity is 200 dogs, with rates varying, depending on breed, from $4 to $9 a day. One owner paid $105 for twelve sun-filled days, and eleven glorious nights for two in a double room—chargeable to American Express.

Basically, this kennel doesn't differ from Aranwood. It's on the up-and-up. The dogs can actually see the trees, bark at wildlife, loll in the sun, or doze in the shade. Not so the typical country kennel. It is enclosed with palisade fencing. The area within depends on man-made shelters for shade. There may be a main building complete with crates plus a few outdoor runs, or there may be dozens of little runs each with its own doghouse. The point is that the owner utilizes the space as economically as possible to accommodate as many dogs as possible, knowing full well as he does that none of his clients will ever see the place where their pet is boarded.

The operator establishes a drop-off point in a major suburban or metropolitan area where he picks up the dog to transport it to the kennel and then returns it on the day promised. This rendezvous could be at a vet's, but more likely it is at a grooming parlor, which he also operates. (In dogs, the profiteers work both sides of the street as often as possible.) The part of the operation the public sees—the pickup point—is where the money goes. Here you'll find the creative decor, the background music, the unusual wall decorations; the money is well spent, for the kennel operators know you'll judge the whole thing by its front.

Those without the money or connections to establish an urban pickup point are not stifled a bit. Using the cleverness and resourcefulness that all who smell a quick buck seem to have in unlimited quantities, the operator initiates a mobile pickup service. He rents or buys a van and picks up and delivers to your door. One such kennel operator offered to drive all the way down from upstate New York to pick up a pair of boarders in Philadelphia. An offer to drive them up to the kennel was turned aside politely but definitely, and a compromise was struck, involving the owner's taking her dogs to Kennedy Airport the day of her flight, where they would be picked up and taken to their country kennel. The one thing a country kennel operation can't afford is on-the-spot visitors, so there is frequently no charge for the pickup-and-delivery service. Which should serve as a tip-off for the wary.

The latest variation on the country-kennel operation is the summer camp for dogs. The first of these camps was the brainchild of a former record producer and dabbler in the commodities and securities market; he started this camp out of desperation when he needed a kennel for his own dogs, according to the *New York Times*. "I went around to all the kennels and saw a lot of lice and fleas and closed-in cages, and I thought, 'There must be some sort of alternative boarding'." Campo Lindo was it. The newspapers covered it in glowing detail: a picturesque, rented farm set a quarter of a mile off a winding mountain road; 75 acres of field and forest with a crystal-clear mountain stream tumbling through it; a pond for the camper's daily swims; no fences, dogs are kept on leashes; no crates, each camper has his own red doghouse, called a bunk. And then there was the program itself:

| | |
|---|---|
| 9:00 A.M. | feed and water campers |
| 9:30 A.M. | check all campers for fleas and ticks and give each a good scratching |
| 10:00 A.M. | exercise and play period, with group activities and training lessons |
| 11:00 A.M. | fresh water |
| Noon | swimming and group activities |
| 2:00 P.M. | rest period and fresh water |
| 4:00 P.M. | play period and training period |
| 5:00 P.M. | dinner and fresh water |
| 8:30 P.M. | bed check and fresh water |
| 11:30 P.M. | final inspection |

The special activities included, according to the owner, "treasure hunts," where the dogs searched for buried bones. And on Sundays, "we have a special barbecue where they are all fed hot dogs and hamburgers." The cost for all this fun and excitement, $40 a week or $150 a month, including door-to-door pickup and delivery in a white van. Special training lessons were extra ($100 a week for obedience training; $125 a week for protection training). For an extra $1 a day, a dog received what is known as "in-house" treatment. "That means the camper will sleep in the house at night, at the foot of a counselor's bed," explained the owner.

There were the Campo Lindo ads in the *New York Post:* "Send your dogs to camp. Seventy-five acres Upstate New York, swimming and other activities, no kennels, no cages, private accommodations for each dog. 430 feet of exercise space, 24-hour supervision. Basic and advanced training available. Pick up and delivery." The Harry Reasoner ABC-TV Show had a great little feature spot showing the waterfall, the fields, the personal attention by girl counselors, ad nausea.

Too good to be true? Just ask the woman from the Bronx who grieves over her "Mickey." Mickey was found dead from exposure and starvation many miles from where he was supposedly cavorting and camping under 24-hour supervision. A Manhattan resident, appalled by conditions at Campo Lindo's New York "headquarters," says it was actually a three-room apartment with "approximately ten dogs tied to various doorknobs and pieces of furniture around a small room. Animal defecation was everywhere." She told the Department of Consumer Affairs that her dog lost 20 percent of its weight in nine days at the camp.

Others contacted Gretchen Wyler, actress, special agent for the American Society for the Prevention of Cruelty to Animals, manager of the Warwick Animal Shelter in Warwick, New York, and vice president of the New York State Humane Association. She, in turn, visited the place, then wrote a five-page report to the New York City Department of Consumer Fraud. The report said, in part:

> In September of 1974 I visited both the original campsite in Arkville, N.Y., and the later established one in Margaretville, N.Y. At Arkville, there were no more than fifteen "coops," each with two sides and a roof, but no floor. A dog was on a rope in front of each coop, about twenty feet apart. [Remember—no kennels, no cages.] A caretaker said there were a couple of guys and gals who came and went, but that he never saw them take dogs for walks. There was a small fenced-in run for exercising and training.
>
> A visit to a local justice revealed that the operators of Campo Lindo had been evicted on a series of complaints from neighbors. The owner of the land said he had leased the campsite to Campo Lindo under lease stipulations which permitted the tenant to "keep and train two or more husky

## 110 THE PET PROFITEERS

dogs, properly enclosed and fenced." The lease covered only some ground adjacent to the two-bedroom log cabin, not the sixty-seven acres which were stretched to seventy-five for the Campo Lindo advertisements. What's more, the waterfall and stream supposedly used for swimming by the campers were not even on the property, but belonged to a neighbor.

At the Margaretville campsite, we counted thirty-eight dogs all tied to similar coops, all splintered, most leaking, and with no floors or bedding. There were thirty-three coops. A woman and her two daughters who were "helping out" said the Labor Day crowd had numbered seventy campers. [Remember—private accommodations.] There was no flea powder on hand. The exercise area had a collapsed fence. And the small house on the property contained two guitars, a hi-fi, and one dirty bed. The girls said they usually kept six or seven dogs in the house at night.

Fortunately, the *New York Times* and *New York Post* have now refused to run any more Campo Lindo ads. But have no fear, ye who wish to let your dogs experience camping next summer. Florida and California may soon have their own versions of Campo Lindo (these areas had contacted the camp owner about buying franchises). And another camp has been opened in New York state by a restaurateur—imagine the doggy bags he can bring home. He acknowledges that he's probably going to lose his shirt ("nobody makes money off it"), but he

*The New York Times*
These young girls were counselors at Campo Lindo, a supposedly pastoral country summer camp for dogs in upstate New York.

is willing to try to be the exception. At his rates, it's going to cost us the coats off our backs: $40 a week (less $2 a day for any days under that, which works out to $20 a weekend) and $5 a day over seven days, or about $160 a month. The pickup and delivery is free, of course, even 400 miles away.

Most people will settle for something less exotic, just so it's closer to home, i.e., the local vet's. Which could be absolutely the worst place to go. After all, would you choose a hospital ward as the ideal place to spend a healthy vacation? Well, that's what you face when you board an animal at the vet's. Certainly, some vets isolate the boarders from the patients, but the same personnel will feed, groom, walk, and clean up after both. Many vets, especially those most desperate for income, such as the newly graduated ones, simply don't have the facilities to do a truly good job of isolating the well from the sick. Then, too, these are the vets most apt to hospitalize every sick animal—especially those too sick to be safe company for other animals—because they desperately need the revenue.

Generally speaking, the vet who needs to augment his income from boarding is not making the money he should rightfully be making from his medical practice. However, like everything else, there are exceptions. For example, there's the vet who decides at midcareer to switch from a small-animal practice to something else. Perhaps he begins manufacturing remedies; or decides to go into animal-control and -enforcement work or head up the local shelter; or simply opts for a different type of practice, such as an equine one. Whatever his reason, the fact remains that his kennel space would go to waste unless he converted his veterinary hospital into a boarding kennel and hired help to run it. (One vet who did so discovered he'd made more from boarding that year than he had from his career.)

Of course, once the vet is not actively practicing, the supposed advantages of boarding with a vet disappear. No longer is quick medical treatment available. No longer is the dog or cat daily inspected by a trained medical eye. No longer will you get medications administered for the cost of the drug itself. Without the practicing vet, this is just another boarding kennel, subject to the same abuses as any other.

Another expert dog person who often takes in boarding customers is the professional dog handler. Ideally, he will have the best facilities to keep dogs in top show condition—he will be able to do an expert grooming job, and he will feed, exercise, and medicate. But the ideal and real seldom coexist. In reality, at the professional handler's, the show dogs come first, boarders a poor second. Which is to be expected; the show dog brings in the big money weekend after weekend, and many stay with the handler all year round. Then, too, the handler's time must be devoted to training, grooming, and conditioning his show dogs; thus grooming of pets will be done either by an assistant or as quickly as possible, using all the shortcuts the pro knows. There are two other disadvantages inherent in boarding with a professional handler. First, most rely a great deal on crating since under normal circumstances a show dog must be accustomed to and spend a great deal of time in his crate. Second, the nature of his business dictates that the professional handler be gone from the premises usually two days a week and sometimes, when following a show circuit, for a week or two on end.

Then again, there are special advantages. For one thing, the kennel must be kept in top-notch shape in case show clients come to call. Also, the health of the show dogs must be protected zealously, which means your dog will get the same close attention.

Still another source of boarding is the serious breeder, perhaps at the kennel from which the dog came. Many such breeders are more than eager to have the chance to see pups they've sold when fully mature. This is the very best way for them to check, first, on their breeding program, and second, on their ability to grade a litter.

At serious-breeding kennels, not puppy mills, every dog gets the same food and accommodations as the breeder's show and brood stock. With the breeder's own dogs' health at stake, he has a bigger stake in the health of all dogs than do those who handle only transients. Since most serious breeders couldn't stay in business without becoming alert to the first sign of a major illness, every dog will be watched carefully. The first sniffle or sneeze or lack of appetite means extra watchfulness. Also, precautions, obviously, are taken to prevent escape or theft of any dog. All in all, this type of boarding kennel should be the very best bet; but beware, remember not all breeders are alike. Some have kennels filthier than the worst boarding kennel imaginable.

It behooves anyone to do some checking of any boarding situation. Perhaps getting references from former clients. Or talking with local vets. Checking to see if the kennel is either state or locally licensed. Best of all, look the place over and see whether you'd like to stay there yourself. If it's not clean enough for you, it's not clean enough for an animal. Above all else, find out who takes care of the dogs, whether he knows dogs, and if he has worked with them. See if he's sober, an adult or a child. One of the teen-agers who worked as a counselor at Campo Lindo said she had only one qualification for the job, "that I love dogs." That's not enough. Not if you, too, love dogs. Especially your own.

## BOARDING-KENNEL TIPS:

1. *What to look for:* clean water or special waterers. No smell, but urine odor is better than disinfectant. Clean runs; one or more may have feces in them, but not all. Something—boxes, boards, shelves—to allow the dog to get up off the floor. Shade, or escape from the sun via indoor/outdoor runs. An isolation area for sick dogs. Adequate ventilation or air-conditioning for summer, heat in winter. Dogproof latches. Extra gates to prevent escape.
2. *Expect them to ask for:* the name of your vet in case the dog becomes ill. Proof of up-to-date inoculations for distemper-hepatitis-leptospirosis. Your own references or identification, an unfortunate necessity caused by those who bring their dogs or cats to board and abandon them.

# IX  BASIC TRAINING

> They spent more than three hours with that dumb poodle puppy and it still can't perform any tricks, so they are going to "get rid of it" and now want to try my breed because they heard they are smarter. Or the Yorkshire terrier that sheds so many hairs; they tried for a year to teach it not to jump up on the sofa, which it had been permitted to do for five years while it was not shedding as much as in its old age. Oh, they hadn't thought of what they would be doing exactly with the Yorkshire. Well, if they don't find another home for it, they are just going to turn it loose where everybody else dumps cat and dog litters. But they would teach my pup from the beginning not to jump on the sofa.
> I took a bitch back this summer who had dared to pee on a Louis Quatorze sofa. I had to refund the money, or they would not bring her back all the way from Maryland, but would rather have her put to sleep by the vet. I had two veterinary references for these people. The one vet told me they were better than 95 percent of all dog owners; the other said they were "absolutely marvelous people." As long as the dog does not pee on a Louis Quatorze sofa. Well, I don't teach my pups the value of antique furniture.
>
> A BREEDER

Buying a pet is easy. It's the training that's hard. Which is why so many pet owners who happen to like their furniture and love their carpeting are now turning to professional help. Wherever they turn, they'll find helpful hands: those of in-home instructors, group leaders, private teachers, or boarding-school heads. The determined do-it-yourselfer will be led by the hand through a maze of training manuals and armed with electronic devices. There are even brand-new helpers: canine psychologists, also known as behavior modificationists.

(They have also been known to refer to themselves as Pet Owner Effectiveness Trainers.) Their new technique is habit breaking, not to be confused with obedience training, which is habit creating. In one sense, obedience training could be considered positive action, in that it teaches a dog new commands. Behavior modification is negative, in that it attempts to undo what has already been done.

The canine psychologist draws most of his clientele from pet owners attempting to cope with their first or second pet, because the seasoned pet owner learns eventually that the easiest way to break a habit is to never let it begin. The next simplest is to scotch it the first time it happens, provided you catch the culprit in the act. But if you're too late, the best use of one's time and energy is in attempting to prevent a duplication of the feat; trying to punish the perpetrator is only self-defeating.

However, like a new pet, a new pet owner has to learn the hard way. And when he's at the end of his tether, when he can no longer face coming home night after night to a pile in the middle of his bed, the canine psychologists come to the rescue. Not only will they cure a dog of that, they'll take on the jumper who can clear entire families at a single bound; the four-legged termite that's finished with the furniture and is taking on the walls; the moocher who makes eating a one-for-you, one-for-me affair; the furniture climber on a continual migration from chair to chair, cushion to cushion, shedding everywhere; the barker who is working on an eviction notice; the runaway who specializes in doing it whenever his master's in a hurry; the sneak thief who could give shoplifters lessons at pilfering items under his master's eye; the nipper who's losing his puppy teeth and—ouch!—the new ones really hurt; and the schizophrenic who only needs to see a leash to think he's a Clydesdale and you're the Anheuser-Busch Budweiser wagon.

Have no fear, just lots of money; the canine psychologists pride themselves on correcting and rehabilitating the problem dog. Pet owners seem to like the idea. So much so that one would have to say this is the "in thing" in dog training. It's being franchised across the country. In 1975 it took $45,000 minimum per franchise, which entitled the franchisee to use the company's name and sales pitch and, if necessary, to avail himself of up to three months of "instruction" at a training "college" on Long Island. In return, the franchisee is assured that his employees will bring in $10,000 to $15,000 a year minimum for simple training, while more difficult training, which requires a training consultant, can add another $15,000–$25,000. The whole operation can be run out of the franchisee's home, at least at the beginning, because the problems that bug owners the most occur in the home, so the canine psychologist does his work there. At the scene of the crime, so to speak. Unfortunately, getting the animal to repeat his crime while the canine psychologist (I'll call him the C.P.) is present is a problem every C.P. faces. An "untrainable" dog always seems to have at least one consistent trait: never, never does it misbehave when anyone is within sight or hearing. Of course, if we could get the dog to misbehave on command, we could train him ourselves.

What the C.P. gets paid for, at an hourly rate, is tricking the dog into doing what it shouldn't do—*when* the C.P. *wants* the dog to do it. Example: He sticks a paper match, tip end up, in the anus to induce a bowel movement. Or he smears a forbidden object with a piece of partially cooked liver to induce chewing. Or he hides bait under the sofa cushions to induce climbing. Of course, once the dog has been tricked into doing what he shouldn't, the trainer may be able to correct him. Then again, he may not. Or the correction may not stick.

The C.P. is a rarity on the dog-training scene. In-home obedience trainers are not. They, too, come to the problems rather than having the problem child brought to them. Obedience training will effectively solve four of those ten basic crimes—pulling on the lead, running away, jumping up, and begging—and the use of obedience commands can help cut down on three others: climbing on furniture, stealing off counters, and chewing. As to housebreaking, well, we're all on our own there.

In-home obedience training has a lot of things going for it as far as both the pet owner and instructor are concerned. For one thing, it appeals to the lazy streak we all have. There's no going out into the rain or rushing crosstown to keep the appointment. The instructor does all that. But that's only fair since the pet owner pays for travel time, expenses, and instructions. The instructor often has no overhead other than a telephone (in his home usually) and perhaps an answering service, which is sometimes free in the form of a wife or husband.

The disadvantage to the pet owner, besides the exorbitant cost of up to $50 a lesson including travel time and expenses, is that there is a natural tendency for an owner to absolve himself of responsibility saying, "Okay, you're in my home, I'm paying you, now do the training." Which the instructor can do. For one thing, it is easy for a stranger, especially a half-way competent trainer, to train a dog to obey. The trick is to train a dog to obey his master, which takes expertise that many in-home instructors simply don't have. What they do have is the gall to suggest that if the pet owner can't get his pet to obey, more lessons are needed. Sort of a "refresher course." At that point, all that's done is to start all over with Lesson #1, but with the owner as the pupil. One instructor who pulls this off regularly claims he got a whole year's worth of weekly lessons out of one lady and could have had more if the dog hadn't been hit by a car.

At the other end of the obedience spectrum is the group lesson. Also known facetiously as group therapy. But the similarities are quite obvious. With both, a group gets together to discover the commonality of their mutual problems. Dog owners quickly discover that problems come in all sizes, shapes, colors, and breeds. Held usually at night and in a rented hall, the lessons last an hour or so and take place weekly for eight to ten weeks. The dogs are taught basic commands: sit, stay, come, heel, down, and (optional) stand, plus the magic word *no*. The cost can be anywhere from $15 to $35—the latter charged by the profiteers, the former by a humane society or other dedicated group.

Ideally, the class is limited to twelve dogs—the most the average instructor can handle with any degree of efficiency. In actuality, many classes will contain as many as sixty dog-owner teams attempting to master the fundamentals under the eye of a whirling dervish known as the instructor. It should be pointed out that the instructor need not be licensed nor have attended an obedience-training school nor have apprenticed under another instructor nor have even trained a dog before. All he needs is to have access to a hall and to place a classified ad in the local newspaper.

It should also be noted that overbooking of a class is done deliberately to compensate for and take advantage of the high drop-out rate common to group lessons, which can be as high as 70 percent. The reasons for it are many, but the most common lies in the psyche of Americans who expect the same results with their dogs' training lessons as with automobile repairs: 24-hour service. In addition, group lessons seem reasonable in terms of cost, which leads people to abandon them quickly if they don't work. In actuality, on an hourly basis, these lessons are quite expensive. For example, in a class of twelve, each pupil can expect to get about five minutes of the instructor's time, individually, per lesson. At $20 for eight lessons, or forty minutes of individual instruction, this is the same as paying the instructor a rate of $30 an hour ($25 for ten lessons works out to be the same). The student in a class of sixty? At $20 for eight lessons, he'll get eight minutes of individual instruction, for which he will have paid at the rate of $150 an hour.

There is absolutely no guarantee that the dog will be any more obedient at the end of all those lessons than when first signed up. You see, the pet owner is the one training the dog. That's the whole idea behind group lessons. First, he has to master the method. Then, he has to parade around in a circle for an hour administering the commands. Finally, he has to devote at least thirty minutes a day in ten-

or fifteen-minute segments to practicing. Otherwise, that dog is not going to be trained, and the pet owner is at fault.

In addition, the instructor has to proceed at a specific pace in order to work in all the commands during the time allotted. If a puppy is more interested in playing, he'll be left behind. If it's an old dog who can't be taught new tricks, given enough time, he too will be left behind. If the dog is a natural, he'll be held back unless the instructor devotes more time to him at the expense of the others in the class, which sometimes happens because the instructor recognizes in this one a candidate for advanced classes.

Furthermore, with a large group—anything over fifteen—the instructor's first concern must be keeping order. One dog out of line can turn a class into chaos. Therefore, the instructor must be quick to intervene when trouble is sensed. And that intervention must be swift and certain. Some dog trainers take physical control of the dog, jerking him and sending him flying. Others throw something in the general direction of the dog. Whatever, the idea is to throw the dog off-balance physically or psychologically, "to show him who's master." The instantaneous effect is normally to restore order, although I've seen a dog turn and run, pulling the lead out of his master's grasp (was that havoc!). Unfortunately, the long-term effects on the reproved dog and its master can be disastrous. Some dogs cower; other refuse to comply when not on a lead; and others will never work in a group surrounding. One that I know of took a violent dislike to skirts. Fortunately, the owner loved pants suits.

There is one decided advantage of this method over all others: it does a great deal to foster "obedience work" in the competitive (show) sense. This because the dog and his master are already competing and have a chance to measure themselves and their potential against others. Which is why many all-breed clubs sponsor such classes.

The way to find a good, effective group class is through someone already in dogs, perhaps the breeder or a vet, or through the local police department, especially in communities that enforce leash laws. Or through the Yellow Pages, but not the classified section of the newspaper. The former can denote stability, the latter transience.

Many established obedience schools offer not only group lessons, but private instruction. The cost is about $75 to $125 for five or six lessons. This may sound pretty steep, but considering how little individual instruction you get in group lessons, it works out to a good buy. The lessons will take half as long as group lessons, and a good instructor will in this time have completed the equivalent of two series of group lessons, taking you through subnovice and novice, or to the point where the dog not only comes, but assumes the proper heel posi-

*Mary Kay Hasseman/Pennsylvania SPCA*
Many humane societies sponsor group classes in obedience for dogs adopted at their shelters, knowing that a well-trained dog is more apt to stay adopted. These dogs are doing a sit-stay as part of graduation exercises at the Pennsylvania SPCA in Philadelphia. Private instruction, although initially expensive, frequently proves to be the cheapest way to get a properly trained dog.

tion, at one's side, on the word "come." The instructor has a greater degree of responsibility in individual lessons than in a group situation, and since he has only the one dog/one owner to train, not 24 or 120, he will be hard put to find a valid excuse for failure. Since his time is his pupil's for that entire hour, one can consult him about other training problems, such as the dog's sneak thievery. Since you are laying out $75 to $125 for the course—many won't have paid that much to buy the dog—chances are you're going to see it through. Besides, with private lessons, one should see immediate results during and after the very first session.

Of course, all of these methods of training a dog have much in common. They cost money. They may not succeed. And they are only as good as the instructors. Fortunately, though, many of the older instructors around can boast of training dogs for the army, the coast guard, police corps, or something similar. (Until recently the military or semi-military was *the* source of good dog-training experience.) If not that, he should have attended a school that teaches a course in obedience instruction or else apprenticed under someone well known. Perhaps he has obtained some degree of excellence in obedience competition, and I don't mean a C.D. (Companion Dog, lowest degree possible) on a single dog. If he talks about his students' experiences rather than his own, take it all with a grain of salt. In obedience showing, the experience that counts comes from doing, not teaching.

The method with the worst instructors and almost a guarantee not to work has got to be doing it by the book. Correction. The worst method is listening to that electronic gimmick, the training tape cassette. Whether it costs $9.95, $19.95, or $2.95, it's a waste of money. If for no other reason than that it lacks the pictures and diagrams that books have. Or should have. Many don't. Many also do not take into consideration the breed of dog being trained—a catlike basenji is a far different problem than an eager Brittany—and that dogs within a breed may differ. And that mixed breeds may not follow traditional training patterns.

Most important of all, many books do not take into consideration the personality of the reader. If he's permissive or authoritarian. If he's not only able, but also willing, to follow the instructions given. For example, one well-known author takes it upon himself to cure the problem dog that digs holes all over the yard. The book's solution: Dig a pit large enough and deep enough to hold the dog with its head at approximately ground level. Fill this with water and keep the hose running while you submerge the dog in the water and push the head under for forty-five second intervals. In between, the dog is allowed up to gasp a breath. This treatment, when tried in an actual situation, not only cured the dog of digging holes, but got the owner in trouble with the law. A neighbor witnessed the procedure and had the owner hauled into court. Although the owner won his case, he lost a neighbor for a friend. And one has to wonder how easy it was after that to give the dog a bath.

Ah, those do-it-yourselfers. They have a tenacity that is above belief, as you may have noticed. Instead of conceding defeat and going for lessons, they will continue in their belief that it is cheaper to go by the book. Thus they will throw good money after bad and buy more books. Of course, during this time the dog is reveling in the attention, and maybe, if an owner is lucky, his dog will stop those bad habits previously used to gain attention. Just in case it doesn't, along comes a twentieth-century reincarnation of Torquemada who promptly sets about reinstituting the Spanish Inquisition, canine style and electronically. The cattle prods, throw chains, and spiked collars were mild compared to his most successful invention: the battery-operated training collar with a remote control. Of which there are many versions—all having two things in common: (1) they're not cheap, and (2) they don't work. Maybe for counterintelligence, but not for dog training.

For one thing, there's no way to predict how a dog will react when given a shock by the collar. Some freeze, seemingly paralyzed, taking long minutes to recover. Others go crazy—freaked out—some never to recover. Still others throw fits, biting themselves and anything nearby —the furniture, curtains, you name it. And still others aren't affected at all. Not one bit. They don't so much as shake their heads or look up or stop what they are doing for a second.

Experts who have experimented with these devices point out that timing is the major problem. It seems there is a $\frac{1}{16}$-second delay between the time the button on the remote control is pushed and the time the shock is administered. Unless one has split-second reflexes, the dog will receive his shock when he's doing something else. But if the collar is not working properly, and contact is not made, then there will be no shock, no correction at all. If the button jams, if the shock continues to be given, what then? Are you prepared to remove a collar from a crazed great Dane or Doberman pinscher?

Not only are these devices dangerous, they're expensive. One collar that is supposed to stop excessive barking, but nothing else, sells for $30. If you want a real electronic trainer, it's going to cost you money. The manufacturer promises that such trainers will save you money. "It can even make you money," one catalog states. "If you are a dog owner, for instance, it can help you turn a practically worthless old trash-runner into a valuable champion worth thousands of dollars." Compared to those thousands of dollars, what's a mere $179.95 or $209.95 or $249.95 for the trainer? A gyp, that's what.

But then, what else should that pet owner expect? As Captain Arthur Haggerty, of the Haggerty Dog Training School, points out, "Would you want your dog trained by an electrician?" To which I add, and your house wired by a dog trainer?

## TIPS ON THE FIVE MOST COMMON TRAINING PROBLEMS:

1. *Housebreaking:* Virtually impossible under six weeks, difficult under three months. One can paper-train, then housebreak, but not vice versa.
2. *Chewing:* Try rubbing the chewed object with something distasteful, such as alum, cayenne pepper, Bitter Apple, even Tabasco. Do not be surprised if it only seems to make the object tastier. Vicks or other foul-smelling stuff seems to be most effective. If nothing works, remember most dogs outgrow this.
3. *Jumping up:* Stepping on his feet takes agility worthy of an Olympic athlete. A knee in the chest works almost as well. Teach him "down" as an alternative.
4. *Climbing on furniture:* Put mousetraps at the ready all over the furniture. Use two-sided tape that sticks to the dog and turns him into a modern mummy. Even try sprays, but test first in case you can't stand the smell.
5. *Excessive barking, crying:* Usually caused by loneliness. Try playing the radio, feeding in the morning so the dog will sleep while you're gone, distracting with quantities of milkbone, or getting it a companion. Even if they don't get along, they'll spend all their time chasing each other instead of bothering the neighbors.

# X  BREEDING

> The dogs sold by Docktors are generally quite expensive and a sales technique used by them, and I'm sure other retailers of dogs, is to convince the prospective purchaser that if he or she breeds the dogs, part or all of the original purchase price will be recouped within a relatively short period of time. However, the purchaser is generally untrained in dog breeding and produces puppies which are not the results of proper mating and therefore unsaleable. This results in puppies which must either be given away or destroyed . . . I would hope that the public could be informed of the inherent problems of breeding and that it is not for the novice.
>
> DAVID A. HUFFMAN, prosecuting attorney, Fraud Division, County District Attorney's Office, Sacramento, California

You don't have to go to California to hear the "Don't think of it as a pet, think of it as an investment" sales spiel. It is employed nationwide by pet-shop salesmen, backyard breeders, and some serious breeders, too.

In one particular case, the pup was one of a litter of six lhasa apsos for sale at $289.95 each in a suburban shopping mall pet shop. The pitch for a bitch went like this: You can get your money back within the year. Lhasas mature at six to eight months, are free-whelpers who don't need Caesareans, have up to nine pups a litter, and can be bred again six months later. And, mind you, you can do the same thing every year for the next ten. As for the males, they can be bred twice a week (at least!) every week for the same ten years. And after the first two stud fees, which pay for the pup, the rest is all gravy.

In case you don't have your computer handy, that works out to $52,191 in potential puppy sales per bitch and $156,000 in potential stud fees per male. That's not buying a pet, that's finding the fabled philosopher's stone that changes things into gold. Of course, as any serious lhasa apso breeders could tell you if they'd just stop the hysterical laughter, alchemy hasn't worked for—lo!—these many centuries and isn't about to start now. Or, to put it another way, have you ever heard of fool's gold?

That's not to say that the pitch is 100 percent phony; it's just not 100 percent accurate. To be specific. A brood bitch's productive life is usually over by seven or eight years. If she is bred but once a year, it is possible to have nine pups in a litter, but the average is more like five. If she is bred twice a year, that average decreases dramatically. Even though this breed is indeed a free-whelping one, it has a higher puppy mortality rate than the usual 10 percent.

Pull that information together, and it doesn't add up to the 180 potential pups dangled before our eyes in that pet shop. More like 24. Nor will those pups bring in the expected $289.95. Instead, they'll go for $150 to $200 when the market is good. However, according to Norman Herbel, of the Tabu Lhasa kennels, the market hasn't been good, "since '71. In fact, the market's been saturated so badly you can't hardly give one away these days." (The puppy millers and backyard breeders make money in breeding by changing with the times. If St. Bernards are in, they breed those; when St. Bernards fall out of vogue, they get out of St. Bernards. Moreover, they don't have the expenses the average amateur breeder does. For example, they wouldn't pay that original $289.95 purchase price—they'd pick up a cheapie somewhere. Maybe at the pound or at a dog auction.) But the amateur has other expenses, such as extra food during pregnancy, veterinarian fees, inoculations, tail-docking if needed, ear-cropping if needed, food, vitamins, stud fees, AKC registration fees, and advertising costs—and that's just for the pups. One also has to consider the annual costs of owning the mother as a pet, her shots, her board bills, her food, her grooming, her everything.

Although dog and cat people are notoriously bad at keeping track of their costs—they belong to the ignorance-is-bliss school—one breeder of English cockers figured her out-of-pocket expenses for a litter of six was $960, or $160 per puppy. Another, with a litter of four, estimated it to be $190 a puppy. Using these figures as a guide, we can see that it would cost approximately $3,600 to produce twenty-four lhasa puppies, excluding any of the costs of caring for the mother or any figure for the pet owner's labor. To make a long story short, the purchaser of that lhasa puppy not only wouldn't realize that $52,191 potential income, he would end up at the end of ten years losing $3,939.95.

That's if nothing goes wrong. And as dog and cat breeders can tell you, there are times when things go wrong more often than they go right. For example, the mother's milk goes bad, and the litter is lost.

Puppies are born with some congenital deformity and have to be put down. The mother turns cannibal—it happens—and eats her puppies. Or the old tomcat gets at the kittens and does the same. Whatever the cause, it is rare that one gets all the puppies or kittens he hoped for. Of course, when he does, it's usually too much of a good thing. That's when the market disappears for that particular breed. One may have had fifty calls for a pup before the bitch was bred, but once she takes, it's as if your phone had been disconnected.

An excess of puppies on the property causes other problems. One breeder of old English sheepdogs had to reimburse his landlord for the cost of a fantastic carpentry job to cover the chewing of woodwork by teething pups. A St. Bernard breeder looked out on his backyard to discover that the dogs had transformed it into a close approximation of a battlefield, complete with enormous bomb craters. A large-hound owner discovered his marriage wrecked by dogs, dogs, too many dogs. And all the time those dogs are eating and eating and eating expensive food. Not to mention woodwork and profits.

What does one do? Cut prices, and cut them again? Or give them away to friends, relatives, anyone who'll take one? Or take the pups to the pound and hand them over along with a donation to get them off your hands? Look to the experts, those whose judgment is so respected that they are given thousands of dollars to buy dogs not yet seen by the new owners. Look to the people with all the connections, who must have buyers besieging them in droves for whatever they'd like to sell. What does expert Anne Hone Rogers Clark do with whippet, Italian greyhound, and miniature poodle pet-quality pups that don't sell? "Put them down."

Wait a minute. Perhaps that friendly pet-shop owner, the one who got you into this mess, will take them off your hands. Not him. He wants his puppies young. Six weeks is best. He wants them guaranteed replaceable by the breeder, which lets out the one-bitch-owning breeder, who can't possibly have replacements on hand. And he wants those puppies cheap. For example, the current wholesale price for a lhasa pup is $100. ("Special for May 16, 1975! Buy 5 to be shipped this week—get 1 free!" reads a wholesale price list from a puppy dealer.)

The buyer of a male pup, who had a potential $156,000 coming to him in stud fees, fares no better than the bitch's owner. You see, to get those stud fees, he's first got to find 104 people per year willing to breed to his dog. That's easier said than done. For example, we get phone calls all the time—and so do others handling every breed—offering us the use of a male at stud. Often it's for free, just so that they can get a pup just like good old Dad. It takes all we can do to

*Evelyn M. Shaffer*
Ch. Balligo's Wingover finishes his championship at the Philadelphia KC show under judge Mrs. Julia Gasow. "Windy," handled by D. Lawrence Carswell, was my first home-bred champion.

explain, without offending them, that first of all, selecting a mate for a bitch is such serious business for a breeder that a breeding may be planned years in advance. Also, that the stud we choose has known virtues and faults. Their dog, we're sorry to say, is just an unknown. In other words, as one breeder put it, "How do you tell a guy nicely that you won't breed to garbage?"

Oh, that poor pet-stud owner. Nobody wants him. Except the canine version of the dating services. For twenty bucks he can register his stud with a California-based service for one year. In return for this, the service promises to "discover a compatible mate for your canine lover . . . arrange a romantic holiday [they book a motel room to do the deed] . . . introduction of the loveliest females to charming (and competent) male companions."

On the East coast, a Marc R. Rapkel harnessed up the "computer" to do the trick. His "Canine Mating Service" offered not just to match breeds (or cross them, if that was your wish) but to find a mate by computer with the same characteristics, idiosyncracies, and temper (including a love of good books—chewing, that is). The interest was so great that the founder began franchising at $1,500 per. He had to. He didn't have a computer. He used 3 by 5 cards. Franchising was to pay for the computer. Ah, me, one wonders how all these enterprising men made an honest, or dishonest, buck in the days P-F (pre-franchising). In any case, to my knowledge, Mr. Rapkel has moved on to better things—at least as far as dogs are concerned. And good riddance —his program sounded more like the source of one-night stands than of steady stud fees.

There is one doggy data bank that is not, per se, a dating bank. That's Professional Breeding Services, Inc., operating out of Hurley, New York. The intention here is to computerize information on the genotype and phenotype * of as many dogs within a breed as possible. It is one of the most ambitious, well thought out operations I have come across. And I'll give you odds that professional breeders will not beat a path to Edward T. Boyle's—the founder's—door. For one thing, his idea is new, and dog people are traditionalists. For another, the program requires that an individual evaluate his own dog, which all other dog people know is impractical, not to mention impossible, because "everybody else but you and I are kennel blind [can't see faults and virtues objectively] and sometimes I wonder about you."

* Genotype refers to the qualities that the dog carries, good and bad, within his genes that can be passèd on to his get. Phenotype refers to the physical appearance —the measurable characteristics—that the dog shows. Sometimes genotype and phenotype are identical, other times, they're not. The tricky part of dog breeding is trying to determine the genotype so as to emphasize good points and avoid bad ones in a resulting litter.

For a third, the program violates one of the basic tenets among dog breeders—that breeding is an art, not a science—a concept that has done more to retard the progress of dogs than anything else. In fact, if anything, the exponents of this "art" have made many breeds worse off than they were 20, 30, or 40 years ago. In sporting dogs, for example, the dual champion is a rarity and confined to certain breeds. In other breeds, there are actually two types in existence: hunting dogs and beauty-contest winners.

For a prime example of man's destroying what nature has created—in the name of art—take the poodle. The poodle is/was a heavy-coated dog. Originally, his trimming was done to make it easier for him to get through the water; a heavy coat was left on the front to protect the vital organs, while the rest was shaved so as not to impede his progress. Pom-poms were left on to protect vital joints.

One who has hunted with such a dog says her champion, Ch. Rimskittle Rampart, a standard poodle retired after winning at Westminster, was four years old before she saw water other than in the bathtub. Now, she's used on upland bird, which she considers legalized chicken chasing, and she's the best duck hunter around. How many owners of poodles, standard or otherwise, have even attempted to test their hunting ability?

Unfortunately, Mr. Boyle's idea of Professional Breeding Services, Inc., was too good to go unnoticed. Thus along comes Canine Genetic Breeding Services, Inc. And if there is a rip-off in the world of dogs, this is it. From the idea to the design to the color selection to the charts to the prices—to the letter, it is the same as PBS, which is not surprising, since the creator of it contacted and got his information from Mr. Boyle and then went from there. At the present time the matter is before the New York state attorney general for fraud; there, hopefully, the best man will win. Until that time, a few tip-offs to tell the good guys from the bad guys. The Canine Genetic Breeding Services kits are unique in several respects: they contain no New York street address, only a postal box. The letter they send is signed anonymously by a "board of directors," not an individual, and nowhere in all the very impressive literature is there a telephone number at which one could contact them.

As a dog lover and a breeder, not simply a writer, this particular money-making rip-off bothers me more than most. An idea that could be of benefit to dogs and to pet owners has been made into a financially rewarding scheme for some joker somewhere. May his next pet poop in his slippers and bite his tail end.

When it comes to money, don't take my word for it that there is none to be made breeding bitches or managing a stud. Just ask any breeder. So, don't fight it. Accept the fact that your pet bitch or dog won't make you a fortune. They can still reward you with that which money can't buy. But if you have a little land you'd like to put to use, K-9 Association, in Kansas City, Missouri, has an idea that should strike a responsive chord in your heart: "Start now raising purebred dogs for PROFIT. Get top . . . prices. We assist all new breeders if qualified. Turn ½ acre of your idle ground into $10,000 income." All you have to do is buy a franchise, and a cheap one, at that. For $490 cash, $506 with $290 down and $18 a month for a year, or $522 with only $90 down but $36 a month for a year.

For this—and I quote Ruth and Sharon Weddle, writing in *Dog Tracks**—you get:

1. Five free litter listings that will be sent to over 400 pet shops. For that you agree to pay the association 10% of the gross selling price for any additional listings requested.
2. Kennel Management Program: you're entitled to a 38 chapter program, covering every aspect of dog breeding necessary to improve your breeding stock and upgrade the dog industry.
3. You're entitled to purchase insurance through the master policy of the association at group rates.
4. You are entitled to buy feed through the association at factory direct prices.
5. You are entitled to purchase supplies through the association at discount prices.
6. You are entitled to receive a complete tax shelter package showing how you can take capital gains and receive full depreciation of your stock.
7. You are entitled to unlimited consultation, by mail, on any aspects of dog breeding.
8. You are entitled to receive a periodic newsletter advising of prices and relating new products.
9. You are entitled to be a member of the board of advisors and as a group offer suggestions to constantly improve the association.
10. In exchange for which you guarantee to supply AKC registered, healthy puppies to each buyer. You will guarantee your offspring for 48 hours after shipment, providing a vet inspects them after arrival.

But over and above that, you will have the opportunity to participate in something truly worthwhile. Or, as the promoters' prospectus says:

For the first time in the history of the dog industry, since the AKC came into existence, someone else has taken the initiative to set up a much needed constructive program of quality control in the vast puppy market.

It kinda gets you right there, doesn't it? If you are ready and eager to sign up and hand over your cash, you have a problem, because the K-9 Association is not that eager to be found. First, their Membership Division, at company headquarters in Kansas City, Missouri, won't answer their telephone. According to the telephone company, there

---

* Reprinted with permission from Weddle Publications.

isn't any phone. Not for the Membership Division. Not for company headquarters. I understand, however, that there are K-9 Breeders' Associations being set up in Ohio and Florida and that a smooth-talking representative has been working the California area; but after months, I have not been able to track any of these down.

It may well be that the company has decided to concentrate their efforts on setting up the retail stores promised to their membership. Twenty-five were to have opened this year in major cities, and another 225 in the near future. Then again, they may have suffered some setbacks in this area. I know for a fact that the only pet shop in my vicinity silly enough to sign up with them folded a couple of months later.

I hope that somewhere out there there is someone whose illusions of quick wealth and wondrous riches have been irreparably shattered. Better by me than Mother Nature, because she is moving in and playing her part in preventing indiscriminate breeding—with a vengeance. Unfortunately, she is working with complete impartiality, affecting the sincere, dedicated breeder and the money-maker alike. More and more breeds are coming up with crippling conditions. More and more birth defects are popping up. Litters are becoming smaller. In collies, for example, which used to average ten to twelve pups a litter, breeders are now pleased to get six or eight. Bitches are coming into season irregularly, going eight and ten months between seasons. Then when they come in and are bred, many don't conceive. Studs suddenly go sterile or are totally disinterested and refuse to breed.

And, of course, Mother Nature still has canine brucellosis up her sleeve. Was it mere happenstance that the disease showed up first in and spread throughout the beagle kennels that produce thousands of dogs for research? Or was somebody trying to tell us something?

THREE TIPS ON GOING INTO BREEDING:

1. Get the best brood bitch you can. Although leasing is the book-method, few breeders will do it, so your best bet is to buy an older bitch, six to eight months at least, whose faults and virtues are already apparent.
2. Breed to a male from a top local kennel if possible; this way the owner will be available for advice at every stage of the proceedings (I've delivered whole litters over the phone), and will, in addition, send prospective buyers to you.
3. Have $1,000 or more in the bank to take care of the expenses so that you are not panicked or enticed into selling when you shouldn't.

# XI  UTILITY

> Exclusive of the pet breeds, not a dozen breeds today live up to the purposes for which they were originally bred.
>
> —MAXWELL RIDDLE, author, judge, and dogman

Man, over the centuries, has looked upon the cat as an animal set apart from all others. In many parts of the world, it was an object of fear—a demon come to earth, the companion of sorcerers and witches. Elsewhere, it was an object of worship. In the Norse countries, the Middle East, and the Orient, it played a prominent role in religions. Nowhere more so than in ancient Egypt, where the goddess Bast was depicted with the head of a cat. Archeologists have, during their excavations of tombs and temples, found thousands of cat mummies, which were, like those of the pharaohs, buried surrounded with objects believed needed in the afterlife. In the case of cats, that meant mice mummified and entombed with them.

The dog, on the other hand, may have been man's best friend, but he was also damn well expected to get off his duff and pitch in with the work at hand. Of the 308 internationally recognized breeds of dogs, fewer than 20 were bred deliberately as pets or ornaments. The others had a purpose. Including being bred especially to do the work of a cat—killing rats. But one would never guess it to look at these rat-killers. One of the best—the papillon—stands but 11 inches high and has strange butterfly ears. Obviously, he doesn't weigh enough to take on a rat in a fair fight. Which he doesn't. Instead, the dog maneuvers its prey into a corner, then worries it until the rodent is too exhausted to fight back. Then, the papillon pounces.

Along came technology, the better rattrap, and D-Con, and suddenly man had no use for rat-killing dogs. Much the same happened to most of the other breeds. For example, who needs a wolfhound to hunt wolves when the world's wolf population has been so decimated that conservationists are demanding that it be saved from extinction?

Another breed that has fallen victim to technology is the St. Bernard. And what a shame it is, for few are the breeds of dogs with such a history of service to man. Although the Alpine pass between Switzerland and Italy was in use in Roman times, it got its name, as did the breed of dog, in the eleventh century. It was then that a young nobleman, later known as St. Bernard of Menthon, founded a hospice at St. Bernard Pass. Since the twelfth or thirteenth century, the hospice has been in the charge of Augustinians whose mother house is at Martigny, at the mouth of the pass. It was they who created the breed, but it wasn't until the 1750s that the dogs first came into real use. First, serving as guide dogs for the monks, then, later, searching for lost travelers, mostly Italian laborers.

One of the most famous dogs was Barry, who in twelve years saved forty travelers lost in blizzards but died under the ice axe of the forty-first, who thought the dog was a bear. (Perhaps if Barry had carried that famous little keg of brandy around his neck—but he didn't. Nor has any St. Bernard before or after him.) It is doubtful that there will ever be a Barry Two. For one thing, the automobile has made the foot traveler a thing of the past. For another, helicopters, with their greater speed and range, can do the job more efficiently. As of April 1975, there were only two dogs left at the famous St. Bernard hospice. When they go, it is feared that it will mark the end of the St. Bernard as a rescue dog.

Man has found another use for him, which is true of several other breeds. Man has converted a dog bred with a specific objective into an object of merriment, with the motive frequently monetary. The St. Bernard is now found participating, at country fairs, in the canine version of that stellar attraction that pulls in the admission-paying customers: the horse or tractor pull. In a dog pull, an individual dog is hitched to a sledge on which carefully weighed bags of sand are placed. The dog is then asked to pull that sledge a given distance. If successful, more bags are added, and he tries again.

Although theoretically any cart dog could be used, the Saint and the Newfoundland—the percherons of dogdom—are preferred. The record-holder, in fact, is a four-year-old Newfoundland who pulled 4,400 pounds over fifteen feet in twelve seconds, in accordance with Sled Dog Association rules. Ch. Bongo Bear, owned by Elizabeth Stackhouse, made the Guinness book of records for that. He himself weighed only 162 pounds.

Sled-dog racing once upon a time was a necessity—a struggle of man and dog against nature. No longer. Now it's against the clock, and the terrain may be snow covered or not. If dry, the sleds are left home and carts are used instead. One sled-dog-team owner collected more than $20,000 in prize money in 1974. Not to mention any bets on the side. Betting, although not organized, does go on, at sled races and at dog pulls. But where the betting action really zings is at professional greyhound races. May that Illinois engineer, Owen Smith, *never* rest in peace. For it was he, at the beginning of the twentieth century, who had the idea of transforming what has been called "the aristocrat of breeds," "the companion of princes," "a god . . . destined to receive homage," into a spectacle. A canine cretin content to live out its life chasing a mechanical hare around a track. All for man's amusement and love of betting.

When Owen Lewis came up with the idea, it was thought to have many advantages over the real or actual coursing of greyhounds, the chasing of a real live hare by two dogs in a race to the hare's death. For one thing, this new version wasn't gory. No hare would die at the end of a professional greyhound race. For another, the race, which is around an oval, could be seen and followed by many who would never otherwise be able to admire the elegance and economy of movement of this—a living, running, exciting machine. The betting? Well, it was like the icing on a cake. Not the main idea, but certainly a sweetener of the whole thing.

That was back in the early 1900s. Today, a greyhound race, with the wagering in the hundred of thousands of dollars, attracts crowds in the tens of thousands. In England, for example, at White City, London, as many as 100,000 have filled the stands. The sport is equally popular in Algeria, Italy, and America. In America, although confined mostly to the South, the idea is spreading, but slowly, thanks to the efforts of animal lovers in the West who are quick to publicize this disturbing fact: studies show that for every dog-racing track in existence, approximately 2,100 greyhounds between two and three years of age will be killed annually because they are not fast enough to win. If one includes the number of culled puppies and aged adults who are also killed each year, the number approaches 4,000 per track per year. California, where legislation to permit such tracks was killed in committee, had planned five such tracks.

Equally as perturbing as the death toll among the dogs is the practice of using live animals to train racing dogs. Although such a practice is not universal and not even—according to many dog racers—necessary, there are those who believe only the real thing gets a dog to do his best. And these people have even gone to court to be able to use their living targets.

In the North, the resistance comes not from animal lovers, but from horsemen who fear that dogs will lower the gate and handle for flat tracks and harness racing. Actually, the two draw a different crowd. Admission at a dog track is about fifty cents and attracts a lower- to middle-class, low-betting crowd. One man, decrying the demise of greyhound racing in France—where the horsemen successfully opposed it—says, "It would be nice, however, to encourage the renewal and development of these exciting shows. They constitute, in fact—like horse racing—a true sport, which implies knowledge and experience as much from the point of view of breeding as from that of selection and training, and also a means of preserving a breed which has remained one of the most ancient, purest and most interesting to preserve."

He is certainly right about one thing. The greyhound race does, indeed, preserve the breed; survival of the fittest is the first rule of the sport. The same law dominates still another sport created for man's amusement: dogfighting. Dating back to the days of Rome, these matches—dog against dog, bear, bull, or man—were especially popular in Elizabethan England. It was not uncommon then for a man to make arrangements in his will to have a dogfight staged in his memory on a given holiday. Although banned in France in 1834 and in England a year later, they continued illegally there and elsewhere for another twenty years. They are still going on today, here in the U.S.A.

If for nothing else, the American dog-show world has dogfighting to thank for two of its indigenous phrases: *fancier,* and *winning at Westminster.* The first originally meant someone who had such a special liking for a dog for its good points that he was willing to back his opinion with a wager. Today, no money need be involved. The second, "winning at Westminster," is *the* goal of today's dog-show people. The absolute epitome of one's show career. More than a hundred years ago, it was also the goal of a dogfighter. Dogfights in London were staged before hundreds of spectators at fashionable sporting places, with "Westminster Pit" being considered the best.

Today, because of the great need in some states for secrecy, the average dogfight audience numbers fewer than fifty. However, in the South, larger affairs, with upwards of twelve matches, have been known to attract enough people to fill that legendary Westminster Pit.

The audience ranges in age from octogenarians to youngsters barely into their teens. Anyone younger than that is discouraged, because kids have a way of talking too much. However, there is no sex discrimination, at least not in the audience. Wives, grandmothers, girls—they're all in attendance and may even be called upon, at the larger conventions, to present the trophies for best dog or bitch of the show. The men range in occupation from physicians to construction workers to just about anything imaginable. For example, there is a veterinarian who not only attends, but also matches his own dogs. Up in Rhode

Island, the dog officer for the city of Providence was arrested in 1974 for possession of fighting dogs.

The Ku Klux Klan's nominee for vice-president of the United States in 1976 is Scott Nelson, owner of Scotty's Yo Yo, a dog he himself described as "a 39-pound dog, 3 years old. Two time winner." In the same advertisement in *Your Friend and Mine,* an underground magazine for dogfighters, he made his position known on at least one national issue. "I don't raise dogs and don't operate a puppy farm and don't peddle dogs. I don't have any beautiful all-purpose dogs for sale. If you want an all-purpose dog or one with hazel eyeballs and pink noses, and a watch dog, contact a Staffordshire breeder or one who peddles dogs. I don't breed for even bites, conformation or pets. Fighting dogs only."

Typically, the fights are conducted in great secrecy. The arrangements are made at the last minute by telephone or word of mouth. Sometimes, strangely worded but carefully timed postcards are used, with a predetermined code word, such as "Coon-on-log," being the signal that a match is on. If not a city fight—like in the basement of a New York brownstone—cars will be told to rendezvous at a preselected point at a predawn hour. There the group is screened to make sure no outsider has infiltrated them. If all's clear, they travel together in a caravan to an out-of-the-way location known only to the men in the lead car.

Watching from above in a spotter plane preparatory to raiding an upcoming fight, Sheriff C. W. "Bill" Porter of Norman, Oklahoma, saw sixty to seventy cars traveling under the cover of darkness: "The traffic reminded me of a football day; the cars were bumper to bumper."

Security checks are made by the participants along the way to be sure they're not being followed. Then each car is checked out before being allowed to park. Again at the entrance, the man at the door checks identification. Only then will he collect the admission charge, ranging anywhere from $5 for a training session to $100 and more for a multimatch event. Once in, no one can leave until the last fight is over.

So secretive and selective are these fights that it took undercover agent Richard W. Knapp many months to successfully infiltrate one dogfight ring. Only after he actually bought a two-time winner (who'd lost one fight in between, which the seller thoughtfully forgot to mention) was he allowed into the circle. Even then, during the fourteen months he worked on the case under the direction of Captain Donald Lambert, Chief Law Enforcement Officer of the Massachusetts SPCA, Knapp heard a lot of talk but saw only three fights.

"Those three were enough," he says. "More than enough. Once I saw a litter of four-month old pups provoked into fighting each other. The men thought it was cute. They did it for the amusement of visiting out-of-state dog fanciers, as dogfighters call themselves."

As for the actual fight, it takes place in a temporary pit about ten or twelve feet square. Atop a canvas floor, plywood walls are quickly erected by the use of metal pins (they can be disassembled just as or even more quickly). The plywood walls are about three feet high, to give spectators an unimpeded view. At the larger, more elaborate fights, there may even be a gate at one end to admit handlers and contestants. At the smaller, sleazier events, man and dog have to climb in, but dead or badly injured dogs, after the fight, get a quick lift out—they're simply pitched over the side.

While the pit is being set up, the spectators drink, reminisce about the great dogs of yore, and wager. Although bets of $20 and $25 are common, at a big match one man might win as much as $12,000, with a total of between $50,000 and $100,000 changing hands.

Frequently, the smaller events are merely "rolls," or training fights. For a fighting dog is tested much like the bulls bred for the corrida. At one year, after six months of training, a dog is matched against another of the same age and weight. Such a match may last anywhere from five to thirty minutes, during which time the dog is not expected to kill, but he must demonstrate the potential for it. Actually, at this age, the dogs don't usually have the jowls and strong teeth needed to kill. If a dog shows any sign of cowardice or no instinct for biting and chewing, he is discarded. Literally. In some areas, such "curs," as they are called, are shot. In another, they're hanged. Other methods include taking an axe and "off with their heads." One breeder used his auto and ran over the cur.

The circles in which Mr. Knapp moved were more practical. "The people whom I associated with," he says, "would tape the dog's jaws shut and pit him against another dog to give the latter dog some practice in killing."

The dogs found at a multimatch event are all proven, having had their first fight at anywhere from eighteen months to two years. But, like any good fight, each event has its "card," with the younger and lighter-weight dogs matched in the preliminaries and the veterans appearing later. Before his match, each dog is weighed in to be sure he is not over the weight. As much as $1/4$ pound too much would call for a forfeiture of $50 to $100 as well as the match. The procedures taken to keep these dogs up to but not overweight could teach many a heavyweight fighter's manager a lesson.

After the weigh-in, each dog is given a bath by his opponent's owner to remove any poisons applied to the coat. This bath may be waived when the two owners know each other well, which is considered to be a sign of good sportsmanship. On the other hand, owners have been known to demand a dental inspection of an opponent's dog, since some practitioners have tried to help their odds by filing their dog's teeth to make them more lethal.

Once these preliminaries are over and the details of the contract repeated and agreed to, the fight is ready to begin. Present in the pit with the two dogs will be a referee and the dogs' owners or handlers. These, according to one set of printed rules, may "encourage the dogs by voice or handclapping or snapping of fingers, but must not touch the dog or use foul, dirty methods." Since there are no rounds (or rest periods) during a dogfight, it's the clock that counts, as in this, an actual account of a dogfight:

> 1:01. Dan is eating Ace's nose off. Ace sings. 1:07 mouth holds again. Up to this time it has been a very fast, hard-fought fight, with Ace continually boring in and Dan punishing him badly with every hold. Now, at about the 1:25 minute mark, the fight seems to turn as Dan lies on the cold

*Massachusetts SPCA*
Two pit bulls in action. Fighting dogs earn reputations as head, ear, or leg chewers, but endurance or "heart" is valued most by their owners.

ground, the strength seems to seep from his body. At about 1:40, Dan barely seems able to come to his feet. He goes back down and at 2:13 Ace lets go and is handled to scratch. Ace runs his scratch and Dan goes down. At 2:16, dogs are handled with Dan to scratch. Satterlee [Dan's handler] lets him go at 2:17. Dan is physically unable to move and takes the count. Ace the winner at 2:17. Ace made a very good courtesy scratch. Dan passed on the following day.

In case we lost you at "2:13 . . . is handled to scratch," an instant replay: When a dog lets go, as Ace did at 2:13, and stops chewing on the other for three seconds, the owners must grab their respective dogs and bring them back to the corners. Then, predetermined by a coin toss, one owner—in this case, Ace's—releases his dog first to see if it will "scratch," meaning to run across the ring at the other dog. If he does, he has made his scratch and the fight goes on. When the fighting stops again, as it did at 2:16, when Dan went down, the dogs are again brought back to the corners. This time the other dog is released first. However, since Dan was unable to move, much less attack, Ace is declared the winner. But only after making a "courtesy scratch," in which the winning dog demonstrates its willingness to go on with the fight by again attacking the loser. If the dog can't or won't, the fight is declared a draw.

Making a good "courtesy scratch" is an important part of the in-pit sportsmanship required in dogfighting. For example, one pit-bull breeder was quoted on the subject in a *New York Times* article in 1974:

> Mr. Bodzianowski (a breeder of fighting dogs for 20 years) likes to tell the story of a dog of his named Peaches. After a fight in Mississippi, which Peaches won by killing the other dog, the loser asked for a courtesy scratch.
> "Her front leg was broke and sticking through the skin at two places [Bodzianowski said]. It would jab holes in the canvas when she walked. The guy said, hell, she couldn't make it over the line again, so I let her go. That dog didn't know what was wrong, she tried to run at the other dog and that stub of a leg would hit the floor and she'd tumble. She finally turned almost a flip into the boards and landed under that dog and dug in. You tell me that dog didn't have heart."

Heart is valued among dogfighters. But stamina is valued even more. In dogfight circles they still talk, with awe, about the man who had a dog who wouldn't let go. Nothing, he claimed, would make that dog break a hold. When challenged, he went even farther. He said that that dog, once it had a hold, wouldn't let go even if "I cut off its legs, one by one." For enough money he was more than happy to prove his point. He was right.

This may be shocking and sickening to you, but not to pit-dog fanciers. Death is nothing new to them. It is estimated that in 40 percent of the fights, both combatants will die; in nearly 75 percent of them, one dog will die. However, the survivor gets more and more valuable. The stakes he fights for get higher and higher. A three-time winner—the equivalent of a champion—is worth as much as $3,000, with his stud fee ranging up to 10 or 15 percent of his value. Pups sired by him are worth between $500 and $1,000. And once a champion, he is a target for every other dogfighter worth the name and with the money—real money, more money than many of those men can make in two or three years on a job.

Because of the money involved, owners hesitate to stop fights too quickly. They know anything can happen. Duncan Wright, president of the American Dog Owners Association (ADOA), can testify to that: "I once saw two dogs fight for about one hour and forty minutes, at which time one of the two appeared to be gone. The second dog, which had been standing over the first, chewing on the head of the downed dog, stopped and stood erect. After a moment, the downed dog suddenly jerked up and disemboweled the standing dog. Within a few minutes, the apparent winner was dead, and the apparent loser became the winner, though he subsequently died."

If there is one place that a bitch gets a break, it is here. Owners are more willing to stop a fight with bitches involved, evidently preferring a live bitch that can bear more fighting dogs to a dead one. Compare, for example, these accounts of two matches. The first, a match of bitches at thirty-four pounds as recounted in *Your Friend and Mine:*

> Bitches down in corner and the handlers urge them on and obstruct view of the spectators. Crowd is quiet as they await the outcome of what has been touted as a master match between two outstanding bitches. . . . Pickup at 46 minutes the red to go. She stumbled and fell and struggled and stumbled all the way across the pit to complete her scratch. The black has a front leg and the red is down but has a foot at 49. Black is going in stifle but the red has a foot. Bitches then work nose and mouth holds at 54 minutes. Pickup, the black to go. Went across like a black streak and knocked the red into her corner. McCaw picks up his little red bitch and gives up the fight at 56 minutes. The black declared the winner in 56 minutes.

The second, two males at forty-one pounds, from *Pit Dog Report,* another dogfighters' magazine:

> Barney has won two prior matches and is known as a skillful ear dog. Tuffy has earned a reputation as a terrible punisher. Both dogs weigh in at 38¾ lbs. . . . A pickup is made at 1 hour with Tuffy to scratch. Tuffy makes a game stumbling scratch as fast as his tired legs can take him across. Barney scratches hard and fast and knocks Tuffy down in his corner and keeps him down biting deep and hard until the pickup at 1 hr. 6 min. Tuffy goes forward at Barney but falls down. Tuffy is looking at Barney

and trying to scratch but he cannot move and is gasping for air. Tuffy takes the count making Barney the winner.

This was a good fight between two strong, hard biting dogs. Tuffy never recovered. He will be remembered as a dead game dog who fought until he could not move and ran out of air and legs but not heart. Barney has 3 good wins now and will be open to match again when he heals up.

Other than the fact that dogfighting is either illegal or considered inhumane in every state, does it actually harm the average citizen and pet owner? Not according to proponents of dogfighting. As Representative George M. O'Brien, Illinois, reported in the House Agriculture Subcommittee hearings:

Fans, owners, and promoters claim we are making a big fuss about nothing. A fellow who refused to identify himself, naturally, told one of my aides recently that dogfights are just good, clean fun, not much different from horse racing. It is just as natural for a pit bull to fight and die as it is for a thoroughbred to race, he claimed.

Of course, he insisted that the dogs don't die very often or even get hurt badly. Reminded that dozens of kittens and dogs are killed in training just one fighting dog for the pit, our anonymous friend suggested that was as good as any other way of getting rid of unwanted pets.

What's that—did somebody say kittens? Sure did. That's how a fighting dog is trained. He's started with cats. The cats are sometimes obtained through classified ads run by unsuspecting citizens and by humane shelters. You've seen the ads: "Cats free to good home." "Cats for adoption—no donation refused, even 50¢." The dogfighters are happy to see your ads. And they love those auctions where litters of kittens are sold for $1 the litter-lot. (Incidentally, the method of training involves putting a cat in a gunny sack with head and feet sticking out and suspending it from a spring above the dog's head. Of course, the claws are removed first to prevent the cat from "messing up" or discouraging the dog. But when the cat gets sufficiently "messed up," the dog is allowed to kill it to sharpen its killer instincts.)

It is estimated that the average fighting dog may kill over 100 cats during his training. A figure pooh-poohed by at least one breeder of pit bulls, who wrote Thomas S. Foley, representative from Washington, chairman of a hearing on dogfighting in 1974. His objection went, in part, like this (his letter is reprinted verbatim):

You have been fed a bigger line on raising a pit dog than the people of this country has been on Watergate and the corrupted bunch of people in Washington.

I'll send you a male, or female pup & I'll have someone from here to Alaska, old mexico—Hawaii or anywhere else send anyone you choose each the same age. Then You and who you choose Raise your dogs just like you would a poodle or any other breed of dog. Love it. Let it. Make sure it gets its shots taken to a Vet when it's needed for 2 years, then make sure they weigh exactly the same. And you take your dog over to where the other dog is and just put them down where they can see each other. And if they don't fight I'll eat a pound of mice, or rats and raw too. Or that mess they've told you that is fed to them to make mean and crave blood. Like the mess I've read on this silly nonsense.

The writer, I hasten to add, is not a fighter of dogs. He says, "I just raise and sell the crazy loveable animals. The American (Pit) bullterrier dogs make wonderful Pet, (house and yard) stock dogs, hunting dogs, and guard dogs."

The writer's contention that these dogs are natural fighters certainly isn't born out by the experiences of Ch. Abraxas Aristotle, a bull terrier owned by Mrs. Sharon Jackson, of Calgary, Alberta, Canada. After going Best of Breed, this $3,500 dog was stolen from a Detroit dog show on a Sunday and recovered on Wednesday in the backyard of a Detroit home, scarred, disfigured, and worthless. Detroit police worked on the theory that in between the bull terrier was stolen by a gambler intent on "making a killing" by entering him in a dogfight. But a major figure in the dogfighting community, when contacted by the ADOA, stated that the "legitimate dog fighters" would not steal a show dog for fighting. After all, as one in-the-know man remarked, putting this show dog into a pit with a fighting dog was "like matching a man in the street with Muhammad Ali."

But not all dogfights are as professional as others. For example, no real professional dogfighter would use a breed other than those bred specifically for fighting. For one thing, as one expert put it, "the fight wouldn't last ten minutes. A shepherd for example will bite and shake, but a bull terrier bites and chews and chews. Much gorier fight that way."

Amateurish matches, though, do go on. At one match, the first event was between two retrievers. When both fought until neither could continue, the bout was declared a draw, and both participants were pitched over the pit wall. The owner of one killed his dog with a heavy blow to the head. The other declined to waste a bullet on his, declaring the dog would die anyway, "why spend another cent on him."

The next match was between two German shepherds. One, after fifteen minutes, turned and attempted to climb the walls. He was pulled back and given another chance. The second chance can last anywhere from three seconds to fifteen minutes, depending on whether the dog is trained or a pet. In this case, the shepherd refused even after fifteen minutes to fight, and he was shot.

The final match was the only one to involve pit bulls, although these were obviously amateurishly trained and handled. The dogs

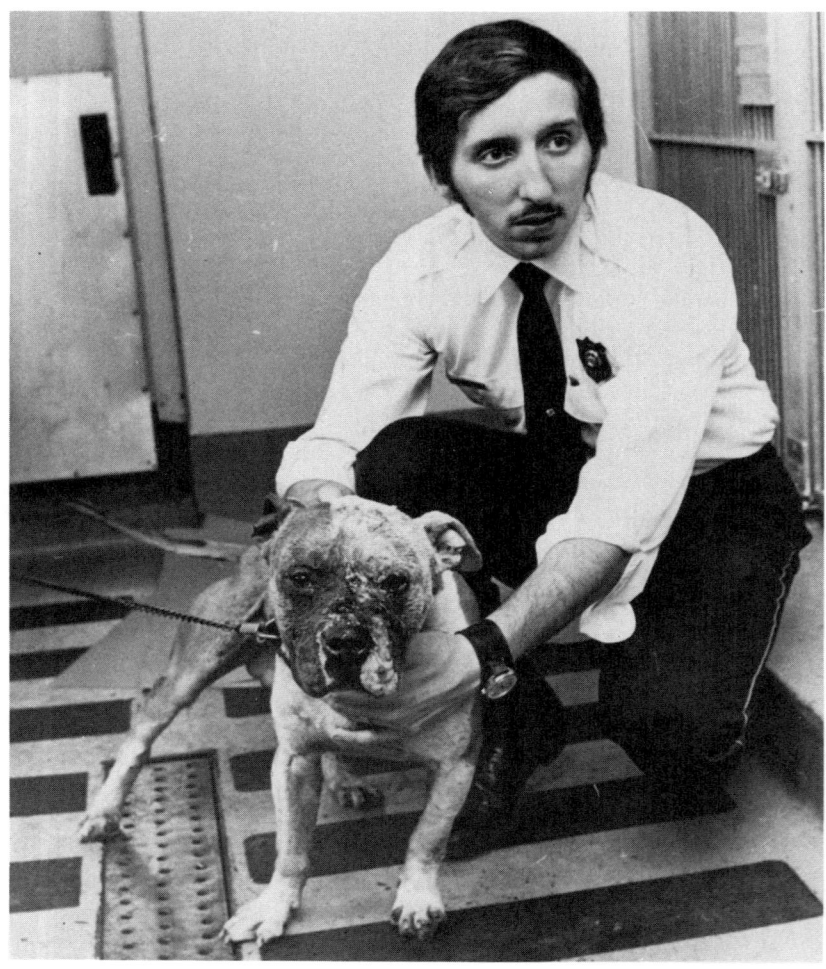

*Boston Globe Photo*
Scarred but lucky, this dog lives. Unlike other pit bulls, he will never fight again. He was captured by agents of the Massachusetts SPCA and is living out his life—peacefully and unaggressively—along with a collie on a Massachusetts farm.

fought silently and savagely for only a little over an hour. Then the match was called.

It should be pointed out that not all "professional" matches are up to par—at least by standards of the editors of *Sporting Dog Journal,* another magazine devoted to dogfighting:

Pennsylvania. The matches saw the debut of 6 out of the 12 participants, matching a dog for the very first time, and as to be expected, not all of the dogs were of first class quality and some of them weren't in top flight condition, but it was clear that they all did their best and are to be congratulated for taking that long hard first step. I'm sure they all learned something and win or lose will be heard from again. L. Jay W. promoted the matches and did a good job getting the newcomers matched as evenly as possible.

Our sport is growing fast and we need these newcomers to keep it going, so let's all give them the encouragement and help they want and need.

Let's don't.

## HOW TO STOP DOGFIGHTING:

1. Since local legislation isn't working, federal legislation is needed, and it may be on its way. In 1974 and 1975, the Honorable Thomas S. Foley, representative from Washington, introduced legislation to amend the Animal Welfare Act and prohibit interstate commerce in dogfighting. As of this writing, it has been referred to the Subcommittee on Livestock and Grains, which is chaired by Representative W. R. Poage of Texas. (Texas, by the way, is one of the five largest centers of dogfighting in the country.) Poage was very much involved in bringing about the original Animal Welfare Act. So there's hope. Whether it will be passed soon enough to prevent the deaths of thousands of dogs, or even if it will pass at all, is unknown. Whichever, it will not stop dogfighting. Only concerned citizens can do that, working through concerned local officials, obeying tough laws passed by concerned legislators. And they will only be concerned if you are.
2. Protest. Make yourself heard. Locally, and in your state House and Senate, and in Congress.

# XII COMPETITION

*To Whom It May Concern:*
Listed below are expenses incurred due to your influence. Please remit partial payment immediately, and balance at your earliest convenience.

| | |
|---|---:|
| Introduction to purebred dogs—one collie | $ 75.00 |
| Introduction to show dogs—one Tervuren male | 200.00 |
| 1st crate | 20.00 |
| 2nd crate | 20.00 |
| 1 grooming table | 30.00 |
| 1 station wagon | 3,600.00 |
| 2nd show dog—one Tervuren bitch | 150.00 |
| 3rd crate | 20.00 |
| 1 van (used) | 3,200.00 |
| Miscellaneous brushes, leads, grooming aids, etc. | 20.00 |
| Winners' pictures | 35.00 |
| Subscription to nine magazines | 16.00 |
| Membership to kennel club | 50.00 |
| TOTAL | $7,436.00 |

A "bill," rendered to the breeder of their first dog, as reported in *Pure-Bred Dogs American Kennel Gazette,* June 1974

About fifteen years ago, it cost $1,500 to finish a champion in the U.S. Today, the best estimates are between $2,500 and $3,000.

Things aren't as bad in England. One dog owner there is quoted in the *British Veterinary Record* as to what it costs him over one year's time to finish, or complete, the championship of a bitch (it's much harder, by the way, to finish a dog in England than here): cost of dog, purchased as adult, $150; entry fees, $130; catalogs, food and drink at shows for owner and wife, $841; supplies, such as grooming tools, $12; food for bitch for a year, $50. Total: $1,183. But note there are no vet fees, no boarding charges, no grooming fees, no photography charges, no traveling expenses, and no payment to a handler to do the actual showing of the dog.

Back here, though, using that low $2,500 figure, it works out that Americans spent $22,752,500 to finish new champions in 1974. With God only knows how much money being spent on dogs that couldn't cut the mustard. First, here's how one goes about finishing a champion.

One needs from the start a dog that is at least good, without glaring faults, and at best spectacular (not that many are). Then one needs to compete against other dogs to win a total of fifteen points. These points, ranging from one to five in number, are awarded according to a chart prepared by the American Kennel Club, based on its records of the previous year's competition within each sex of each breed in each region of the country. These figures, by the way, are manipulated by the AKC in order to achieve what is, in their opinion, the right kind of show results. For every breed, the AKC's ideal is to have 5 percent of all shows awarding no points at all, around 20 percent (but closer to 18) awarding three points, and 2 percent awarding five points, the maximum number that any dog can win in any one show.

In amassing those fifteen championship points, the dog must have at least two majors (awards of three points or more) under two different judges. To get such a major, one must defeat a given number of dogs according to the AKC's sliding scale. Consulting one, you'd find that the least number of dogs a potential champion would have to defeat to get three points is four, and the most (in the case of German shepherd bitches) is thirty-eight.

Obviously, the more dogs you have to beat, the higher the odds are against you, and the more unlikely it is that you will get that champion at the $2,500 figure. But the serious breeder tries because, in these days when dogs have no real use other than as pets, the dog show offers him a proving ground for his breeding program, a chance to see how his dogs stack up against the rest. For others, it's the competition itself, the American love of winning, that keeps them coming back year after year, dog after dog, dollar after dollar, in search of a 9- by 12-inch certificate with a small gold seal in the corner, or some Best of Breed and Best in Show rosettes or silver.

No one in dog-show circles would be shocked to hear that one woman has an annual dog-show budget in seven figures; this is no surprise, since five of the six top-winning dogs in the country in 1974 were purchased and owned by individuals who were "well-off," to put it mildly. For those who collect trivia, I should like to point out that all six dogs were owned by women, and that two of those dogs were owned by the same woman.

Some would say it is the love of competition that accounts for the huge investments; others would say it is the love of the adulation Americans lavish on those who back winners. Some might even call the whole business an ego trip. Why else would someone own dog after dog that he or she never sees except from ringside? And if that dog doesn't win, no one will see him ever again.

But others, the newcomer, novice, or naive dog owner, are drawn by the possible financial remunerations involved. For example, one big winner, retired young, is supposed to have serviced more than 300 bitches, at $300 per. Figure it out: $90,000 can pay for an awful lot of campaigning. Unfortunately, the stud fees don't come the way of the average big-time winner. The intelligent breeder goes to the father of

*Atlantic City Press Bureau*
The Boardwalk show in Atlantic City, New Jersey, is fairly new on the dog show calendar, yet it attracts nearly 4,000 dogs each year to the huge Convention Center. There is talk that the show may have already outgrown its present quarters.

the dog, the male who produced this great phenom. There's always the chance that a male who breaks every conceivable record is sterile. One of the all-time great dogs never sired a puppy, although he tried—and tried. He may have enjoyed certain benefits in life, but his owner never made a cent in stud fees. As a matter of fact, since most stud contracts call for a repeat service in case the bitch misses (and a refund only after a second miss), the owner had spent the original stud fees and had one heck of a time coughing up the money a year later to repay the people who'd come to his dog.

If not for the money, then what? Dog-show people like to think of showing as a hobby (I call it an addiction). Or better yet a game. A game that involves pouring lye on a dog, drugging a dog's water, or giving a dog a hypo that makes him temporarily sterile (that happened at prestigious Westminster Garden). Sometimes it seems as if the name of the game is "Skillful Skullduggery." Or so one would assume, what with all the dirty tricks and fakery going on these days.

One terrier owner ruefully admitted, "A friend taught me how to show my bitch, but the dirty tricks I learned from having them done to me in the ring." There she was, after only nine times in the ring, already a master at crowding out another dog, throwing another dog's movement off, and diverting the judge's attention from another dog to hers. Give that woman another month of seasoning and she'll know how to spook any dog in the ring, temporarily cripple the dogs in front or behind her, and agitate any competitor in the ring. Since she's in terriers, she probably won't need to know how to double-handle like the people do in the bigger breeds, such as German shepherd dogs. Double-handling is a lot of fun to watch; it's like watching a dual track meet. Inside the ring, the dog and his handler are told to gait, or run around the ring, to show off the dog's movement. That is the signal to an owner or friend to run around the outside of the ring, urging the dog on.

This type of trick, like so many others, is easy to detect if one just keeps one's eyes open. The sophisticated dog people are more apt to go in for fakery, also known as cosmetology and/or cosmetic surgery. For example, dogs have their ears put into "molds" of one kind or another at eight weeks to insure that they "develop" properly. Other top winners walk around with half a pound of antiphlogistics on their ears for five days a week and half a pound of metal filings for two days—this to correct "flyaway" ears that don't fold over properly.

Now, since the beginning of that new veterinary specialty, dentistry, rarely do dogs come into the ring with homemade braces on their teeth. Instead they sport caps. Tails are fixed surgically or weighted down, sometimes even broken and reset and broken and reset again, in an attempt to get them to conform to whatever the standard calls for. Have you ever seen a dog with a cast on his tail? He's the most woebegone soul imaginable, and terribly frustrated, because suddenly that tail doesn't wag freely and properly.

Eye operations are commonplace, with haws (the inner eyelids) clipped or tattooed to get the right shape or color. Even the shape of the eyes can be altered to correct a fault or get the right expression. One owner of a dog took along a close-up of the top-winning dog in her breed and asked the surgeon to make her dog's eyes look just like that. He did. Dogs with yellow eyes appear in the ring dark-eyed thanks to drops administered just before show time.

Dogs with too much skin under their throats have their throats lifted, so to speak, and the excess cut out. For the dog born lacking a testicle or two, the vet just implants an artificial one or two. This particular gambit backfired on the owner of one monorchid (a dog with only one testicle descended into the scrotum). After the artificial one was implanted, the second one came down naturally. And there he was with the only three-testicled dog in town.

Such dirty tricks, such elaborate and frequently expensive fakery, can be explained by statistics supplied by David Wachsman, of the AKC. In 1974, there were 799,612 dogs shown, an increase of 6.5 percent in number of dogs competing over 1973. In that same year, 1974, there were 9,101 champions, an increase of only 4.6 percent over 1973. However, in relationship to the total number of dogs shown, the actual number of new champions *decreased* by 1.7 percent. And this has been the trend over the past twenty years. Putting it another way, the probability of any one dog in any given show becoming a champion, as computed by a computer expert, is between 10 and 15 percent. Or, to make the same point still another way, the odds *against* a dog becoming a champion are 8 to 1. So, the only chance of improving those odds are to, first, have the best dog around or, second, make him look like the best dog around with a little veterinary voodoo or, third, make all the others look worse by playing dirty tricks on them.

Once one gets that champion, by hook or by crook, then comes campaigning, wherein one champion competes against other champions. At the normal all-breed show, a dog would be shown first within his own breed in the "Specials," or champion class. If he won that and went Best of Breed (or Variety), he would go into a class with all the other BOBs in his Group—Sporting, Hound, Working, Terrier, Toy, or Nonsporting. Then the winners of each group, six of them in all, compete against each other for Best in Show.

Once one is into campaigning a dog, one has graduated to the big time, to the big expenses, to where the real money is to be made. But not by the dog owner. By everyone else. Beginning with the show-giving club. It will collect an entry fee of approximately $10 for every dog competing (of which 16 to 18 percent will be champions being campaigned). In 1974, show-giving clubs made close to $8 million from their shows. Of course, they had expenses; they had to pay to have a superintendent send out entry blanks or premium lists and then to print a catalog of all those completed entries (for which the show charges the public anywhere from $1.50 to $5). Also, there was a charge for renting the tents, portable johns, and other apparatus, including seldom enough chairs.

After all those and any other incidental expenses are paid—such as the judges' salaries, expenses, and transportation—there is always a tidy sum left over. For example, one show-giving club in the Midwest isn't a club at all; it's a profit-making corporation that discovered there were such profits to be made in dogshows, it's gone from giving one show per year to two. This is a trend that will be seen more in the future as others want to cash in. Already the three-day-weekend has been created to accommodate all the shows these clubs want to give. It would not be farfetched to suppose that at some point we will have dog shows every night of the week as well—if only they can find the space. Who knows, maybe we'll have dog-show stadiums and arenas someday, as we do for other organized sports.

There are others standing there with outstretched hands willing to separate a dog owner from his money. The handlers, for one. To have a handler at one end of the lead in the Best-of-Breed competition will cost anywhere from $25 to $50, say $35 average. If the dog wins and goes into the group competition, there may be another charge, say $15, for handling him. If he wins, the handler collects a bonus, $50 for first place, less for second, third, or fourth. The winner of the group is now eligible for Best in Show, and most handlers will take him into that for free (it's good publicity). If the dog wins, there's another bonus. Usually $100. The total handler's fees for one Best-in-Show win could come to $200.

Understandably—they don't want to frighten newcomers away—most handlers are reluctant, to say the least, to discuss how much money they make in their profession. But in the early 1960s *Sports Illustrated* ran an article on the top female handler—maybe the top handler, period—of that time, Anne Hone Rogers, who had to be making $50,000 a year. More recently, Ric Chashoudian was the subject of an in-depth article by the *Los Angeles Times*. It was an eye-opener. For one thing, he grossed $150,000 one year, with $20,000 coming from one owner for handling her dog, the lakeland terrier that was the top dog in the U.S. in 1974. Very few handlers do as well, but few are starving, either (witness the lavish motor homes many use to take themselves to and from the shows).

Then there are the photographs taken to commemorate each win. They'll run as much as $10 per in color, but one will have to buy extra black-and-white transfers for magazines that don't print color.

Speaking of magazines, it is here that one separates the rich from their money. I refer to advertising. And advertising is an absolute necessity if one really wants to succeed in a big way. For a starter, one runs one picture a month—can't run more, as of 1975—in the dog-show bible, the AKC *Gazette*. This will cost around $500 a year depending on the size of the photographs, and I'm not talking full-pagers, either. Next, you have the magazines that admit, "yes, we send complimentary copies to all group and most all-breed judges, about 2,000 in all." To reach those judges and impress them, full-page ads are the thing. They can set one back as much as $350 per page per issue, and one must be in at least three national dog magazines per month, and plan to take regular ads in all the specialty breed magazines and in the dog-show programs. Add all that up, and one can readily understand how one owner could spend almost $30,000 in one year advertising one champion.

Then there are those costs one doesn't declare on one's income tax: the charges for fixing shows. Especially paying off judges. For example, although judges do get paid for their work at shows, some have been known to live on spaghetti while waiting for the judging assignments to come through. So, yes, some judges are not above accepting "gifts," especially the monetary kind. However, smart judges don't take checks that can be shown to others—or do they?

There are other ways of fixing a show besides buying off the judges. There is, for example, the reappearance of that Elizabethan novelty, the paid claque, which applauds when *the* right dog is moved before the judge, just in case he forgot those thirty-six full-page ads the owner bought. This only costs a cocktail party after the show to "celebrate," which could even be tax deductible.

One of the most interesting, visually, of all the devices used to influence judges was one employed by a Pembroke Welsh corgi owner, known professionally as "Irma the Body." Each year, they say, she sent those favored judges on her Christmas list a card showing herself in all of her natural glory. And in those pre-*Oui* days, such a card was treasured.

Speaking of spectacles, from the spectator's point of view you get more for your money at a cat show than at a dog show. For one thing, a cat show is colorful; a dog show is not. The cat people go to great lengths to decorate the cages the cats are kept in. Some go in for

Oriental motifs, such as topping the cages with pagoda roofs. Others make "Swiss chalets" out of the crates. Almost all, if they have nothing else, are elaborately swathed and draped with colorful hangings, with plush cushions on which the cats languorously recline. And then there are the cats. Cats and more cats, in an unbelievable range of colors and color combinations.

As far as the actual show itself is concerned, it is a strange, contradictory combination of absolute chaos and complete inertia. By that I mean there are many, many people rushing hither and yon as they go from show ring to show ring, but the cats themselves do nothing, not even when shown. The cat doesn't take a step. It doesn't meow. It doesn't move. All it has to do, as one cat owner put it, "is be a rag. It also helps if it is alive and breathing and of the proper coat, color, and conformation for its breed." Not necessarily in that order.

The actual judging procedure is quite simple. The judge removes the cat from a cage; puts it on the judging table; runs his hands over it to judge its bone structure, coat, and condition; then puts it back into the cage. That's that.

The cats themselves look indifferent, if not outright bored. And one seldom sees or hears a happy cat at a cat show. But there are loads of happy exhibitors. That's because the cat-show people get their money's worth at every cat show. Walk down the aisle and see cage after cage with ten or twelve ribbons and rosettes proudly displayed. On a good day, a truly good cat might have fifteen to eighteen rosettes awarded in the course of one show. Correction. Not one show. For what is going on is actually several shows simultaneously.

Cats, although classified, like dogs, by breed, are divided for show purposes into two groups, or categories: longhair and shorthair. In the usual two-day show, two judges will each judge all of the longhairs, while another pair of judges are each judging all of the shorthairs. Thus, at the cat's very first show, he is actually entered in two specialty shows depending on his breed's length of coat. Then, at the shows, there are two all-breed rings, wherein shorthairs and longhairs compete against each other, again doing it twice under different judges. So, the cat has now, in one show, competed under four different judges. Since all it takes to become a champion is six winner's ribbons (but under three different judges), it is conceivable that a good specimen could finish after attending two events, that is, two 2-day shows. Then he can go on to win his grand championship. This requires 150 grand-champion points, garnered by getting one point for every champion defeated at a show, but of necessity scored under three different judges.

These can be accumulated in three steps: (1) Going best champion in his breed in his ring, which will net him one point per champion of his breed entered and thus defeated. (2) Continuing on to compete against other breed champions in his group. Going Best Longhair or Best Shorthair Champion will allow him to pick up one point for every longhair or shorthair champion entered, and thus defeated, within his group. (He must thus relinquish those points achieved by going Best of Breed, otherwise there would be duplications of points.) (3) Going on to become best champion in the all-breed ring, which means getting one point for every champion defeated in the other group. Or, in effect, for every champion entered in that all-breed ring.

Since each champion competes twice within his breed and twice within his group, and then again in the all-breed competition, he can conceivably double the number of points he won. Thus, it is possible to achieve a grand champion in one two-day show. However, that is a grand championship in only one association. If one wishes really to do the thing right, one must register one's cats with all nine cat registry associations and make one's grand championship (under differing rules) in each.

There are certain essential differences between cat and dog shows. For one thing, there are no professional handlers in cats; none are needed, the judge does it all. If one wishes to have a cat campaigned, one has it agented—an informal arrangement usually made between friends. Also, if one's goal is winning enough ribbons and rosettes to paper one's walls, then the cat show is the place to go. It is not unusual to see more ribbons and rosettes handed out in a class than there are entries.

A third, but very essential, difference between the two is in regard to their position on altered animals. Recognizing a very basic fact of life—that we are experiencing an agonizing pet population explosion—the cat people have opened their shows to neutered animals. The spay works toward and wins his premiership and grand premiership exactly like his whole brothers and sisters.

This would not go down at dog shows. The AKC, while it publicly deplores the population explosion among dogs, continues obstinately to consider the dog show as the breeder's showcase. (If this really were the case, then the biggest class in any breed would be the Bred-by-Exhibitor class. More than half the time there isn't a single entry in that class, which to my mind kills the AKC's theory.) No dog that is neutered can be shown in point competition; however, they are allowed in the obedience rings. Without commenting for the moment on hypocrisy on the AKC's part, suffice it to say that their position is a combination of old-fashioned tradition and facing the economic facts of life: the production of puppies and their registering are the AKC's largest sources of income.

If one has had it with the high cost of dog shows but is not prepared to switch to cats, there are alternatives. The dog people themselves have decided to find other sources of pleasure in their dogs besides show potential. To do so, they have gone back to the original purposes for which those dogs were bred. (Hurrah!) For example, amateur whippet racing. Although touted as something new, it is actually quite an old sport, at least in this country; it was the province of the rich in the early part of this century and a casualty of the Great Depression. Only in the Baltimore-Washington, D.C., area did much whippet racing occur after 1929. From then on, about 75 percent of all whippets in the country were located in that area. Then, by 1948, all whippet racing disappeared. It wasn't until the mid 1950s that it was revived, and then through the efforts of Mrs. Wendell Howell of California, who believed that a dog wasn't complete unless it was more than a pet or beauty-contest winner—it had to be utilitarian, too.

Although whippet racing is not an official sport of the AKC, race meetings are held under official rules and regulations of the American Whippet Club and are operated by local individuals and clubs. To acknowledge expertise in this area, an Award of Racing Merit is given, and although not an official AKC title, many a whippet owner is prouder to have an A.R.M. after the name than a Ch. in front of it.

Inspired perhaps by the success of the whippet fancy in obtaining multipurpose dogs, fed up with comments like "you call *that* a dog?" and others that are unprintable, and desirous of proving that the Afghan, too, has a heritage and abilities beyond just looking pretty, an association was formed called the American Sighthound Field Association. In the 1970s rules and regulations were drawn up for holding gazehound races in America. Taking a page from the whippet group's experience with the AKC (The American Kennel Club does not wish to take part in racing of any type), this group called their races "lure coursing" or "lure field trials." Actually, these are much more accurate names, for the fastest dog in each race may not be declared the victor unless he has shown: enthusiasm and follow (worth 30 points), agility (25 points), and endurance (20 points) and has escaped a pre-slip penalty or a recall penalty, each costing 10 points per judge. Speed is worth only 25 points out of the possible 100 points a dog might get.

The first such licensed Lure Field Trial in the northeastern U.S. was run on November 17, 1974, under the sponsorship of the Delaware Valley Afghan Hound Club and the Borzoi Club of Delaware Valley.

By all accounts, it was quite a day. Verbal enthusiasm from all quarters had been great for months, but until the entries closed, no one realized just *how* eager eastern sighthound owners were for the ASFA events. An astonishing entry of eighty-four Afghans and borzois (forty-two of each) was recorded. Area newspapers had provided extensive coverage, and calls from all kinds of dog owners and non-dog owners alike gave a clue to the amount of public interest in the sport.

A few weeks before, someone had suggested the ambassadors from Afghanistan and Russia be invited. The Field Committee agreed to the idea with a bit of amusement, expecting that no ambassador would drive all the way from Washington just to watch the sighthounds run. There was near panic when His Excellency Abdullah Malikyar from Afghanistan accepted, saying he would arrive about 10:00 A.M. There was no reply from the Russians.

At 10:15 A.M. a big black car arrived at the entrance, and the teen-age parking detail signaled it toward the cornfield across the street where they had been told to park the public. The driver strenuously objected, and just in the nick of time, one sharp-eyed kid spotted the DPL license and escorted His Excellency up the drive to his reserved spot. Fortunately, the ambassador has a good sense of humor.

Thirty-seven Afghans were present for the draw, followed, at the end of their three stakes, by three pups. The rolling Pennsylvania countryside around Norma and Bob Sellers' Vale Vue Kennels reverberated with cheers for the coursing hounds all day long. Each hound was carefully muzzled personally by Norma and adorned with the proper racing blanket. Almost one-third of the dogs running were AKC champions, several of them currently active in breed rings. None of these owners would take a chance on their dogs being ripped up during a heated dispute with another dog over a few strips of white plastic. Five years of experience with many breeds at Vale Vue has shown that a hound either will chase the lure or not, regardless of a muzzle. Taking the muzzle off a reluctant hound doesn't seem to help.

The following spring, not only forty Afghans and thirty-six borzois were brought, but so were fifteen whippets, five Scottish deerhounds, six Irish wolfhounds, eleven Salukis (including a National Specialty Winner), and one greyhound. Representatives of all seven of the breeds that hunt by sight performed well and delighted the crowd, which included, as special guest, AKC prexy John LaFore.

Not only the hound owners and breeders are interested in testing their dogs. In the West, there is an organization called the Stock Dog Fanciers of Colorado, which holds trials to test the working or herding ability of dogs. Some of the dogs entered are just continuing their day-to-day life, herding farm animals together. Others, such as breed champions and obedience-titled dogs, may never have seen a ranch before. Some of the breeds eligible for these trials would surprise you. The old English sheepdog, living up to his name; the Briard; the standard schnauzer; the puli; even a samoyed, a dog used in the old days for herding reindeer. (One such dog in the Boulder area happened on the scene when a cattle truck overturned, allowing its occupants to escape. The helpful samoyed, without training, rounded up and held the cattle.)

The terrier people have formed the American Working Terrier Association. Begun in 1971 to keep alive the natural abilities for which these dogs were bred, the trials attempt to duplicate natural conditions, but without bloodshed or damage to either the terrier or his quarry. The tunnels (or "earth," as they are called) are lined on the top and two sides with wood. For new or novice dogs, these tunnels are ten feet long; for more experienced dogs, the tunnels are thirty feet long. At the end of it is a caged quarry, either a rat, raccoon, or badger. The idea is for the dog to find the tunnel, go to earth after a quarry, and then work it (chase it, giving voice as he does). At one such trial, more than 25 percent of the entries were show champions or on their way to their championships. Among the breeds being worked are wire fox terriers, Australian terriers, Lakelands, Norwichs, Sealyhams, Bedlingtons, Westies, miniature schnauzers, cairns, smooth foxes, and Scotches; and, with great democracy, the terrier people opened their arms and admitted a non-terrier to their group: the dachshund, both long- and wire-haired. Again, the natural ability of the dog counts more than speed. Although a working certificate is awarded, the coveted award is the Certificate of Gameness, given to a dog scoring 100 percent on willingness to go to ground without the assistance of the handler, creep down the thirty-foot-long and nine-inch-wide tunnel, handle the three ninety-degree turns, face the quarry, and give voice.

Not to be outdone, the working-breed owners have formed a group, or I should say many groups, that hold Schutzhund Trials. At these, a dog must excel in (1) obedience, much of it more advanced then the standard AKC obedience work; (2) tracking, again harder than the AKC version; and (3) "man work," or protection, which involves the greatest amount of cooperation and control between handler and dog.

Naturally, there is enthusiasm for anything new. What is more surprising is the continuing popularity of regular field trials. From 1964 to 1974, according to the AKC, beagle field-trial-attendance statistics maintained themselves, while all others either doubled or increased by better than 100 percent. Examples cited in the AKC

*Gazette* include: basset hound trials and starters doubled; retriever trials increased by 25 percent, but the starters increased by 100 percent; English springer spaniel trials doubled, and the starters increased by 100 percent; and pointing-breed trials doubled, and the starters increased by 118 percent.

I would be remiss if I did not point out that the term "starters" can be misinterpreted (and frequently is). The AKC does not count the number of different dogs entered in field trials (nor shows for that matter). What it counts is the total number of entries. Therefore, if a dog is shown more than once, he's counted more than once. And since, for example in beagles, a dog must win three licensed field-trial classes, in the process collecting 120 points or one for every dog he beats, a dog may have to be shown dozens of times. So, don't be discouraged by the idea that you might have to face as many as 1,811 competitors at any given field trial. It's not so.

What should discourage you is the fact that there are thousands, if not hundreds of thousands, of men who've devoted all of their adult lives to attempting to turn a hunting dog into a field-trial champion. They have not managed to do so. Not even running against other amateurs. For example, in 1973, Vizla owners were the only ones to have more amateur field champions than regular champions. In 1974, the situation was reversed, but the Brittany and Labrador people upheld the honors for amateurs.

If you are still not discouraged and still want to give it a try, then go to it, provided you've got the financial backing. Don't let anyone tell you the training of a dog is a backyard, shoestring operation. Take it from the pros, the people at the AKC, who hand out the field-trial-championship certificates. They maintain that "Buying, rearing and training a dog to its field championship is a gamble at best, a true labor of love and one that may require a grubstake of some $10,000." Many field-trial men consider this to be a very conservative estimate, especially since no value is given to the time spent, which could, over the four years involved, be counted in thousands of hours. And dollars.

It should also be noted that buying a ready-made field champion, such as a Labrador, can cost a small fortune. For example, in 1973, you could have bought a Mercedes-Benz 450 SL-C for the same price you'd pay for a top-caliber Labrador retriever. In 1968, promising swamp dogs, as they're called, were in the 5, 10, and 15 class— $5,000, $10,000, and $15,000, that is. As in every other area, inflation has set in here, too. The $15,000 (1968) models were going in 1973 for $20,000. In 1980, who knows? The top price paid, to my knowledge, still remains $22,000. (The top price asked is a different story.) For that $22,000 you get no guarantees and no warranties. But if you can

*The New York Times/Barton Silverman*
A relay race of obedience-trained dogs is, obviously, serious business for animals and animal owners alike.

afford that much, you'll undoubtedly acquire a dog in good running order.

It is a strange commentary on dogs, and what man has done with them, that the ultimate achievement these days was at one time commonplace. I mean by that owning a dual, or field/bench (show), champion. At one time, it wasn't unusual for a dog to be hunted all week, given a bath Friday night, and put into the show ring the following day to hold his own with all the other dogs. Today, the dual champion is a true rarity.

## TIPS ON PLAYING THE SHOW/FIELD-TRIAL GAME:

1. Get an honest evaluation of your animal before you do anything else. A professional handler will usually be happy to look your dog over. The really top ones, the ones who lay their reputations on the line every time they enter the ring or take a dog into the field, will give you the most dispassionate evaluation. They may charge for it, too. If so, it could save you a potful. The cost? No more than the entry fee for the first event they will discourage you from entering. As Bill Trainor, president of the Professional Handlers' Association, puts it, "for every dog that I agree has show potential, I turn away eight or nine."
2. If you are determined to show or field trial, don't throw away good money. Keep the rejected dog as a pet and buy another, one with real potential—verified by a pro. Again, the handlers can steer you to a good one. Although the initial cost of such an animal may seem steep ($750–$1,000 for a nine- to twelve-month-old field prospect, as much for a similarly aged show prospect), in the long run you'll spend less, because this money is truly an investment, one that can eventually pay off.

# XIII   REGISTRIES

> If a breed isn't recognized by the AKC, to me it's a mutt, it isn't a breed. The American Kennel Club—that's what it's all about.
>
> A TERRIER BREEDER

> It's high time the AKC gets off its registration-only policy and does something for a change.
>
> A BASSET BREEDER

Most Americans will never have any contact with the AKC. Not even those who should. The AKC itself estimates that at least 40 percent of all owners who could register their dogs with the AKC won't. It is evidently good enough for them to have AKC papers\*, which are proof positive that the dog is purebred. For other owners, it's enough to know that the AKC is there, serving as a better-business bureau of dogs, a canine consumer advocate, and a court of last resort.

That is not the case. These are all misconceptions that are fostered in large part by the AKC itself, which for years has been mysterious, devious, and generally inaccessible to the masses. Occasionally they have come down from Mount Olympus long enough to mingle with members of the fourth estate and feed bits of information to their

---

\* "Papers" is dogese for the blue slip, or individual registration application, provided each member of a litter born of parents already AKC registered if the breeder (the owner of the dam) fills out, has signed, and files a litter application, and pays the fee. The blue slip is then given to each puppy's buyer. It allows them to choose and have registered with the AKC any dog name, provided it is not more than twenty-six letters long, the name of a celebrity upon whom it might pass ridicule, or the same as that of another dog of the same breed. Filled out and accompanied by another fee, this brings the owner a purple and white permanent registration certificate. "Papers" should not be construed to include health certificates and/or pedigrees.

worshipers everywhere. Thus it was in 1954 that a reporter for *The New Yorker* magazine wrote a two-part profile of the AKC. According to William F. Stifel, executive secretary of the AKC, the reporter "was good at telling stories that were funny at the expense of the dog lover. But he finally confessed to members of the staff that there was one thing he hadn't done—he hadn't found a good scandal."

That story was written more than twenty years ago. Today, that reporter would not lack for a good scandal. For example, "AKC Reg." was once the dog world's equivalent of the Good Housekeeping Seal of Approval. No more. As Alexander Feldman, chairman of the board of AKC, said in 1973, "AKC registration is not a guarantee of quality." Mr. Feldman has also described the steps that the AKC has taken to prevent people from making such a mistake. They include running classified ads in major Sunday newspapers; printing posters, some 100,000 of which you can bet will never find their way to the place they're needed—the pet shop; and enclosing a leaflet on responsible dog ownership along with every puppy's new permanent registration certificate, i.e., weeks too late to do any good. But nowhere in the ads or on the poster is the buyer warned that a puppy's eligibility for "AKC registration is not a guarantee of quality." Only in the leaflet, that always-too-late leaflet, and on the last page at that, does the AKC reveal what dog fanciers have long known—that being AKC registered is no measure of quality. In fact, it isn't even a guarantee that a dog is purebred.

The most recent proof of that, to my knowledge, came out of a small-claims court in Grand Rapids, Michigan. The dog in question was purchased and registered as a purebred basset, but it didn't grow up to look like one. When it was shown to another basset breeder plus other dog experts, the consensus of opinion was that this was a beagle/basset cross. The puppy's breeder, according to all reports, held that the litter was AKC registered and that therefore she was not the one at fault.

Although the AKC, after viewing pictures and hearing the story, did write the owners stating that the ancestry of the dog was questionable, they took their blessed time doing something about it. In the meantime, the owners took the case to court, where the judge ruled that "the ad in the paper offering the puppies for sale stated that they were AKC registered; it did not say that the puppies were purebred, and since when they bought the puppy they were presented the blue slip, they did in fact have an AKC registered dog."

The irony of all this, however, was that the alleged sire of the puppy was only $4\frac{1}{2}$ months old at the time of the breeding—$2\frac{1}{2}$ months younger than the minimum age accepted by the AKC for breeding purposes. By their own rules and regulations, the AKC should have

## REGISTRIES 161

rejected the litter application before a single puppy received its blue slip. For the AKC then to sit back and many months later say that they would have to investigate the matter is a farce.

The AKC does admit, reluctantly, that AKC registry is no proof of being purebred. In an attempt to remedy that, the AKC now has a new individual puppy "Registration Application." On it, most of the potential color possibilities of the particular breed are listed so as to enable the owner to circle the right one.

Are they using this to check each offspring against the parents' coat colors to determine by genetics whether those parents could have produced these pups? *They are not.* (Even though they have the information on the parents in their computers and a book on coat-color inheritance in their library.)

Are they using those color choices to screen out those dogs disqualified by their breed standards? *They are not.* White German shepherds, white boxers, and dogs of any other off-color you can think of are, under AKC rules, registrable if their parents were AKC registered. By this token, any "sport" of any kind—dwarf great Danes, long-haired Weimaraners, polka-dotted poodles, or anything else under the sun—is as much qualified for registration as any champion-of-record of any breed.

Are they demanding, as the horse people do, a picture of the "tie," or actual mating, to prove that these parents were indeed mated? *They are not.*

Are they requiring photographs of each dog being registered to ascertain visually that the dog is indeed a member of the breed? *They are not.* Except when registering a dog presently registered with another registering body, foreign or domestic. (These dogs must be photographed, in color no less, from the front and side. The photographs submitted must be no smaller than 3 inches by 4 inches, and the application accompanying them must be notarized.) This holier-than-thou attitude toward foreign-bred dogs seems out of place, since an AKC-registered dog is less apt to be purebred than, for example, any dog bred in West Germany, where breeding is stringently controlled.

Are they requiring impartial witnesses for each breeding, who will swear that it occurred? *They are not.*

Are they requiring notarized signatures on the litter application? *They are not.*

Are they checking signatures to make sure no signature is a forgery? *They are not.* Even though one of the easiest ways to fake good papers is to pick a stud's name from an old show catalog and scribble the owner's signature on the litter application blank. The chances of being caught are practically nil. For one thing, the AKC doesn't play handwriting expert and attempt to verify signatures. And then, even if the dog is dead, the AKC probably doesn't know it. The vast majority of dog owners refuse or don't bother to return the AKC registration certificates to the AKC if the dog dies. It happens to be an AKC rule, but they don't bother to enforce it.

As for the pups, are they requiring that each pup be identified by sex and color at birth on the litter application blank to prevent a dead pup's papers being sold or used for another? *They are not.* It is true that they ask for the number of males and females living at the time the application is filed, but they make no effort to find out whether or not that number is accurate.

Naturally, the AKC has a ready explanation for what it does and does not do. "But how far can the AKC go to correct the wrongs that have been, and are being, perpetrated upon the unwary public?" asks Roy H. Carlberg, vice-president of the AKC. "Many people believe that the AKC is all-powerful, all-knowing and in complete authority over all aspects of the dog game. This, needless to say, is erroneous. We are limited to the provisions of our charter and to the enforcement of those registration rules and regulations governing the registration of individual dogs and litters."

Poor, helpless AKC. Its hands tied by its own charter. One hates to kick a full-grown body when it's down, but "limited to the provisions of our charter"? I suggest they read the foreword to their own booklet of rules on registrations and dog shows, which specifically states that in Section 2 of that charter, the objects of incorporation are described and include: "to regulate the conduct of persons interested in exhibiting, running, breeding, registering, purchasing and selling dogs. . . . to detect, prevent, and punish frauds in connection therewith." Which gives them exactly those powers that they have chosen not to exercise.

It was not the AKC that brought suit against those California Docktors Pet Centers for misrepresentation and fraud in connection with the ten-year unconditional guarantee—that just happened to be as conditional as could be—that Docktors was offering the purchaser of a puppy. It was the ADOA, another organization with no more ability than the AKC to, in Mr. Carlberg's words, "usurp the functions of federal, state or local agencies, that, under law, are empowered to take remedial or punitive action in matters involving dogs." (By the way, the ADOA won a settlement for $51,000.)

The AKC, understandably, doesn't want to get bogged down in legal proceedings. But it isn't as if there is nothing else they could do, even though there are thorny problems. For instance:

*Idea:* Issue breeding permits only after the dog's health and genetic soundness have been proven or certified by a vet. *Problem:* All those blank puppy health certificates presently being signed by vets.

*Idea:* Require each parent to have one or more championship points before allowing its get to be registered. *Problem:* A dog's appearance does not determine what genes it passes on. A dog may have a problem that would disqualify him from being shown and yet be able to pass on some tremendously desirable characteristics to its offspring.

*Idea:* Do as Canada does, and have two types of registration. And let the breeder determine whether the pup should be bred or not. (Actually, the AKC is indeed considering such a system—and has been for years. Mr. Feldman, chairman of the board, said as much back in 1973, when he revealed that the board of the AKC had under consideration "the possibility of a graded system of registration for breeding and show on one hand, and pet-only on the other." The board, as of this writing, has not put such a system into practice.) *Problem:* Only concerned breeders would bother to do it, and they already are selling their nonsuitable pups under a "must spay or neuter" agreement.

*Idea:* Limit the number of litters any one individual could breed in a year to fewer than ten. *Problem:* Easily circumvented by using family members' names or even false names. In fact, when it comes to the products of fake papers—the poor-quality pups churned out by puppy mills—the AKC, in the words of its board chairman, takes this position: "I feel strongly that a well-organized, dedicated local club can be far more effective in combating the puppy mills than the AKC. However, I also feel it is AKC's responsibility to assist and provide guidance in every way possible."

Bravo, Mr. Feldman. The only trouble is that local clubs don't approve litter applications; the AKC does. They don't register individual dogs; the AKC does. If the AKC were willing to abdicate this responsibility to the local clubs, then I agree, a local club would be far more effective. But is the AKC willing to give up the revenues from litter applications and individual registrations—the $6,467,818 it received in 1974, or 86.5 percent of its total income? They are not.

(It might be wise to point out here that the AKC, according to its annual report, spends more than 68 percent of its total revenues for "payroll and related expenses." Which does not include the payroll for those publishing the *Gazette,* show awards, or the *Stud Book Register.* Add those in, and an estimate of 75 percent for payroll would not be unreasonable.)

To understand why the AKC acts or does not act as it does, one must understand that when it was founded, more than 90 years ago, its purpose was to "referee" a gentleman's game. It was founded by a group of amateur sportsmen, and to this day it is run by amateurs who brag that they maintain the amateur tradition. Unfortunately, today there are people in the dog business whose livelihood depends on selling dogs, and these are not gentlemen by any stretch of the imagination.

The AKC, those rich, old men in their gold-domed (literally) ivory tower, may well have been jolted out of their complacency by a scorching letter written back in mid-1972. It came from a staff veterinarian at the Illinois Department of Agriculture. In it, David R. Bromwell, D.V.M., carefully spelled out what Illinois was doing to govern the licensing of pet shops and dog dealers. He then challenged the AKC to pitch in and do its part.

Specifically, Bromwell accused the AKC of being blind to its responsibilities, of talking a good game while doing nothing constructive. He particularly singled out for criticism the fact that (at that time) the AKC had no personnel assigned to investigate, document, and verify the breeding, transferring, and other operations of the nation's puppy mills.

The AKC got the message. At least enough to appear to do something about it. It hired two field agents (and has since doubled that number) to police puppy mills and related operations all over the country. When queried as to what the agent does when he "investigates" a complaint about a puppy mill, an AKC official at New York headquarters cited but one thing: "Educate them on record-keeping."

Now, anybody with half a brain knows "educating" a puppy-mill operator into proper record keeping à la AKC regulations isn't the answer. Look at one Midwestern operation with 1,400 brood bitches. It's so systematized that it purchased a large, used mail-sorter (the cubbyhole type) once used by the U.S. Post Office. When one of the bitches gets bred, her name goes up atop a cubbyhole. And into that cubbyhole go all the pertinent data on the breeding. Once the bitch whelps, any further papers, such as vet certificates and AKC registration forms, go into that cubbyhole. Which certainly has the AKC's own recommended record book beat all hollow. In fact, this kennel could teach the AKC a thing or two about record keeping. They, at least, are efficient.

By the AKC's own admission, the above-mentioned type of breeding operation is not uncommon. A new AKC computer system regularly updates a printout naming those individuals applying for ten or more litter registrations per year. One printout shows that in Iowa, out of 14,656 litters registered in 1974, only 500 breeders accounted for more than 56.5 percent of the total. In Kansas, those registering ten or more accounted for 60.4 percent. But these were admittedly the high ones. A more normal figure would be that of Arkansas, where only 37 percent of the litters registered came from breeders of ten or more litters a year.

According to the AKC, the largest number of litters registered in one year by any one breeder (as of April 1975 in those states checked) was 284. Using the AKC's average of 4.7 puppies per litter, that was at least 1,335 puppies wholesaled in one year by one breeder. But this was just a drop in the bucket compared to the Illinois woman who sold 3,500 pups out of her basement in one year. Between the two of them, these two breeders produced more than half a million dollars worth of pups in one year. And those same two individuals produced potential revenues for the AKC of $90,957, or 1.4 percent of their total budget.

The AKC says it takes an average of three weeks to process a litter registration. Puppy mills ship out their products at four weeks with papers. Allowing for weekends and post-office misroutings, the only way to get papers on four-week-old pups is by registering them the day they're born (or before). Yet studies show that pup mortality in the first two weeks of life is high, which means that at least 10 percent of all puppies registered by large-scale operations will be dead before their papers arrive. As a result, those papers could be used to move other pups than those for which the papers were issued. There have even been auctions of excess AKC papers. Two for a dollar is cheap compared to paying the AKC's fees, which, as of this writing, are $7 per litter application. At their own average rate of 4.7 pups per litter, that works out to $1.49 per pup. But at 50 cents for fake papers, puppy millers save 99 cents. And pet producers who refuse to spend $2 on temporary shots until a pup is ordered sure aren't going to pay a dollar more than they have to.

The AKC says that once they have all breeds computerized (not just on their first-stage computers, but on the more complex ones), processing a litter registration will be merely a matter of days. The beneficiary then will not be the individual who sells his pups at eight weeks and up, but the ones who ship their pups out of the Topeka airport at four weeks of age. (Over 800 went out in one day, by the way, according to the AKC.)

What the AKC is doing is simply good, solid business practice: identifying their customers, determining their needs, and satisfying those needs as efficiently as possible. Unfortunately for the AKC, they have two very different groups of customers: the puppy millers who produce most of the revenues and the dog fancy that use it via *expensive* shows and field trials.

When you get right down to it, the puppy mills are the most reasonable. All they ask of the AKC is to be left alone, to get their papers processed quickly, and to have the AKC continue sponsoring all those dog shows and field trials so that "AKC" continues to mean something to the gullible public.

The dog fancy is not so cooperative. It is, in fact, downright pugnacious. It wants "AKC registered" to really mean something, and it wants those who demean it put out of business—by the AKC. At the same time, these people want to go on enjoying shows, being awarded championships, reading the *Gazette,* and acting as if they were really pulling their weight. The irony of all this is that the dog fancy need the puppy producers more than the puppy producers need the snob appeal of "AKC reg." And the AKC knows it. The AKC also knows that without the puppy producers and their registration fees, the dog-show game couldn't be played, nor could the amateur sportsmen and ex-politicians running the AKC enjoy the prestige and perquisites derived from the game.

Hoist by its own petard, the AKC has no choice but to attempt to satisfy both of its masters without antagonizing either. Thus, they educate the puppy mills and show them how to live within AKC regulations while at the same time boasting to the dog fancy that they cancelled 300 litter registrations for "cause" in 1974. (A whole 300 out of more than 418,000 granted.) Then they computerized their record keeping, enabling them to process papers faster and also spiel out impressive statistics about the size of the dog-show game. At the same time, of course, they are increasing their fees—computers are expensive, you know, and so are M.I.T. graduates to work them. Two-facedly, the AKC tells the puppy mills those fee increases are for services rendered; to the dog fancy the AKC says it imposes those higher fees to hurt the puppy mills: litter registrations up 40 percent, change of ownership up 100 percent—a stab at the heart of the puppy mills.

The idea of the AKC "coming to the fancy" instead of remaining untouchable behind its metropolitan walls was indeed a historic event, which occurred when an AKC-sponsored talkathon got under way at Atlantic City, New Jersey, in December 1973. A potentially worthwhile meeting, which wasn't. First of all, only known dog people were invited to attend and have a free lunch on the AKC. Of course, the public was not barred, but reservations were required and ads weren't run in the general media. So naturally, only dog people came. But *dog people already know the problems* in dogs. They have been the ones yelling for action. It is the puppy-buying public that needs to be educated and helped and protected.

The speeches were on dog shows, field trials, the duties of an AKC field man (one who attends shows, not polices puppy mills), and on the AKC—its size, history, and workings. And especially its good works. The prepared text of the proceedings, which does not include the scripts of all the films shown, runs twenty-four pages long. Each page is two columns wide, single-spaced, and printed in hard-to-read-but-gets-more-words-to-the-inch eight-point type. For many of those who attended that meeting or those like it in the months to come, it meant spending at least one night in a hotel. That alone should give you some idea of the type of people the AKC is attracting. Not many puppy millers, cutting corners wherever they can, can dole out $25 to $35 to spend a night in a hotel in order to spend a day listening to the AKC pat itself on the back.

That isn't to say that the AKC avoided pointing out problem areas, because they didn't. Take, for example, research. Dr. Priscilla K. Stockner, an advisor to the AKC, noted that "Research money is not readily available in any medical discipline, therefore the competition is keen. We are not looking for projects, they are looking for us. There is no shortage of capable investigators or problems which need solutions . . . I propose that there is a way for these questions to be answered. I propose that national breed clubs, kennel clubs, and obedience clubs can take an active part in canine research. I know that there are millions of dollars in just such club treasuries."

Meanwhile, the AKC, the biggest club of them all, the one with the 500-plus employees and the more than $7,476,000 annual income, boasts of having contributed a couple of hundred thousand dollars to the support of basic canine research. They spend twice that amount each year on stationery, telephones, postage, and similar staples. In 1974, the rent for their sumptuous quarters at 51 Madison Avenue in New York was 38 percent higher than their basic appropriation for "educational purposes and research on dog health"—$276,175 for rent, $200,000 for research.

Included in the latter are the costs of publicity, advertising, public relations, films shown here and abroad, and, of course, the costs of putting on those elaborate symposiums known as "A Day with AKC." Of what's left after that, not one cent went to help control or combat hereditary defects such as juvenile cataracts or progressive retinal atrophy, which cause blindness; heart defects, which kill; or hip and elbow dysplasia, which cripple. Instead, the AKC boasts of funding research on frozen canine semen, early detection of rabies, and heartworm prevention. Laudatory efforts indeed, but only the first should be of primary concern to the AKC. (The other two are also heavily funded by others, including drug companies.)

As for the research on frozen semen, it's a project long overdue, which is the direct result of the AKC's own rules and regulations against artificial insemination. The AKC, with its admittedly amateur sportsmen preserving the AKC's traditional amateur leadership, has been dragging its feet against a program that has revolutionized the cattle and dairy industries. Yet here, quite possibly, could be the salvation of purebred dogs. A puppy mill would not have to maintain a kennel full of money-eating stud dogs when they could buy—cheap—vials of semen from top-quality dogs. They would also be able to sell all of the get without replacing their studs periodically. They would be able to compete, quality-for-quality, with the best breeders in the country. The puppy-buying public as well as the stud-dog owners would benefit.

The AKC does not see it in this light. Instead of welcoming it with open arms, they note that "The application of this data poses several difficult and complicated questions for the AKC. The Board of Directors is already involved in discussing these questions and formulating well thought-out opinions and policies." It is questionable that these amateur sportsmen are the right ones to do so. In fact, the emphasis on amateurism and sportsmen may be the basic problem with the AKC.

With the pet population explosion a reality, more than 75 percent of AKC's twenty or thirty key executives should not be devoting their full energies to shows and related activities. Admittedly, the show game—if one can call it that—is useful in promoting the breeding and registering of dogs. It is, to rephrase the AKC's own words, the proof of the breeding. However, it is not profitable to the AKC. Despite the popular misconception, the AKC does not get a "take" from every dog-show event or match. Those $10 and up entry fees are the property of the show-giving club.

It is true that the AKC receives dues from its member clubs plus license fees for the holding of specified show events by member and nonmember clubs. Although it is impossible to ascertain from the AKC's financial sheet just how much was raised from these sources, a little detective work and one small calculator puts the total at less than 3 percent of the AKC's total income in 1974. In return for this miserly sum, the AKC is expected to maintain a staff of field representatives who attend almost every show to see that everything is up to snuff, keep and record show results, issue championship and other certificates, publish the *Gazette* and the *Stud Book*, issue judges' and handlers' licenses and, in the words of one official, "underwrite the vast expenses associated with the sport."

In reality, though, it is the puppy producers who are underwriting the sport. The 400-plus member clubs have made no effort to accept the financial responsibility of their sport. No wonder AKC officials, off the record, speak bitterly about the "contributions" their member clubs are making to purebred dogs.

The AKC's membership is composed of clubs, no individuals allowed. These are the parent clubs that write their breed's standard of perfection; local clubs that try to preserve, maintain, or attain a breed's standard; all-breed clubs that give shows that allow breeders and exhibitors to demonstrate their progress within that standard; and obedience- and field-trial clubs sponsoring events that give dogs a chance to do their thing. The way the AKC tells it, the organization is a simple thing: Each member club elects a delegate to the AKC, these delegates elect the board of directors, and the board of directors appoints the AKC executives. Obviously, from this, the delegates are in control of things. Only that isn't quite the way it goes.

For one thing, the AKC determines which clubs shall become members, and it accepts or rejects their constitutions. They also say who may or may not serve as a delegate. Witness this historic announcement made by the chairman of the board in 1973: "What I believe is most indicative of the Board's intention to meet all important problems 'head on' is the amendment to Article VI, Section I of the Constitution and By-Laws of the American Kennel Club. . . . I am proud to be the chairman of the Board that has the courage of its convictions by submitting to the Delegates an amendment which would delete the word 'male' before the word delegate." Bella Abzug, Shirley Chisholm, Margaret Chase Smith, what are you waiting for? Women's Lib has arrived at the AKC. Only something funny happened on the way to complete equality—one of the first women delegates duly elected to represent her all-breed club (which gives one of the largest shows in the country) was deemed unacceptable to the other members of the "club" and wasn't allowed to serve.

The male-chauvinist attitude of this good-old-boys club even extends to the working part of the organization. In the very expensive film made by the AKC, entitled "Inside the AKC," there are lots of females typing, filing, answering phones, and checking registrations. The only female "executive" shown is in charge of personnel. This despite the fact that in the dog business, and particularly in the show end of the business, there are as many females involved in breeding, training, showing, handling, stewarding, judging, and photographing, as there are males, perhaps more.

The AKC, however, is more than willing to capitalize on female labor. Take, for example, the *Gazette,* a magazine published monthly purely for the dog fancy. It is not available to the general public via newsstands. At $1 per copy and $20 for a three-year subscription, this one-inch-thick compendium of news has to be one of the big bargains in dogs. It brought in revenues of $432,654 in 1974 (before the one-photo-per-dog-per-issue rule went into effect). It costs $901,995 to publish—and that without paying the breed columnists one cent, even though they make the book worth subscribing to. Those columnists included, in one typical issue, two husband-wife teams, seventeen men, one initials/sex-unknown, and *sixty-six* women.

While the AKC may be a monolith, it is not a monopoly. At least not so long as the UKC has a say. Of course, to complicate matters, there happen to be two UKCs. One is the United Kennel Club, Inc., a privately owned, nonmember, profit-making organization located in Kalamazoo, Michigan. The other is the Universal Kennel Club, a door in the Washington Building in Washington, D.C., and also a privately owned, nonmember, profit-making organization.

UKC #1, The United Kennel Club, Inc., is the second-oldest registering body in existence. As is the case with the AKC and UKC #2, most of its revenues are derived from registrations. Moreover, it also licenses 2,400 different events in the United States and Canada, receiving twenty-five cents per dog entered (just as the AKC used to do) to compensate it for the forms and record keeping involved. When one registers a litter with UKC #1, each puppy must be designated by sex, color, and name. That puppy is then given a registration number. If sold, the new owner has the right to change the name. The UKC #1 also accepts individual dog registrations; however, a color photograph is required as well as proof that the parents were registered with some registering body other than UKC #2.

It recognizes all breeds recognized by the AKC and many that the AKC doesn't. For example, it recognizes the American Eskimo, the miniature boxer, the Columbian collie, the toy fox terrier, the Arctic huskie, the American toy terrier, and the English shepherd. It was first to recognize the American (pit) bull terrier, later accepted for registry by the AKC as the American Staffordshire terrier. Whereas the AKC recognizes only one coonhound breed—the American black and tan—the UKC #1 recognizes six such breeds.

Probably the greatest single difference between UKC #1 and all other registry bodies is its policy on "family breeding." This all-inclusive term refers to the breeding of closely related individuals. Many breeders also frown on "inbreeding," which is the canine version of incest. "Linebreeding" is, however, another story and the backbone of the best kennels in the country. Here, granddaughter is bred to grandsire, niece to uncle, aunt to nephew. Such breeding is totally unacceptable to UKC #1 (not to AKC or UKC #2). Special exceptions are sometimes made, but only after pedigrees have been reviewed and reasons —such as preventing the end of a strain—have been carefully documented, even to the point of consulting with university geneticists.

Interestingly, the AKC does not provide a pedigree with its registration certificate. The United Kennel Club does: a three-generation pedigree, at no cost, and either a six- or seven-generation pedigree if one or both parents are Purple Ribbon—already UKC registered—registrations. In contrast, the most the AKC can or will provide is a five-generation pedigree; for that you pay $10. (By the way, a seven-generation pedigree lists the 254 closest ancestors of the dog being registered. Imagine *people* paying that kind of attention to what and how they propagate. Can't you just see the prospective father-in-law putting off the young suitor who has asked for the hand of his daughter by saying, "I'll have my lawyers examine your pedigree, and we'll let you know in a few days.") The UKC #1 also publishes two magazines: the monthly *Coonhound Bloodlines*, for the six coonhound breeds it registers, and the bimonthly *Bloodlines*, for all other breeds it recognizes. Each costs less than a dollar.

One other point of difference between the United Kennel Club and the AKC is that UKC #1 encourages dog owners to have their dogs tattooed and registered with their UKC #1 registration number. The AKC still has not seen fit to participate in the finding of missing and stolen dogs via a tattooed AKC registration number.

Since the United Kennel Club did not, until recently, believe in promoting itself to the total dog fancy, let alone the public at large, not many people know of it. Or where to avail themselves of its services. You can write to its Registration Office at 321 West Cedar Street, Kalamazoo, Michigan 49006, for free registration-application papers and for additional information.

Unlike the UKC #1, the Universal Kennel Club accepts any purebred dog or "any recognized new breed of dog." (The only requirement is that a photograph, "to verify their breed," be attached to the application form if neither parent has been recognized by either the AKC, UKC #1, or UKC #2. Once the pet, via this photograph, is ascertained to be purebred and registrable, the parents are assigned registration numbers, too.) As they themselves put it, "And here's our 'bottom line': UKC will save you money and make it easier for you to sell your dogs." Which it is certainly. After all, all one needs is the signatures of the seller and buyer. Their fees are nominal, and most of the cost is borne by the buyer, not the seller or breeder. Those fees are $3 for a pup less than three months old, $4 for a pup between three months and one year, and $5 for older dogs.

The one thing the UKC #2 does require, however, is for one to show the markings, if any, on a dog diagram on the application form. Also one is asked to indicate if the tail or ears have been cut off or trimmed.

This is not for verification of the breeding, but for use in their lost-dog registry. When they register a dog, they issue a tag with their registration number on it. In addition, they also print the name, address, and telephone number, not of the UKC, but of the owner. This saves them the expense of hiring a telephone operator to take calls on lost dogs.

The solution to this whole mixed-up registry situation in dogs is complex. UKC #1 has taken the first step: It has taken legal action against UKC #2, which will begin to develop when and if it can locate the owner. As for the AKC, that's a difficult nut to crack. They, to their credit, are trying to do something about the situation, but they have their hands tied by the disparity between the source of their funds and the major cause of their expenses. How much longer they can let their registration system subsidize their show-sponsoring position, I don't know. But they may have their hands forced: When and if the term "AKC reg." loses its appeal to the public, and thus to the puppy millers, the resulting drop in revenues could bring about the demise of the whole organization.

The cat-registration system, in comparison, is small potatoes, financially and geographically. It also affects fewer people. But when it comes to number of registries and resulting red tape, cat people have the dog people beat easily.

There are nine different registries: the American Cat Association, Inc. (ACA); American Cat Fanciers Association (ACFA); Cat Fanciers' Association, Inc. (CFA); Cat Fanciers Federation, Inc. (CFF); The National Cat Fanciers Association, Inc. (NCFA); The United Cat Federation, Inc. (UCF); International Cat Federation (ICF); Crown Cat Fanciers Federation (CROWN); and CCA, meaning unknown. Of these, only two, ACFA and CFA, have permanent addresses and office staffs. All the rest have to be tracked down through a fancier, one of the two registry bodies one can find, or *Cats Magazine*.

There are some arguments in favor of the proliferation of cat registries. *Cats* credits the registries with many worthwhile ideas that have "flowed through them into the mainstream of Cat Fancy thought and practice. While there are great differences in each registry, even that works to some people's advantage. Personality conflicts, or political differences, can be resolved simply by the aggrieved parties leaving the registry in question and joining another." Some of the more radical groups are given credit for helping establish interesting new cat breeds. When it comes to shows and judging, the differences are fewer, and a winner in one association usually has no difficulty winning in another association's domain. Judging and exhibiting procedures seem to be fairly uniform.

Probably, for the benefit of all concerned, the nine groups should get together on some sort of cooperative registering venture that would still allow each association to maintain its identity. Single registration of an individual cat would save at least $25 per cat over the current method of having multiple registrations required.

Cat registrations are growing. CFA installed a computer system when it got large enough. ACFA has already passed them in size, but has no computer yet. Put all the others together, and they are approaching that level. Likely, the high cost of computer rental and operation will force the creation of a central registry before long. The total savings each year for cat fanciers could run to $100,000 or more. And, with diligent work by association officers, the mechanization of a central registry need not alter the personalities of the various cat registries as they are now constituted. They could still have their officers, run their shows and other events, publish their literature, and maintain a loyal following. But, as has been the case with banks and other businesses, the sharing of computer time could make for more efficient service to the people footing the bill.

Proponents of maintaining the status quo cite the notion that the associations exist for the single purpose of being registries, that turning into a central registry would be an irreversible step. They do not see how conflicts regarding the status of breeds unrecognized by some associations and recognized by others could be reconciled. Then, too, most associations are convinced that CFA, the only one with a computer capability, is out to do in the other associations.

Incidentally, it is revealing to compare the CFA financial statement with that of the AKC. The former is a model of rectitude, while the latter seems intent on fudging figures and categories. With a lot fewer dollars to play with, CFA still produces a multipage yearbook containing its annual report, which reveals the most minute details. I defy anyone, even those rival cat registries, to find much fault with the CFA's record keeping in terms of its finances. This kind of open-minded communication with the cat fancy should help resolve the problems of multiple associations, multiple registration fees, differing breed regulations, and interclub jealousy.

The yearbook, by the way, would put many college yearbooks to shame. It is nearly two inches thick, weighs more than five pounds, costs about $10, and is beautifully gold-stamped and embossed on the cover. It is published in lieu of a magazine, wrapping up the year's events and news, complete with winning cats, ads, CFA business and financial reports, and so on. The center spread, à la *Playboy,* features the Best and Second-Best Cats of the year in glorious color.

# XIV  LOST AND FOUND

> Has anybody here seen Duffy?
>
> Duffy is a miniature poodle who left his home . . .
> and never returned.
>
> *The Ambler Gazette,* Ambler, Pennsylvania

A self-styled dognapper, speaking pseudonymously in a national dog magazine, elaborated at great length on the profitability of stealing dogs for ransom (up to $2,500) or resale to private parties. In describing why he chose this particular form of larceny over others, he pointed out another advantage besides money inherent in his profession: safety. Dogs can't "finger you" in court, and the vast majority of dog owners can't legally identify their own dogs.

Owners may know Frisky by sight, and he may know them, but that's not a legal identification. Unless a dog has very distinctive markings—which rules out 99 percent of all purebreds and at least 75 percent of the mongrels—there is only one other acceptable form of identification: tattooing. But for every dog that's stolen, hundreds of pets will get lost on their own: a hole under a fence, an open door, a passing challenge of a tom, the inviting scent of a bitch in season, a friendly child who'd just love to be walked to his home, or just plain freedom and the open road. Whatever the case, the problem is how to find him. Once found, a tattoo will serve to identify him.

Getting a tattoo on a pet is no big deal, unless one owns a critter who just can't stand vets. Otherwise, the vet simply shaves the inside of the left ear and tattoos it. Alternately (and many people prefer this—especially fearful vets who like to stay as far away as possible from the biting end), a spot on the inside of a rear leg is used. The flank-over-ear advocates feel that no honest-to-goodness vivisectionist or unscrupulous researcher would have any compunctions about cut-

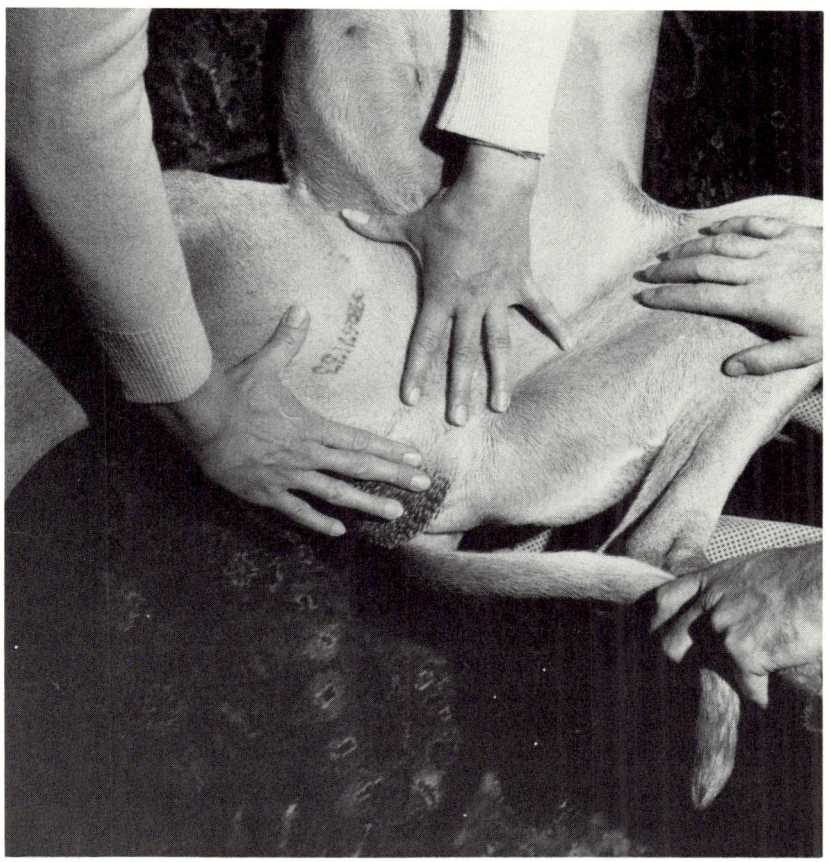

*The New York Times/Meyer Liebowitz*
Tattooing a dog on the inner flank, or inner ear, is one of several ways to protect a pet in case of theft or loss. It is also the only acceptable proof of ownership in a court of law.

ting off an ear to remove the tattoo, whereas they would stop at a leg.
    That is nonsense. In the first place, the tattoo on the flank can't be seen unless one looks for it deliberately; a hundred dogs in a laboratory could have such tattoos and no one would know it. But a pet with only one ear is a dead giveaway. Besides, laboratories wouldn't dare jeopardize government grants of enormous sums for the sake of getting a stolen pet cheap. Quite the contrary: It's cheaper for them to buy beagles bred for the purpose. If anything, an ear tattoo is a far better safeguard that a stolen pet won't be sold for research purposes. Then, too, if the pet is picked up by the local authorities or simply a con-

cerned person, the tattoo on the ear is readily seen, since the hair there—at least on all cats and those dogs with other than pendulous ears—is naturally thin. The tattooed area on the flank, on the other hand, has to be kept clipped or shaved for the tattoo not only to be read but even to be seen.

There are alternative solutions for owners who want to avoid the average $10 charge for having the vet do the tattoo or who have vets who prefer not to do the job, as many do. For example, many SPCAs and other animal-welfare agencies sponsor tattooing clinics because they have a big stake in the future of local pets. What it boils down to, in a cold-blooded, calculating way, is that every pet returned to its owner is one more they don't have to euthanize. Local breed clubs, which are also concerned about the fate of their members' dogs, also sponsor such clinics, and most are willing to accept any pet for tattooing, provided the owner is willing to pay a small fee. Still another possibility, one utilized by puppy millers and brokers who use tattoos as positive identification in the event of loss, casualty, or death during shipment, is to buy one's own machine. One can be had for about $65.

Making the decision to tattoo and getting it done are easy compared to deciding what to tattoo on the animal. The owner's social security number is the most common choice. But there are drawbacks. Some people don't want their social security number in other people's hands. The social security number also is of no use in tracing the dog back to its owner. The social security administration will not give out the name and address of the holder of a particular number—and who'd want them to? They also refuse to contact that holder to notify him to contact the finder of the pet.

Another choice is a telephone number, complete with area code. But that is a problem if you move, or if the telephone company decides to change your number, or if you decide to go the unlisted route. Of course, it would certainly come in handy if one's dog is dognapped; the thief would know just exactly how to get in touch with you to collect ransom—or a "reward." I suppose one could just make up some digits, if all that was desired of the tattoo was that it serve as legal proof of ownership. That is, if one could identify it without seeing it. Which assumes your record of it hasn't been misplaced (as you know it will be) over the years.

The problem of what to tattoo on a pet may well be decided by the registry service the owner decides to patronize. But apparently many people just go ahead and tattoo without following through and registering the tattoo with one or more registries. Registries claim to have had many pets reported to them bearing tattoos which, along with their owners, have never been listed. Obviously a tattoo is only effective if it is registered with an effective registry, and the registries seem to be as elusive and difficult to find as any lost pet itself.

Take Petfinders as an example. This Los Angeles-based lost-pet search operation started out well, but now it seems to have faded away. According to published reports, Petfinders started about five years ago, when Mrs. Paul King lost a cat and it turned up at a shelter twenty miles away. A year of research and planning followed. Then Petfinders went into business with a rented office, hired help, and six telephones. Petfinders charged $15 for a one-month search. You filled out detailed information forms and included a photo of your lost pet. The search entailed a daily check at shelters and in the newspapers. Eventually, costs forced the Kings to move the operation into their home. But mail addressed there now comes back marked "moved . . . no forwarding address."

Another registry, with a remarkably similar name—Pet Finders, Inc.—was set up in 1973, utilizing a nationwide toll-free telephone number for the reporting of lost pets around the clock. The cost for the service was $12 for a three-year period. The firm promised to utilize the latest sophisticated computerized technology, excluding tattooing. Instead, they provided a registration number printed on a blue and white aluminum identification tag to be attached to the pet's collar. The tag also bore the message, "I'm Lost, Please Call Toll Free." Well, now Pet Finders, Inc., is lost. At least the Better Business Bureau of Metropolitan New York, Inc., couldn't find them in 1975.

A Berkeley, California, firm with the impressive name of United States Pet Registration apparently doesn't want to be found. Nor does the Universal Kennel Club (the UKC #2, remember?), in Washington, D.C. And there's a third firm I'm still trying to track down, the CBI, who got their start tattooing seamen so the bodies could be identified if washed ashore after a shipwreck. One has to wonder how they made the transition from corpses to canines.

The one dog registry that is not only national but gives forth promise of permanence is the National Dog Registry, in Carmel, New York. In business since 1966, NDR uses the social-security-number system and recommends having the number tattooed on the inner right thigh of the dog. The one-time, lifetime cost is $15. The problem so far as I can see it is a question of endurance: how long can Mrs. Dagmar Swanson, owner and tracer of lost pets, continue to go without sleep in the cause of finding and tracing dogs. You see, the National Dog Registry has a twenty-four-hour hot line, 914-277-4485, that can be called any time of day or night to get not only an answer but some action. And the person answering night and day is Mrs. Swanson, who has an extension phone alongside her bed to take the wee-hour calls. Fortunately, she recently agreed to get an in-case-of-emergency answering machine, which will record incoming messages.

The point of all this is, so far as I can determine, that only those registries run by dedicated individuals seem to succeed. At least in staying in business, if not in making a profit. "In fact," says Abraham Sunny Pure, one of the individuals about whom I speak, "I'm losing my own shirt . . . but I'm staying in it because I believe in it."

Pure is owner/one-man operator of a local firm, Pet Guard Registry, in Philadelphia. Pet Guard charges $4 per dog for the lifetime of the dog. Included with the registration is an identification card for the owner and a tag for the dog's collar. The latter discourages the thief and helps the "finder." This is one service that will accept dogs registered with other services, something quite unique.

Pet Guard, incidently, uses what Pure regards as superior methods. For one thing, his tattoo device does all the digits simultaneously, not one at a time as most do. He says that this method is less painful than others. Second, he accepts any coding whatsoever, not just a social security number. Which means one could change to his registry without having to retattoo the dog.

One of the problems with pet registries, Pure points out, is that people don't know about them, not until they've lost the dog and discover how much they really need one. Another is lack of cooperation on the part of veterinarians in informing their clients about the registries. For example, Pure made an offer to all veterinarians in his area. He gave them tattoo equipment, renewal equipment, and a supply of registry cards—all this for only $10. Many vets wouldn't even take him up on his offer. Hundreds of others did, but have never even used the equipment. Or, at least, they have never sent back a single registration card.

Mr. Pure questions whether a national registry is the right registry route for everyone. Obviously, for the owner of a pet who gets left behind accidentally when a family moves cross-country, a national registry is an absolute necessity. But for every case like that, there are thousands of pets who will stay fairly close to home. In fact, most of the services quickly admit that the vast majority of recoveries occur within 200 miles of the loss.

That is a fact that the latest registry on the scene seems to be using to its advantage. The firm is Ident-a-Pet, in Brooklyn, New York. In its first two years, it registered over 6,000 pets, and it is now attempting to branch out nationally. Although not going the franchise route, they're doing something quite similar. A classified ad in *Pets/Supplies/Marketing* magazine seeks pet shops, groomers, dog clubs, and vets to "make high profit offering a unique service that takes only five minutes." The service is to become an agent for Ident-a-Pet.

Ident-a-Pet claims to have a tattoo machine that is revolutionizing the whole industry. It is, they declare and witnesses concur, absolutely painless and, if anything, feels more like a tickle than a tattoo. They have their own numbering system, each number starting off with an "X"; that's because everybody who finds a lost pet is supposed to know immediately that X stands for love, which stands for Ident-a-Pet, which is a bit doubtful. The fee is $20 per animal, and at that rate, they ought to do better, at least financially, than the rest of their competition. Whether or not one can make a "high profit" as an agent for them, I don't know, but if the idea does work out and more pets get registered, we'll all have gained something.

TIPS ON HOW TO LOCATE A LOST PET:

Tattooing and national registries are not the only solutions to the lost-pet problem. There are many things one can do to try to recover a pet, even if the pet is neither tattooed or registered:
1. Drive or walk around the neighborhood in the immediate vicinity of where the pet was last seen.
2. Make some telephone calls—to animal shelters, the local police, and neighbors who might keep an eye out for the pet. Give them the details, including past history (if any) of escapes and where found.
3. Place a classified ad in the lost-and-found column of your newspaper. Give approximate location lost so people in that area will be alerted. Offer a reward, but don't spell out how much. One doctor who offered $1,500 for the return of his Irish setter soon found a procession of setters brought to his door. When he finally got his own back, it quickly disappeared three more times, only to be returned for the reward each time.
4. Call or write the American Humane Association in Denver, Colorado, for its list of 600 radio stations across the country that belong to the Pet Patrol Radio Directory. These stations will gladly broadcast lost-and-found-animal notices as part of their public service contribution. Select the two or three nearest your home or the point where you lost or found a pet, and telephone them. They'll do the writing while they interview you on the phone. There's no charge for this service. Some 35,000 lost-pet spots were broadcast in a recent year.
5. Don't overlook this important step: Remedy the situation that permitted the pet to get away in the first place. Even if the pet never shows up again, chances are about 4 in 5 that it will quickly be replaced with a similar one.

# XV DEATH

> Death is sad for the one it leaves behind.
>
> GRETCHEN WYLER

The end comes, in fiction, with the dog's age-grizzled muzzle resting on his master's slippered foot. The eyes slowly, almost imperceptibly, glaze over, then close forever. There is that respectful silence death always imposes, to be broken, finally, by someone who says, in a hushed tone, "He's gone. But only to that Erin-Heaven in the sky reserved for the noble Irishman."

Would reality could be so. But it's a fact that old age and natural death take very few dogs; nor do self-sacrifice and heroic deeds, as so many authors would have us believe. Instead, most animal deaths are accidental, accompanied by a blast of a horn, a squeal of brakes, and a dog-sized thump. Or they are deliberate—done by the owner, the owner's agent, or the local animal shelter.

Some owners try to avoid the fact of death. When they can no longer keep an animal, for whatever reason, they surrender it to a local animal shelter, convincing themselves that someone there will see to it that the pet is quickly adopted. Of course, no one does. One shelter worker told me of a given weekend when, out of 200 dogs and cats surrendered, 195 were put down immediately as being unadoptable. Other owners, faced with the problems inherent to old age—incontinence, blindness, or deafness—and unwilling to have the animal put down, commit the ultimate cruelty: They turn to those shelters that offer geriatric services. Here, for a weekly, monthly, or annual fee—usually paid in advance—the animal will be able to live out its life. But what a life that is: confined constantly to a cage, unloved, unpetted, unplayed-with, cared for impersonally (one animal in such a shelter was found with five pans of food in its 3-foot-by-4-foot cage, no water, and no place to sleep except in its own fecal matter).

The well-intentioned owner doesn't know this. Quite the contrary, most believe that they have done their pets a great kindness. Fortunately, word about such abuses does get out, and when that happens, the shelters have been forced by public pressure to abandon their service. But it is the poor pet owner who feels most guilty. He had hoped to repay the years of love given him with at least a last few years of life. Years of comfort in which that pet would be cared for by humanitarians not just willing, but also physically and medically able, to cope with the problems of the geriatric pet.

There are alternatives to the shelter with the geriatric service, one of which is Barkwoods, the nation's first canine/feline geriatric home, which opened in September 1974. Barkwoods, a family-run operation headed up by Mrs. Eleanor C. Lillesand, is a boarding kennel/retirement home with facilities for thirty animals. Plans call for expanding the facilities with another building that could hold forty more dogs. Although many aged animals have come for short- and long-term boarding, the first lifetime resident didn't arrive until March 1, 1975. ("Grandma" is her nickname, Cha-Cha her real name, twenty-one her age. Arthritis, cataracts, deafness, and bladder problems made her retirement from apartment life to an old-age home inevitable.) However, she will undoubtedly be followed by many others.

The charges at Barkwoods are $90 to $140 per month, depending on size and geriatric problems. Included in these charges are bathing and grooming as needed, one monthly visit by a vet, and the administration of medications. However, emergency care, medications, and—in case of death—cremation and burial are extra and billed as incurred. Although the charges sound steep when paid in a monthly lump sum, they actually work out to less than $3 a day for a small dog or cat—less than the standard boarding rate in the same area.

If the owner is living, he must pay at least one month's fee in advance. This is not the case, however, where the owner is deceased and has set up a trust fund to care for his pet until its natural death. And this is the real service offered by Barkwoods: solving the problem of what to do with a pet or pets after the owner dies.

Not a month goes by that we don't read about some animal or animals that have inherited thousands of dollars from their deceased owners. In fact, these cases are so common that it takes a bequest in the hundreds of thousands of dollars to make the front section of the newspaper these days. When seventy-five dogs, after a protracted court battle, inherited close to $9 million, it inspired one steak-lover to figure out how much meat that money would buy. It worked out to over 60,000 rib steaks per dog.

What we don't read about is how many of those well-laid and well-

*Associated Press (Wide World Photos)*
Four employees and one veterinarian pamper 81 lucky dogs in Florida who inherited $14.5 million from their late mistress, Eleanor E. Ritchey.

financed plans go astray after the reading of the will and all of the publicity. Note that there was a "protracted court battle" before those dogs could eat steak. For example, one famous breeder provided in her will that none of her money could go to any of her natural heirs "until the last of my dogs is dead." The heirs cleared that stumbling block with one phone call to a vet, and within 24 hours after the will was probated, the last of her dogs was dead.

Another, thinking that she had found a way to ensure the proper care of her dogs, stipulated that upon the death of the last dog, the money was to go to a nonprofit organization. Until then, a trusted employee was to have the use of the funds for all reasonable expenses. When the last dog finally died, the funds turned over to the organization amounted to merely a pittance. The "reasonable expenses" had included, thanks to a clever lawyer, such things as yearly transportation charges to and from the vet's. In a new Cadillac, every year.

Because of all these ploys, Mrs. Lillesand recommends that if you are considering making some arrangements for the eventual care of your dogs after your death, you should consult a lawyer; set up a trust fund to be executed by the bank, which will make an accounting to your executor yearly; and not name an individual or a kennel to handle those funds. (She does not want her name mentioned in wills.

What she would like is for you to name Barkwoods in Egg Harbor, New Jersey, as the place for the dogs to stay.)

Whatever you do, it is important that you make sure that upon your death the fate of your animal is predetermined. Take, for example, the case of a Doberman pinscher. He was a one-man dog. The owner worked the dog, showed him, groomed him, and campaigned him, but the wife wouldn't give him houseroom. Instead, he was out in the kennel all the time. Unexpectedly, the owner died—and the dog went bananas. The kennel man, who had known the dog since he was a puppy, went to the widow and suggested the dog be put down. She refused. She was going to keep the dog in memory of her husband, as a living tribute.

The kennel man contacted the woman's vet and had him call her about putting the dog down. She refused adamantly. By this time, the dog had become uncontrollable; the combination of grief, the sense of fear in those around him, and the lack of discipline and purpose all combined to turn him into an untrustworthy, snarling beast. Members of the local Doberman Club contacted the woman. After seeing the dog, each advised that he be put down. But no, she knew better than they. By that time, the kennel man had left the scene, and no one was around to feed, much less groom and handle, the dog. One day when she opened the pen and leaned down to put the food dish in, the dog struck—and savaged her.

But for every animal that outlives his owner, there are millions who will be put down beforehand. The reasons for doing so vary, but in most cases I couldn't question the fact that it should be done. In fact, the knowledgeable animal lover frowns not on the person who puts a pet down, even for just a semigood reason, but on the person who allows a dog to age and degenerate to the point where it cannot function even as a pet. The dog who cannot hear or see or smell and who defecates anywhere at will and then mishmoshes and patty-cakes his mess is hardly *living*. The true animal lover recognizes that animals enjoy a privilege that many people have fought in court to achieve and enjoy: the right to have their suffering and pain ended abruptly and painlessly.

The question is not whether an animal should be put down, but where and how. Nor is there truly much controversy over the where. "To those who think the thing to do is leave the dog at the local shelter or pound," says one breeder, "all I can say is don't! No matter how good that facility may be in your area, that is not the way you treat a loving and faithful friend when it needs you the most. You don't need to add fear and the feeling of being abandoned to the problems of the very old or the very ill. We make the arrangements in advance with our vet, going quietly in the back door of the clinic to avoid the crowded waiting room, and it is done quickly and skillfully while I hold the dog in my arms. The veterinarian doesn't attempt any conversation with me, but he says a lot of kind and comforting words to the dog long past the point the dog can hear them."

Actually, much the same thing can be done at a reputable animal shelter. An appointment can be made in advance, the dog or cat can be held in your arms, and death can be administered quickly and skillfully. The trouble is that there are just too many unwanted pets in this world, with owners who cannot or will not be present when the animal is put down. For these animals, death may be entirely different and not at all painless.

As in almost anything else, money plays a part in this problem. It costs the people of the United States, either through taxes or donations, approximately $5 per dog or cat that is euthanized. This works out to more than $85 million per year just to dispose of pets that people became tired of. Add to that the fact that there is no perfect method of euthanasia; multiply it by the attempts of animal-welfare agencies and public pounds (and anyone else you can think of) to dispose of the greatest number of pets in the shortest period of time and at the smallest amount of money; and you can see why death for some will be long and agonizing, not true euthanasia or "happy death."

The method most preferred by humanitarians is the injection of a drug, such as phenobarbital, into the bloodstream. However, this requires the skilled and expensive services of a veterinarian, and few vets are willing to spend their days killing, not healing, dogs. Also, the dog itself must be calm and still—which is just the opposite of what a dog in a strange place surrounded by strange people will be. If the dog struggles, it is quite conceivable that the solution will not be deposited into the bloodstream. In that case, according to Robert L. Hummer, V.M.D., M.Ph., "if even a small portion of the solution is deposited in the tissue surrounding the vein, a severe burning sensation will be experienced by the animal."

Since finding the vein is time-consuming and laborious, many vets take the quick and sloppy way, going the intracardial route directly into the heart. This method is especially favored with dogs that are struggling since presumably they can be held down long enough to get the task over with quickly. However, this method, too, has its problems, according to Dr. Hummer: "The vet is disregarding, from a humane viewpoint, the sensitive tissue that must be penetrated before reaching the heart. This procedure is especially painful if several jabs of the needle must be made before the needle is introduced into one of the chambers of the heart."

Forced by economics and the sheer number of animals that must be put down, most shelters turn to the high altitude-low pressure method. (This method, the invention of Dr. Sigmund Rascher, was developed for testing the effects of high altitudes on German pilots in 1941. He refined the method by using captive Jews as guinea pigs in a decompression chamber at Dachau.) It has certain great advantages for those who use it. A veterinarian need not operate the machine, which saves money. The person who does operate it need not be highly educated, and that saves money. With it, several dogs or cats can be done at one time, and that saves money. What happens occurs within a soundproof metal chamber, so that no one can either see or hear what is happening, and that saves money because it prevents a large turnover in operator personnel.

Fortunately for the poor animals, the death has not been proved to be as painful as some humanitarians would have us believe, except—and that's important—when the equipment has been overcrowded,

*The New York Times/Jack Manning*
A typical decompression chamber used for euthanizing cats and dogs in an SPCA "lethal room." In rooms like this all over the country about 37,000 cats and dogs will die every day of the year.

when it has not been maintained properly, or when the operator, either through ignorance or haste, does not adhere to the complete operational profile as recommended by the American Humane Association's scientific advisory committee.

But the Euthanair, the glorified decompression chamber, costs money to buy and maintain; thus many shelters have tried other methods, the most common being carbon monoxide. Opponents refer to it as the "gas chamber," which has obvious emotional connotations. Actually, this can be a painless method, as evidenced by the number of people who are deliberately or accidentally killed by it each year. If handled properly, CO will cause unconsciousness in approximately forty seconds and death within two to three minutes. But it's how it's handled that counts. And the hose hooked between a car exhaust and an oildrum is another story altogether.

Electrocution has even been tried by some budget-conscious shelters. Fortunately or unfortunately—I'm not sure which—the danger to the humans proved so great that personnel developed certain prejudices against it. There have been other methods, such as the use of drugs that are derivatives of curare; these slowly paralyze the pet to death—a gruesome death the description of which gives me nightmares that I shall spare you.

In stark, happy contrast to this is nitrous oxide, better known as laughing gas, the closest thing I've come across to a "happy death." Perhaps you're already familiar with it. Many dentists use it. As one humane worker/dental patient described it, "It's just fantastic. You're really high. It's a trip. And I said to the doctor, would this kill me? I said, if you took me up with this and then turned it off and I was still up there and was lacking oxygen, would I die? And he said, of course. Well that's all I had to hear." And somewhere in a humane shelter, small animals are experiencing truly "happy death." Unfortunately, it's against the law. It seems nitrous oxide is a "controlled substance" and may only be used by medically certified individuals. It also is prohibitively expensive for all but the small, well-endowed shelter.

However, many anesthesiologists feel that nitrogen inhalation, also known as nitrogen flushing, may have exactly the same euphoric results. It has been studied by Colorado State University using a total of 400 animals. Electroencephalograms, electrocardiograms, and arterial-blood-pressure recordings were used to determine whether the animals suffered unduly. The findings concluded that nitrogen inhalation was:

> effective, humane, safe and economically feasible. EEG's showed patterns characteristic of the change from the conscious to the unconscious state in

an average time of forty seconds, the same time span as that required for "free standing" animals to "collapse." . . .

The humaneness of this method of euthanasia is demonstrated by the fact that animals became unconscious and collapsed [not keeled over, but gently crumbled, according to Snyder Manufacturing Company's public-relations chief] in less than one minute. Moreover, we observed no signs of pain in any animal in this study prior to unconsciousness during euthanasia, specifically including those with severe upper respiratory disease. We observed no signs of bloating in any animal euthanized by this method; indeed, one of the virtues of this technique is that it is physically incapable of causing bloating.

Some limb twitching and other evidence of impaired muscular control did occur. However, since the animals were unconscious, they were totally unaware of this activity and death took place without any apparent painful sensation. Some animals displayed symptoms such as gasping, muscle tremors, convulsions or yelping, but these events always took place after unconsciousness, as determined by our detailed physiological data.

One of the basic advantages of this method is that it is now available through the Snyder Manufacturing Company at a price practically any shelter (or practically any vet) can afford. Four units are in operation right now, and unlike the high-altitude decompression chamber, which looks like a torpedo—all metal and with a solid door—the nitrogen-flushing unit looks like a regular grooming cage except that the door is not wire but transparent plastic. Also, the process is completely automatic; no room for an employee to go wrong. One pushes a button and everything proceeds as it should with safeguards against anyone turning it off before the necessary five minutes are up.

Here, indeed, could be the answer to our search for painless, inexpensive death for our unwanted pets in the future. One thing I know: the longer and the more you are aware of our tragic excess of animals, the more realistic and practical you must become about facing up to the realities of their deaths. What so many people cannot seem to come to grips with is why so many were ever born to begin with.

# XVI POSTDEATH

The [Heinkels'] Sealyham lay on the draining board beside the sink. Dennis [Barlow] lifted it into the container. . . .
"I have our brochure here setting out our service. Were you thinking of interment or incineration?" [Dennis asked.]
"Pardon me?"
"Buried or burned?"
"Burned, I guess."
"I have some photographs here of various styles of urn."
"The best will be good enough."
"Would you require a niche in our columbarium or do you prefer to keep the remains at home?"
"What you said first."
"And the religious rites? We have a pastor who is always pleased to assist."
"Mr. Barlow, we're neither of us what you might call very church-going people, but I think on an occasion like this Mrs. Heinkel would so want all the comfort you can offer."
"Our Grade A service includes several unique features. At the moment of committal, a white dove, symbolizing the deceased's soul, is liberated over the crematorium.
"And every anniversary a card of remembrance is mailed without further charge. It reads: *Your little Arthur is thinking of you in heaven today and wagging his tail.*"
"That's a very beautiful thought, Mr. Barlow."
"Then if you will just sign the order." . . .

Reprinted from *The Loved One,* by Evelyn Waugh, by permission of Little, Brown and Co.

To dispose of a dead goldfish can cost as little as four cents, the estimated cost of flushing it down the toilet. To dispose of a pet fish—there is a difference—could cost as much as $99.75 for a proper burial at a pet cemetery. (Which is exactly what one young couple spent.)

There are also people who couldn't care less what happens to their pets' corpses, such as those who go in for on-site burial of their pets (which in many states is illegal) or who latch onto the trash idea. Although not feasible for a Newfoundland or other large animal, it works quite well for cats and toy breeds as well as terriers. They simply put them in a leaf-and-garden bag or any other plastic sack of the proper size and stick it in the nearest garbage can, not necessarily their own. Grisly, but true. Operators of landfills can tell hair-raising tales about the quantities of dead animals that appear in any given day's truckloads of trash. If the weather is hot, the chances are good that all such animals will be covered with dirt before the rats get at them. In cold weather, when the ground is hard to work and objectionable odors are not as great a problem, the pet may be recycled by rodents or other carrion-eaters, including feral (wild) dogs and cats.

Recycling, but not at the dump, is the usual destination of those dead animals picked up by firms working for that purpose under contract with metropolitan areas. Although they are supposed to pick up any dead animal anywhere within the community, their primary job is to haul away the remains of animals euthanized, but not cremated, in local shelters and pounds. Depending on frequency of pickup, the bodies may be stored almost anywhere in trash cans or kept in refrigerated rooms. Once picked up, they are taken to a rendering plant. There they are dumped into a gigantic bone-crushing and cutting machine along with carcasses of diseased livestock and offal, bones, and fats from slaughterhouses and/or meat-packaging firms (not to mention your neighborhood butcher). Slop, such as grease from restaurants, is added to the concoction.

After being chopped and shredded and minced up fine, the mixture is transferred to a cooker, where it is boiled under pressure to eliminate all traces of bacteria and render the stuff sterile. Once cooked down, the basic composition is bone-and-meat meal and tallow.

A team of reporters working for "Chicago Today," part of *The Chicago Tribune,* followed that meat and tallow even farther:

> From extensive interviews with [a renderer,] industry brokers, officials of the National Rendering Association, and cosmetics and pet food experts, it was learned that:
> - The processed meat meal and tallow . . . becomes an ingredient in dry pet food. This was confirmed by a spokesman for a leading pet food company. About 15% of the dry pet food consists of the by-products of the rendering company.
> - The fatty acid derived from the tallow is used to give cosmetics their oily characteristics and as a mixing agent, according to Dr. Joseph Kalish,

technical editor of the *Drug & Cosmetic Industry*, a major trade paper. Kalish is considered an expert in the use of fatty acids.
- He said the fatty acids are used in:
  - Handcreams and face creams in which the processed tallow is the agent that keeps the oil and water in the cream from separating.
  - Toilet and bath soaps.
  - Shampoos, hair colorants and dyes, rinses and hair-setting lotions.
  - Makeup creams and as a "sticking" agent in face powders.
  - Lipstick as a hardening agent.
  - Mascara and eye creams.
  - Shaving soaps and creams.
  - Bath oils and cream deodorants.
  - Baby toiletries and sun-tan lotions.
- Tallow also is used in textile softeners, gasoline additives, tires, batteries, paints, missile lubricants, and printing inks. The meal and tallow are most commonly used in feed grain for livestock.
- A spokesman for a pet food company said that rendering-industry by-products are generally labeled on packages of pet food as "meat by-products," but there is no elaboration as to the type of meat.*

Just think of that the next time you see an ad for makeup with a "new, richer, creamier formula." For that matter, the next time you reach for the lipstick, hand cream, or baby oil—it may contain a touch of Spot or Tabby.

Unless you have a great financial stake in a makeup company, you might wish to have your pet avoid such a fate. In which case you should have the remains of any euthanized pet returned to you. If the pound, shelter, or veterinarian has a crematory, the ashes can be returned to the owner, if he brings his own jar. Some people go a step farther and choose an airtight urn suitable for their mantlepiece. Others, feeling that animals are a part of nature, sprinkle the ashes on a favorite piece of greenery or, aware that the ashes are quite mineral-rich, use them to aerate garden soil.

Some vets can't own a crematorium because of zoning or ecological reasons. If the vet is near a large metropolitan area, he may be able to use a communal crematory.† For example, the Pet Crematory Service of America, in Farmingdale, Long Island, services over half a hundred pet hospitals as well as individual pet owners. Their fee schedule for individual owners is determined by the size of the animal, just as is done with boarding rates. A sampling of those rates includes $10 and up for birds; $75 and up for large animals, such as German shep-

---

* Copyright 1973, Chicago Tribune Company. World Rights Reserved.

† No people crematorium approached by this author would agree to do or admit that they had done an animal cremation, although one did state that he had been approached about doing a joint owner-pet cremation—and he refused. It is not against the law for them to do so, but most felt it unethical or bad public relations.

herds; and $85 and up for great Danes and other giants of dogdom. However, they do offer a multiple-cremation service. In this, three to five animals at a time are reduced to ashes, which are divided equally among the owners. So is the fee, beginning at $60.

If such a crematorium is not available, a vet may be able to offer something completely new, called "farm burial" by those in the cemetery business and the big R.I.P rip-off by me. For about $10 in the Midwest, more on the East and West coasts, you can supposedly give "your loved one the dignity and decency of a burial out in the tranquil countryside." The fee is split fifty-fifty between the vet and the operator of the farm-burial service. The vet gets his for pushing the service plus storing the animals until the farm-burial operator can make his weekly or semiweekly stop at the hospital.

The farm-burial operator, in return for his 50 percent, provides the trucks that pick up the remains and take them to a farm, out where land is cheapest to buy or rent. There, a backhoe has already dug a community trench into which 100, 200, or more animals will be dumped. However, precise records are kept—not of where an animal was buried, but of who his owner was. This so that each owner can receive a most dignified and sincere record that Rover or Poopsie or whoever had, on such and such a date, solemnly received a farm burial.

In the first year of one such operation, pickups averaged 300 to 350 a week. Once the word got around, not about the circumstances under which the animals were buried but about the idea of a farm burial as compared to the dump, the operators began to be contacted directly by pet owners. However, they still charged the same fee as when the vet was the middle man.

Nowhere have I found records to prove that the farms upon which these animals were buried had been rezoned as animal cemeteries of record; nor had provisions been made to keep them as such in perpetuity so as to protect the remains buried thereon. Of course, there are legitimate "farm burials," but these are actually commercial pet cemeteries that have been converted from a farm but have retained the farmland feeling. With this type of farm burial, one not only knows the exact location of the cemetery itself, but exactly where on it the pet is buried. The animal does not share a communal grave but has his own plot. But like anything else connected with pets, money is a big, big factor here. For example, the rip-off costs only $10 to $15; the farm cemetery costs ten to fifteen times that much.

Going to a regular commercial cemetery, one could conceivably spend 100 times that much. For example, Kurt Unkelbach, in *How to Make Money in Dogs* (Dodd, Mead, Inc., 1973), gives the following costs (as of 1973) for burial in a 250-acre modern commercial cemetery:

1. Burial plot (fifteen square feet), $200 to $400, depending on location.
2. Annual care of plot, $75. Perpetual care, $600.
3. Metal casket, $200–2,500, depending on size, style, and lining. Wood caskets start at $300. In stock.
4. Headstones, $200 and up; monuments, $500 and up. In stock.
5. Estimates given for special designs on either of above.
6. Lettering. Depends on style, size, and number of characters. Minimum $75.
7. Chapel service (optional), including organ music and services of minister, $150.

Fee schedules for parks I have contacted vary considerably among themselves and from the one above.

Plot—Depends on size and location. A 12-by-12-inch plot for birds or ashes ranges from $12 to $20. A 2-by-3-foot plot, suitable for a cat or small dog, goes from $60 up. The same plot in a two-tier burial park (where one animal is buried beneath the other) can cost anywhere from $30 to $65 per animal. One expert on pet cemeteries figures the national average to be around $50 per plot. However, those who own an animal as big as a horse (and horses have been buried in pet cemeteries) may have to buy two, three, or even four plots to accommodate it.

Annual care—Depends on the cemetery. Some include the cost of the care within the plot price. But this is generally only in those parks that ban tombstones and other protruding memorials. Elsewhere the annual fee runs between $2 and $5. Perpetual care is another story. At some cemeteries it is based on a percentage of the cost of the plot or of the funeral itself. It can conceivably be as little as $25 and definitely as much as $500, but that's for extra-special care. A high of $200 would be more normal.

Caskets—Can run as little as $2.75 (turtle-size) to as much as $185, wholesale. However, it is possible, according to one casket manufacturer, to "manufacture a line of your own inexpensive caskets. This can be done by simply nailing together boxes made of pine or redwood, and a simple lining can be installed." He also suggests using infant (people) caskets, which can, in the case of deluxe units, run into several hundred dollars. "The only trouble with using infant caskets," he cautions, "is that they are quite narrow, and it is difficult to fit a pet in properly." Although no funeral home that I spoke to admitted selling infant caskets for pets (one out of the dozen did recall that many, many years ago a woman sent her chauffeur down to pick up an infant casket in the family limousine), a people-casket manufacturer found there was indeed a great demand for its product for use by pet cemeteries. Thus, it manufactures high-impact polystyrene caskets that range in price from $40 to $115 (the latter with white velvet lining, in the largest size) wholesale. This particular casket includes a small pillow, a fabric overlay, and a built-in vault so no other container is needed. The latter (needed to waterproof wooden caskets) can cost an additional $25 to $50, retail, depending on size. By the way, the normal markup for caskets for pets, unlike those for people, which the funeral director usually sells at or slightly above cost, is at least 50 percent more than—and as much as two and one-half times—the wholesale price.

Headstones—For a flat plaque, the cost can run anywhere from $15 for a tiny one to $165 for a bronze one. The usual run of markers includes: flat marker, $28.60; slant marker, small $55.00, medium $65.00, large $100.00; pillow marker (not flat, but not as slanted as the slant marker), $37.00; tablet, in your choice of three styles, $54.50; and base for tablet, $17.40. No one could call those prices unreasonable, especially since they include freight, lettering, and a selection of design engravings. But those are wholesale prices. The retail prices are another story: $28.60 flat marker, retail $85.00; $55.00 slant marker, $165.00; $65.00 slant marker, $195.00; $100.00 slant marker, $295.00; $37.00 pillow marker, $111.10; $54.50 tablet, $163.50; and $17.40 base, $52.50. Of course, these are simply run-of-the-mill markers. John Lux, a monument maker whose own pet monument contains the pictures and names of four animals—three not yet dead—has worked on markers that have gone as high as $3,500.

Estimates for special designs—Unless the monument is specially designed, for a standard run-of-the-mill monument, an artists' charge of $15 is added to wholesale prices for the reproduction of any specific pet or animal. This charge will, in the nature of things, be jacked up 300 percent, or to $45. One special design feature now being used by many monument people is a small, wallet-size photograph of the dog enclosed within a special frame. It costs but a few dollars to have added to the monument. Of course, to protect the photograph from fading, there should be a special metal cover. That'll cost a few bucks extra.

Lettering—Depends on style, size, and number of characters. It is included in the charge for the standard plaques, tablets, and markers.

Chapel service—First you have to find a priest, rabbi, or minister to agree. Many pet-cemetery owners can find one. Just ask. As late as the Middle Ages, church masses were said for man's animals, especially his dogs. But those days have passed. So uncommon is it, that French novelist Antoine de La Salle found it good fiction material. In *Cent*

*Lee Edwards Benning*
The resting place of Checkers, former President Nixon's famous black cocker, in the Bide-A-Wee Home Association Pet Memorial Park, Wantagh, Long Island. His is but one of the many famous-owner pet graves that receive appropriate-to-the-owner perpetual care.

*Nouvelles* he creates a parish priest who, upon the death of his dog, decides to give it a Christian burial, which angers his bishop. The priest, ordered before a tribunal to defend himself against a charge of sacrilege, ends his speech thusly: "And you will understand, my Lord, that I was able to put this dog, who was worth more than a good number of Christians, in a discreet position. The dog gave me many instances of its wisdom in life, and above all in its death! It even wished to leave me its will, at the head of which is the name of the bishop of this diocese, to whom it bequeaths 150 crowns, which I have here for you now." He was, of course, cleared of the charge.

There are other charges that I haven't touched on. For example, interment fees (opening charges), which can range from $5 to $25 or be included within the cost of the plot; pickup charges, $5 and up; Christmas decorations, $5 and up; other seasonal decorations, $15 and up. There is also the cost of flowers for those cemeteries where artificial decorations are banned during the year or during the spring and summer.

One of the more ingeniuous ideas, which is widespread across the country, is to allow the owners of pets to pay for any improvements and beautification projects. According to one pet-cemetery owner, "There are memorial structures at cemeteries throughout the United States which run into many thousands of dollars, and the customers are happy to have the opportunity to contribute to a project such as this."

What the average pet funeral would cost is difficult to ascertain. Mr. Unkelbach, who came up with the original set of cost figures says, "the least any dog can cost his owner, if chapel is omitted and annual care is desired, is a fat $750." He may be right. At Bide-A-Wee Home Association Pet Memorial Park, in Wantagh, Long Island, one young couple paid $250 for a plot, $125 for a Philippine mahogany casket, $200 for perpetual care, and the $15 interment fee, plus $20 for a marker—all for a parakeet.

E. C. Jordan, president of the National Association of Pet Cemeteries, the organization that represents the majority of the approximately 400 pet cemeteries in the country, notes two basic differences between pet and human cemeteries: (1) Pet cemeteries pay real estate taxes assessed to them, which human cemeteries do not. (2) People bury people because they have to bury people. People bury pets because they want to bury pets. "There are no unloved pets in a pet cemetery," he says.*

A visit to any cemetery is an experience, but one to a pet cemetery is surprisingly interesting. Although most of us would find visiting those around the world—the several in England, the one at Monte Carlo, another in Japan, still another in Brazil, and the three in France—rather a far piece to go, America has many fine and interesting ones. One of the most famous of these is Bide-A-Wee. Here is where former-President Richard M. Nixon's famed Checkers is buried as well as Charles Atlas's Smokey and Hermione Gingold's threesome: Yorkshire Pudding, Fido, and Mr. Poodle (but you can't find them— she hasn't gotten around yet, after ten years, to getting a marker).

In another section of the twelve-acre site is buried a rather different assortment of pets, all owned by one man, including: one old English sheepdog; one spitz; one Persian cat; one bush baby; one Pookie Pig, the guinea pig; and Gary the grasshopper. Another section is dedicated to "Sarge," a Belgian shepherd, the mascot of the World War II Canine Corps. In this section, so that Sarge's upright memorial is not obscured, only bronze flat plaques may be used. Behind what was

---

* One of the newest trends in people cemeteries is to set aside a portion for pets. This, as Mrs. Maria Garber, manager of Whitemarsh Memorial Park, outside Philadelphia, put it, "is by popular demand. So many people want to have their pets buried with them—which of course we could not do—that we decided to honor their request the only way we could."

once the chapel but is now the future columbarium lie three veterans of the New York City mounted-police unit. The three, victims of incurable equine infectious anemia—swamp fever—were taken to the cemetery in February 1975, where a large grave, ten feet deep, eight feet wide, and nearly twenty feet long, had been dug for them (the equivalent of twenty-one regular graves, at an average cost of $60 apiece, which was donated by the cemetery). At one end, a long ramp had been prepared. One at a time, the horses were led down into the grave, humanely destroyed by a veterinarian, then covered with a tarpaulin and dirt so as not to distress the next horse to follow. Each of the three—Shalom, age fourteen, Sundance, eleven, and Wilkinson, seventeen—was buried with its departmental bridle bearing its name. Peter Marmorato, owner of the Art Stone & Memorial Company, is donating a suitable memorial, which will bear their departmental shields. And the three will not lack for equine company, since adjacent to their grave is one of a horse buried in November 1974 with plastic bags containing hay, carrots, apples, and oats placed next to its head.

A walk through the cemetery provides proof that the animals here are beloved. One has a mausoleum in the form of a doghouse, another a statue, still another a food dish bronzed and converted into a flower holder/plaque for Chipper. And towering over all is a column bearing a replica of a fireman's hat—a memorial to the dog's kept by New York's Fire Department.

There are shrubs and greenery everywhere, as well as elaborate seasonal decorations including an Easter bunny. One gravesite is covered with artificial grass and contains a statue of St. Francis.

Perhaps more than anything else the epitaphs are revealing. Many are repetitious: "Gone but not forgotten," "forever in our heart," "my seeing eye dog, my eyes, my treasure"—the standard suggestions of the memorial-manufacturing company. Others are more innovative. "An Angel Touched Her and She Slept," is the favorite of the manager, Mrs. John Barry Sheehan. Probably the most famous ran in Louis Sobel's column and appears on the memorial of Sir Richard Henry Winston, owned by Mr. and Mrs. Herbert. It reads, in part, "For when you spell dog backwards, you'll get the name of God." Another quotes Lord Byron:

> To mark a Friend's remains
> These stones arise.
> I never knew but one,
> And here he lies.

Many have been the famous epitaphs written for dogs and cats found in cemeteries throughout the world. In Queensland, Australia:

> In memory of Ranger. Died May 8, 1938.
> If there be an afterworld for such as thou;
> may the juiciest of bones be thy reward.

Inscription on the marble mausoleum built at Abbotsford, England, for Maida, a Scottish deerhound owned by Sir Walter Scott:

> *Sit tibi terra levis* (May the earth lie lightly on you)

By John Greenleaf Whittier:

> Bathsheba:
> To whom none ever said scat,
> No worthier cat
> Ever sat on a mat
> Or caught a rat:
> Requis-cat.

An old standard with a new twist:

> Her cup of love runneth over . . . by a hit-run driver.

In the "Dog That Bit People," James Thurber may well have written the funniest dog story ever. As its title implies, Muggs, the Airedale, bit postmen, meter readers, salesmen, friends, family. No one escaped him. Especially, and literally, the hand that fed him. Thus, he ate family-style at the table. And the Thurber family not only tolerated but loved Muggs. When he finally died, he was buried beneath a simple wooden marker with a two-word epitaph. "Mother," remarked Thurber, "was quite pleased with the simple dignity of the old Latin epitaph." It read: Cave Canem. Or "Beware of the dog."

# Appendix I PUREBRED DOG AND CAT PRICES

Based on a national survey, this is a price comparison of the thirty-seven most popular breeds and/or varieties of dog and cat currently being sold in pet stores. Note that in every case the retail pet store charges more for a pet-quality animal than does the private breeder; that in six cases, the pet-shop pet costs as much as the private breeder's top show-quality prospect; and that in nine cases, the pet-shop pet costs even more than a top show prospect.

| BREED | PET SHOP | | PRIVATE BREEDER | |
|---|---|---|---|---|
| Dogs | Wholesale | Retail | Pet Quality | Show Quality |
| Afghan | $100–130 | $350 | $150 | $250 |
| Airedale | 60 | 175 | 150–175 | 250–300 |
| Alaskan malamute | 75–85 | 175 | 85 | 100 |
| American Eskimo | 40–50 | 200–300 | 85 | 100 |
| Basset | 85 | 129–225 | 125–200 | 125–350 |
| Cocker | 85 | 225–265 | 125–200 | 350 |
| Collie | 65–75 | 150–200 | 100–200 | 350 |
|    "Rare" white/merle | 40 | 100–150 (rare) | culled | culled |
| Dachshund, miniature | 85 | 200 | 165—smooth<br>175—long<br>185—wire | 175—smooth<br>250—long<br>300—wire |
| Dalmatian | 60 | 150–175 | 125–150 | 200–300 |
| Doberman pinscher | 100 (cropping $25 extra) | 150–500 | 250 | 350 |
| Fox terrier, toy | 45 | 100–150 | Not recognized by AKC | Not recognized by AKC |
| German shepherd | | | | |
|    Male | 70 | 200 | 150–250 | 300–350 |
|    Female | 50 | 150 (known to be sold for as little as $25) | 150–250 | 300–350 |

## APPENDIX I

| | | | | |
|---|---|---|---|---|
| Irish setter | 50–65 | 350 | 250 | 500 |
| Labrador | 50–65 | 300 | 200–250 | 500 |
| Lhasa apso | 100 | 300 | 150 | 250 |
| Maltese | 125 | 200–325 | 200 | 250–400 |
| Old English sheepdog | 125 | 350 | 250 | 350 |
| Peke-a-poo | 65 | 150 | — | — |
| Pekingese | 85 | 100–190 | 125–500 | 500 at 6 mos. |
| Pomeranian | 90 | 135–150 | 150 | 250 |
| Poodle, miniature | 65 | 35–150 | 150 | 250 |
| toy | 85 | 50–200 | 150 | 350 |
| Pug | 85 | 200 | 150–200 | 300–500 |
| Samoyed | 75 | 180–250 & up | 150 | 250–375 |
| Schipperke | 80 | 150–250 | 150–200 | 250–350 |
| Shetland sheepdog | 85 | 165–175 | 150–200 | 250–300 |
| Siberian husky | | | | |
| Brown eyes | 65 | 150 | 85 | 100 |
| "Rare" blue eyes | 95 | 200–250 | 85 | 100 |
| Silky terrier | 100 | 150–275 | 150–200 | 250–300 |
| Welsh corgi | 70 | 175–250 | 125–175 | 300 |
| Wire fox terrier | 85 | 150–175 | 175–200 | 200 & up |
| Yorkshire terrier | 125 | 350 | 150–250 | 350 |

*Cats*

| | | | | |
|---|---|---|---|---|
| Persian | 70 | 75–100 | 35 | 125 |
| Siamese | | | | |
| Sealpoint | 20 | 100 | 50 | 150 |
| Others | 25 | 100 | 75 | 150 |

# Appendix II DOG BREED POPULARITY CHART

From 1964 to 1974, purebred dog registrations with the AKC increased overall by 72 percent. Of the 121 breeds involved, three showed little or no gain, four were recently admitted to recognition and thus must be discounted, 14 decreased in registrations, and 100 increased. However, few breeds grew at the overall average, some increasing more than 2000 percent. Therefore, the average increase for those 100 breeds was not 72 percent but 360 percent. A lesson can be learned from this: A decrease in face of a pet population may mean trouble within the breed, or fly-by-night operators and puppy-millers have decided the profit was nil and pulled out. An increase of 72 percent or thereabouts means the breed is holding its own and not experiencing overpopulation. An increase of 360 percent or more is a danger signal—the breed is either in danger of, or already has been, exploited.

| Breed | 1964 AKC. Reg. | 1964 Rank | 1974 AKC. Reg. | 1974 Rank | Change | |
|---|---|---|---|---|---|---|
| Affenpinscher | 36 | 100 | 72 | 109 | increase | 100% |
| Afghan hound | 1,242 | 43 | 10,918 | 28 | increase | 779% |
| Airedale terrier | 3,138 | 30 | 7,088 | 37 | increase | 126% |
| Alaskan malamute | 772 | 50 | 8,416 | 34 | increase | 990% |
| American foxhound | 33 | 104 | 55 | 112 | increase | 67% |
| American Staffordshire terrier | 143 | 85 | 647 | 73 | increase | 352% |
| American water spaniel | 198 | 75 | 291 | 92 | increase | 47% |
| Akita | * | * | 1,057 | 61 | | |
| Australian terrier | 312 | 66 | 1,291 | 57 | increase | 314% |
| Basenji | 1,681 | 35 | 2,348 | 47 | increase | 40% |
| Basset hound | 13,716 | 10 | 17,251 | 21 | increase | 26% |
| Beagle | 53,353 | 3 | 51,777 | 4 | decrease | 3% |
| Bedlington terrier | 732 | 51 | 515 | 79 | decrease | 30% |
| Belgian malinois | 4 | 111 | 9 | 119 | increase | 125% |
| Belgian sheepdog | 211 | 73 | 511 | 80 | increase | 142% |
| Belgian tervuren | 69 | 93 | 467 | 82 | increase | 577% |
| Bernese mountain dog | 11 | 109 | 198 | 97 | increase | 1,700% |

* Not accepted for registration by AKC in 1964.

# APPENDIX II

| Breed | 1964 AKC. Reg. | 1964 Rank | 1974 AKC. Reg. | 1974 Rank | Change | |
|---|---|---|---|---|---|---|
| Bichon Frise | * | * | 1,022 | 63 | | |
| Black and tan coonhound | 155 | 83 | 239 | 94 | increase | 54% |
| Bloodhound | 391 | 62 | 1,337 | 55 | increase | 242% |
| Border terrier | 61 | 95 | 71 | 110 | increase | 16% |
| Borzoi | 330 | 63 | 1,656 | 51 | increase | 402% |
| Boston terrier | 12,231 | 12 | 11,200 | 27 | decrease | 9% |
| Bouvier des Flandres | 118 | 87 | 735 | 71 | increase | 523% |
| Boxer | 8,872 | 15 | 12,552 | 26 | increase | 41% |
| Briard | 45 | 98 | 205 | 96 | increase | 356% |
| Brittany spaniel | 7,247 | 18 | 19,368 | 17 | increase | 167% |
| Brussels griffon | 154 | 84 | 196 | 98 | increase | 27% |
| Bulldog | 3,597 | 27 | 6,465 | 41 | increase | 80% |
| Bullmastiff | 258 | 70 | 588 | 78 | increase | 128% |
| Bull terrier | 219 | 72 | 641 | 74 | increase | 193% |
| Cairn terrier | 1,899 | 34 | 7,339 | 36 | increase | 286% |
| Cardigan Welsh corgi | 194 | 76 | 325 | 89 | increase | 68% |
| Chesapeake Bay retriever | 721 | 52 | 2,214 | 48 | increase | 207% |
| Chihuahua | 40,966 | 5 | 20,639 | 15 | decrease | 50% |
| Chow Chow | 924 | 47 | 4,016 | 44 | increase | 335% |
| Clumber spaniel | 7 | 110 | 45 | 113 | increase | 554% |
| Cocker spaniel | 15,632 | 8 | 35,492 | 9 | increase | 127% |
| Collie | 18,424 | 7 | 28,068 | 11 | increase | 52% |
| Curly-coated retriever | 2 | 112 | 36 | 116 | increase | 1,700% |
| Dachshund (all varieties) | 48,569 | 4 | 47,581 | 5 | decrease | 2% |
| Dalmatian | 3,108 | 31 | 8,596 | 33 | increase | 177% |
| Dandie dinmont terrier | 167 | 82 | 190 | 99 | increase | 14% |
| Doberman pinscher | 4,815 | 22 | 45,110 | 6 | increase | 837% |
| English cocker spaniel | 442 | 60 | 800 | 69 | increase | 81% |
| English foxhound | 0 | 115 | 7 | 120 | | |
| English setter | 839 | 48 | 1,561 | 52 | increase | 86% |
| English springer spaniel | 5,181 | 21 | 14,389 | 25 | increase | 178% |
| English toy spaniel | 30 | 105 | 41 | 115 | increase | 37% |
| Field spaniel | 0 | 113 | 24 | 118 | | |
| Flat-coated retriever | 27 | 106 | 90 | 108 | increase | 233% |
| Fox terrier | 9,713 | 14 | 6,516 | 39 | decrease | 33% |
| French bulldog | 72 | 91 | 171 | 101 | increase | 138% |
| German shepherd dog | 63,163 | 2 | 86,014 | 2 | increase | 36% |
| German shorthaired pointer | 5,908 | 19 | 15,284 | 24 | increase | 159% |
| German wirehaired pointer | 180 | 79 | 958 | 64 | increase | 432% |
| Giant schnauzer | 70 | 92 | 386 | 87 | increase | 451% |
| Golden retriever | 3,993 | 26 | 20,933 | 14 | increase | 424% |
| Gorden setter | 317 | 65 | 1,072 | 60 | increase | 238% |
| Great Dane | 3,467 | 28 | 20,319 | 16 | increase | 486% |

* Not accepted for registration by AKC in 1964.

| | | | | | | |
|---|---|---|---|---|---|---|
| Great Pyrenees | 263 | 68 | 1,493 | 53 | increase | 468% |
| Greyhound | 40 | 99 | 229 | 95 | increase | 473% |
| Harrier | 34 | 102 | 42 | 114 | increase | 24% |
| Irish setter | 4,015 | 25 | 61,549 | 3 | increase | 1,433% |
| Irish terrier | 449 | 59 | 344 | 88 | decrease | 23% |
| Irish water spaniel | 75 | 90 | 108 | 106 | increase | 44% |
| Irish wolfhound | 138 | 86 | 1,347 | 54 | increase | 876% |
| Italian greyhound | 536 | 55 | 626 | 77 | increase | 17% |
| Japanese spaniel | 263 | 68 | 393 | 85 | increase | 49% |
| Keeshond | 1,366 | 41 | 5,535 | 43 | increase | 305% |
| Kerry blue terrier | 1,099 | 45 | 833 | 67 | decrease | 24% |
| Komondor | 12 | 108 | 100 | 107 | increase | 733% |
| Kuvasz | 19 | 107 | 134 | 104 | increase | 605% |
| Labrador retriever | 10,340 | 13 | 36,689 | 8 | increase | 255% |
| Lakeland terrier | 117 | 88 | 190 | 99 | increase | 62% |
| Lhasa apso | 598 | 54 | 17,692 | 20 | increase | 2,859% |
| Maltese | 1,531 | 37 | 5,766 | 42 | increase | 277% |
| Manchester terrier | 1,279 | 42 | 630 | 76 | decrease | 51% |
| Mastiff | 79 | 89 | 641 | 74 | increase | 711% |
| Miniature pinscher | 1,571 | 36 | 1,085 | 59 | decrease | 31% |
| Miniature schnauzer | 13,593 | 11 | 41,392 | 7 | increase | 205% |
| Newfoundland | 490 | 56 | 2,157 | 50 | increase | 340% |
| Norwegian elkhound | 2,039 | 33 | 9,034 | 31 | increase | 343% |
| Norwich terrier | 191 | 77 | 304 | 91 | increase | 59% |
| Old English sheepdog | 473 | 57 | 16,050 | 23 | increase | 3,293% |
| Otter hound | 48 | 96 | 32 | 117 | increase | 33% |
| Papillon | 175 | 81 | 460 | 83 | increase | 163% |
| Pekingese | 23,989 | 6 | 23,631 | 12 | decrease | 1% |
| Pembroke Welsh corgi | 1,416 | 38 | 2,374 | 46 | increase | 68% |
| Pointer | 323 | 64 | 405 | 84 | increase | 25% |
| Pomeranian | 13,960 | 9 | 16,433 | 22 | increase | 18% |
| Poodle (all varieties) | 178,401 | 1 | 171,550 | 1 | decrease | 4% |
| Pug | 7,284 | 17 | 7,607 | 35 | increase | 4% |
| Puli | 294 | 67 | 758 | 70 | increase | 158% |
| Rhodesian ridgeback | 252 | 71 | 817 | 68 | increase | 224% |
| Rottweiler | 178 | 80 | 883 | 66 | increase | 396% |
| Saint Bernard | 4,098 | 24 | 31,361 | 10 | increase | 665% |
| Saluki | 66 | 94 | 729 | 72 | increase | 1,005% |
| Samoyed | 2,106 | 32 | 10,203 | 29 | increase | 384% |
| Schipperke | 1,028 | 46 | 1,332 | 56 | increase | 30% |
| Scottish deerhound | 34 | 102 | 157 | 103 | increase | 362% |
| Scottish terrier | 4,677 | 23 | 8,819 | 32 | increase | 89% |
| Sealyham terrier | 203 | 74 | 130 | 105 | decrease | 36% |
| Shetland sheepdog | 7,533 | 16 | 22,944 | 13 | increase | 205% |
| Shih tzu | 2,811 | 43 | 9,690 | 30 | increase | 245% |
| Siberian husky | 1,406 | 40 | 18,473 | 19 | increase | 1,214% |
| Silky terrier | 667 | 53 | 3,038 | 45 | increase | 355% |
| Skye terrier | 185 | 78 | 284 | 93 | increase | 54% |

\* Not accepted for registration by AKC in 1964.

## APPENDIX II

| Breed | 1964 AKC. Reg. | 1964 Rank | 1974 AKC. Reg. | 1974 Rank | Change | |
|---|---|---|---|---|---|---|
| Soft-coated wheaten terrier | * | * | 486 | 81 | | |
| Staffordshire bull terrier | * | * | 371 | 86 | | |
| Standard schnauzer | 465 | 58 | 919 | 65 | increase | 98% |
| Sussex spaniel | 0 | 114 | 6 | 121 | | |
| Vizsla | 799 | 49 | 2,197 | 49 | increase | 175% |
| Weimaraner | 5,398 | 20 | 6,961 | 38 | increase | 29% |
| Welsh springer spaniel | 35 | 101 | 60 | 111 | increase | 72% |
| Welsh terrier | 1,214 | 44 | 1,126 | 58 | decrease | 7% |
| West Highland white terrier | 1,409 | 39 | 6,493 | 40 | increase | 361% |
| Whippet | 429 | 61 | 1,043 | 62 | increase | 143% |
| Wirehaired pointing griffon | 46 | 97 | 168 | 102 | increase | 265% |
| Yorkshire terrier | 3,412 | 29 | 19,223 | 18 | increase | 463% |

* Not accepted for registration by AKC in 1964.

# INDEX

Abraxas Aristotle, Ch., 141
Accessories, x, xii, 75–87
  for owners, 80–81
ADOA, *see* American Dog Owners Association
Adolph's Meat Tenderizer, 55
Adoption agencies, 33–50
  abandonment to, 4, 36, 39
  care in, 48–49
  *See also* Shelters
Aennchen Dancers (Maltese line), 18
Agway (company), 61
Air Transport Association, 17
AKC, *see* American Kennel Club
*AKC Complete Dog Book*, 83
Allied Mills, 61
*Ambler Gazette, The*, 174
*American Blue Book of Dog Breeders*, 84
American Cat Association (ACA), 172
American Cat Fanciers Association (ACFA), 172–73
American Dog Owners Association (ADOA), 139, 141
  Docktors Pet Center suit by, 162
American Humane Association, 179, 186
American Kennel Club (AKC), 11–12, 21, 30, 129, 148, 155
  authority of, 159
  Best of Breed award of, 145, 148
  Best of Show award of, 145, 148
  blue slip of, 159$n$, 160
  Bred-by-Exhibitor class of, 152
  breeding bias of, 152
  championships of, 18, 145, 148, 156
  *Complete Dog Book*, 83
  constitution and bylaws of, 169
  fees of, 124, 168
  founding of, 163–64
  *Gazette*, 150, 163, 166, 167, 169–70
  income of, 167, 170

investigators of, 164
licensed shows of, 184
obedience-work standard of, 155
papers of, defined, 159$n$
Racing Merit awards of, 153
Registrable of, 8, 84
referrals from, 28, 30
registration with, 159–73
requesting information from, 82
selection of delegates of, 169
support of canine research by, 166–67
talkathon sponsored by, 166–67
American Shetland Sheepdog Association, 27
American Sighthound Field Association, 153
American Society for the Prevention of Cruelty to Animals (ASPCA), 109
  SPCAs licensed by, 46
  *See also* Societies for the Prevention of Cruelty to Animals
American Veterinary Medical Association (AVMA), 51–52
American Whippet Club, 153
American Working Terrier Association, 155
Anable, David, 3
Animal Gourmet, 73
Animal Specialties, 86
Animal Welfare Act, 143
Ankeny Kennels, 9
Aranwood, 102–4, 106–7
"Are Animal Welfare Societies a Rip-Off?" 41
Argus Archives, 36
Arkansas, AKC registration in, 165
Art Stone & Memorial Company, 196
Arthritis, 53, 181
ASPCA, *see* American Society for the Prevention of Cruelty to Animals

# 206 INDEX

ATA (Air Transport Association), 17
Atlantic City Boardwalk show, 146
Atlas, Charles, 195
AVMA (American Veterinary Medical Association), 51–52

Baggie, 77
Baillargeon, Barbara, 88
Balligo's Wingover, Ch., 126
Barkwoods, 181
Barnes, Tommy, 96
Barry (St. Bernard), 132
Berg, Paul, 55
Bernard, St., of Menthon, 132
Best in Show, 149
Best in Specialty Shows, 26
Best Longhair Champion, 152
Best of all Working Dogs, 26
Best of Breed, 145, 148
Best of Show, 145, 148
Best Shorthair Champion, 152
Better Business Bureau, 22
*Bibliography of the Dog* (Jones), 82
Bide-A-Wee Home Association Pet Memorial Park, 42, 44–45, 94, 195
Birthday parties for pets, 72
Bitter Apple, 55
*Bloodlines* (magazine), 171
Blue Book Information Center, 84–85
Blue slip of the American Kennel Club, 159$n$, 160
Boarding, x, xii, 102–13
  Aranwood a model of, 102–4, 106–7
  in "camp," 109–10
  charges for, 105–6
  in-home, 106–8
  by local vet, 111
  by professional dog handler, 111–12
  by serious breeder, 112
Boardwalk show (Atlantic City), 146
BOB (Best of Breed), 145, 148
Bongo Bear, Ch., 132
Books on pets, 82–86
Borzoi Club of Delaware Valley, 153–54
Boyd, Stephen, 46–48
Brandt, Barbara, 7
Brandt, Fritz, 7
Bred-by-Exhibitor class, 152

Breeders, types of, 23–32
Breeding, 123–30
  franchise for, 129
  lemons from, 22–23
  services for, 127–30
  for show and racing, 153
Brewster Pedigrees, 21
*British Veterinary Record,* 144
Bromwell, David R., 164
Brucellosis, canine, 58–60
Burial
  cemeteries for, 191–97
  cost of, x, 180–81, 184, 191–95
  on "farm," 191
  services for, 192–94
Byron, Lord, 196

Campbell soup, 61, 63, 68
Campo Lindo, 108–10, 112
Canada, dog registration in, 163
Canine Genetic Breeding Services, 128
"Canine Mating Service," 127
Canine psychologists, 114–16
Cardinet, Dr. George, III, 48
Carlberg, Roy H., 162
Carnation (company), 61, 68
Carswell, D. Lawrence, 126
Caskets, 192
Cat Fanciers' Association (CFA), 28, 172–73
  yearbook of, 173
Cat Fanciers Federation (CFF), 172
Cats
  in competition, 151–52
  killed for dogfighting, 140
  prices of, 199–200
  *See also specific topics*
*Cats Magazine,* 172
Catteries, sale and ordering by, 22
CBI (dog registry), 177
CCA (cat registry), 172
Cemeteries, 190–92
*Cent Nouvelles* (La Salle), 193–94
Center for Disease Control, Brucellosis Surveillance report, 59
Certificate of Gameness, 155
CFA, *see* Cat Fanciers' Association
Champion Valley Farms Recipe (dogfood), 63
Chashoudian, Ric, 149
Checkers (dog), grave of, 194, 195

*Christian Science Monitor*, 3
Clark, Anne Howe Rogers, 125
Clip Joint, The, 88
Collins, Donald, 64–65, 72
*Collins Guide to Dog Nutrition, The*, 64
Colorado State University, 186
Competition, xii, 144–58
   cats in, 151–52
   charges for, 148–50
   fakery in, 148–50
   field trials in, 155–58
   finishing a champion for, 145
   judging of, 151–52
   remuneration in, 146–49
   working/herding dogs in, 154–55
Consumer protection, 109
Contraceptives, 76–77
*Coonhound Bloodlines* (magazine), 171
Coprophagy, 55
Cosmetic surgery on dogs, 147–48
Cremation, 190–91
Cromwell, J. M., 85
Crown Cat Fanciers Federation, 172

Dachau, decompression chambers at, 185
Dahm, John, 7
Dahm, Sandi, 7
Danenhower, Eloise G., 36
Delaware Valley Afghan Hound Club, 153–54
Delicatessen for dogs, 73
Diet change, 55
Digitalis, 54
Docktors Pet Centers, 16, 22, 123, 162
Dogfighting, 134–43
Dog Lovers International Club, 81
Dog pull, 132
Dog racing, 132–34, 153, 157
*Dog Tracks* (Weddle and Weddle), 129
*Dog World* (magazine), 11
*Drug and Cosmetic Industry* (trade paper), 190
Du-Say's, 75, 86

Ear mites, 53
East, Edward M., 38
Ecology of surplus dogs and cats, conference on, 40

Edwards, Albert Ingalls, ix
Egypt, ancient, 134
England
   competition in, 144
   racing in, 133, 134
Estrus, 56–57
Euthanair, 186

"Family breeding," 170
Federal Trade Commission (FTC), 68, 70
Feldman, Alexander, 160, 163
Flea and tick collars, 76
Foley, George, 84, 85
Foley, Thomas S., 140, 143
Foley Organization, 85
Food, *see* Pet food
Food and Drug Administration (FDA), 70
Forbid (coprophagy remedy), 55
Ford, Gerald, 19
France, 134
Freda, Joan C., 4, 6–7, 20
Friends of Animals, 49
Funerals, 193–95
   *See also* Burial

Gaines Dog Research Center, Small Animal Nutrition Workshop, 71
Garber, Maria, 195*n*
Gasow, Julia, 126
*Gazette* of the American Kennel Club, 150, 163, 166, 167, 169–70
General Food, 61, 62, 63
   FTC prohibition against, 68
Geriatric services, 180–82
Gilbride, Anna P., 71–72
Gingold, Hermione, 195
Giuliani, Lillian, 54
Glendening, Sharon, 98
Glick, P. R., 59
Good Housekeeping Seal of Approval, 160
Graham, Ellen, 73
Greyhound racing, 133
Grooming, x, 88–101, 102
   accidents during, 90–94
   do-it-yourself, 100–1
   need of, 96–98
   prices for, 98–100
   schools of, 94–96
   tranquilization during, 89–90, 99

# 208  INDEX

Grooming (cont.)
    what to look for in, 98–100
*Growling Gourmet, The*, 73

H & M Pet-A-Rama, 4, 7, 20
Haggerty, Capt. Arthur, 121
Haggerty Dog Training School, 121
Health certificate, 6
Healthy pets, how to tell whether you are getting, 20, 32
Heinz, H. J. (company), 61, 68
Herbel, Norman, 124
Hills Division, Riviana Foods, 100
Hodge, Guy, 42
Horsemeat in pet food, 70
Horses of New York City mounted-police unit, 196
House Agriculture Subcommittee, 140
House Subcommittee on Livestock and Grains, 143
*How to Make Money in Dogs* (Unkelbach), 191–92
Howell, Mrs. Wendell, 153
Huffman, David A., 123
Human Information Services, 41
Humane Society of the United States, 19, 39, 42
Humane society poster, 43
Hummer, Robert L., 184
Hybrid corn, 38

Ident-a-Pet, 178–79
Illinois, AKC registration in, 165
Illinois Department of Agriculture, 164
International Cat Federation (ICD), 172
*International Encyclopedia of Dogs*, 85–86
Iowa, AKC registration in, 164
Irma the Body, 150

Jackson, Sharon, 141
Jay Jay (Afghan puppy), 3–7
Johnson, Patty, 11
Jones (geneticist), 38
Jones, E. Gwynne, 82
Jordan, E. C., 195

K-9 Association, 129–30
Kalish, Joseph, 189–90

Kansas, AKC registration in, 164
Kansas State University, 48
Kennels
    advertising by, 29
    disposal of stock by, 15–16
    growth of, x
    lemons from, 22–23
    pricing by, 31–32
    referral to, 29
    species degeneration by, xii
    stocking of, 21
    *See also* Puppy mills
Keystone Veterinary Association, 54
King, Mrs. Paul, 177
Knapp, Richard W., 135–36
Kohl, Sam, 96
Ku Klux Klan, 135

LaFore, John, 154
Lambert, Donald, 135
La Salle, Anthony de, 193
Latimer, Heather, 78
Lethal room, 185
Lewis, George E., 58, 60
Lewyt, Alexander, 44
Liberty (Ford's dog), 19
Liggett & Myers, 61, 63
Lillesand, Eleanor C., 181
Lipton, Thomas (company), 61
Lost pets, 174–79
    lack of results in finding, xii
    registries of, 177–79
    tips on finding, 179
*Los Angeles Times*, 149
*Loved One, The* (Waugh), 188
Lure Field Trial, 153
Lux, John, 193

Maida (Scottish deerhound), 197
Marmorato, Peter, 196
Mars (pet-food manufacturer), 61, 68
Massachusetts Society for the Prevention of Cruelty to Animals, 135, 137, 142
Meason, Robin, 98
Medical tests, 57–60
Megahan, Margaret M., 34
Michigan Grooming School, 95
Mississippi, municipal pound in, 46–48
MIT, 166
Morris Animal Foundation, 48–49

Nabisco, 61
Nash, Ogden, 33
National (pet-food manufacturer), 61
National Association of Pet Cemeteries, 195
National Association of Trade and Technical Schools, 96
National Cat Fanciers Association (NCFA), 172
National Conference on the Ecology of the Surplus Dog and Cat Problem (1974), 40
National Dog Groomers of America Association (NDGAA), 88, 96, 100
National Dog Registry (NDR), 177
National Rendering Association, 189–90
NDGAA (National Dog Groomers of America Association), 88, 96, 100
Nejdl, Robert, 8
Nelson, Scott, 135
New York City
  Department of Consumer Affairs, 109
  Fire Department, 196
  Police Department, 196
*New York Post,* 110
New York School for Dog Grooming, 96
New York Society for Prevention of Cruelty to Animals, 42, 46
*New York Times,* 9, 78, 108, 138, 175
*New Yorker* magazine, 160
Nixon, Richard M., 194, 195
North Shore Animal League of Long Island, 42–43
Novak, Kim, 19

O'Brien, George M., 140
*Old Dog Barks Backward, The* (Nash) 33
Olin, John, 48
Onassis, Jacqueline, 19
"Open Litter" (Doberman pinschers), 26
Orthopedic Foundation of America, 48
*Our Puppy's Baby Book,* 86
Overpopulation of pets, xii, 40, 152, 201
Ownership, responsibility of, 4

Papers for dogs
  AKC, 159–73
  fake, xii, 162
  health certificates, 6
Parent-breed clubs, 28–29
Penicillin, 56
Pennsylvania Department of Agriculture, 54
Pennsylvania Society for the Prevention of Cruelty to Animals, 36, 46, 54, 119
Pet Crematory Service of America, 190
Pet Finders, Inc., 177
Pet food, x, 6, 7, 12, 61–74, 189–90
  analysis of, 71
  canned regular, 65–66, 70
  cat salad greens, 67–68
  cereal in, 68–70
  dry, 66–67
  horsemeat in, 70
  kidney flavored, 69
  milk as, 68
  protein in, 69, 70
  semimoist, 66, 68
  snacks, 67
  vitamins, 67–68
Pet Food Institute, 60–61, 70
Pet Guard Registry, 178
Pet legislation, xii
*Pet Mass Marketing* (trade magazine), 63
"Pet Owner Effectiveness Trainers," 115
Pet Producers of America, 27
Pet shops, 2–20, 35
  markups by, 15
  papers of sale by, 7
  proliferation of, x
  puppy mills and, 8–15
  sales by, 16, 18–20
  shipping to, 16–18
  species degeneration and, xii
  "testimonials" of, 19
*Pets/Supplies/Marketing* (trade magazine), 67, 88, 96, 178
Phenotype, defined, 127
Philadelphia Kennel Club show, 126
*Pit Dog Report,* 139
Pitman-Moore, 58–60
Plots, cemetery, 192

Poage, W. R., 143
Poluto Mats, 78
Poodle Perfect, 98
Pooper-scoops, 77–78
*Popular Dogs* (magazine), 85
*Popular Dogs' Dog Lovers Complete Guide,* 85
Porter, C. W. "Bill," 135
Pounds, 33
  See also Adoption agencies
Prices of purebred dogs and cats, 199–200
Professional Breeding Services, 127–28
Professional Handlers Association, 158
Psychologists, canine, 114–16
Puppy farms, *see* Puppy mills
Puppy mills, x, 3, 8–15, 124, 154–67
Puppy Piddle Pads, 78
Pure, Abraham Sunny, 178
*Pure-Bred Dogs American Kennel Gazette,* 144
Purebreds, registration of, *see* Registry
Purina Puppy Chows, 14
Purple Ribbon, 171

Quaker Oats, 60–61

Racing dogs, 132–34, 153, 157
Ralston-Purina, 14, 61, 63, 68–70
Rapkel, Marc R., 127
Rascher, Sigmund, 185
Referral services, states offering, 29–30
Registry, 35, 159–73
  "AKC Reg," 160
  Canadian, 163
  of cats, 172–73
  computerized, 164–65, 177
  fake papers in, xii, 162
  tattoo for, 176–77
  of UKCs, 170–72
Recycling of animal bodies, 189–90
*Report to Humanitarians* (quarterly newspaper), 41, 48*n*
Restaurant for pets, 72–73
Rhode Island, 134–35
Riddle, Maxwell, 131
Rimskittle Rampart, Ch., 128
Ritchey, Eleanor, 182

Rival Pet Foods, 63
Roeglin, Marguerite, 9–11, 13
Rogers, Anne Hone, 149
Rome, ancient, 132, 134
Roundworms, 54

Sachs, Ann, 102–4
Sachs, Arthur, 102–4
St. Bernard hospice (Switzerland), 132
Sarge (World War II mascot), 195
Sargeant's (company), 76
Schutzhund trials, 155
Scott, Sir Walter, 197
*Secret of Cooking for Cats, The,* 73
Senate Select Committee on Nutrition and Human Needs, 72
Sex life, 56–57
  contraceptives and, 76–77
Sharon's Poodle Shoppe, 98
Sheehan, Mrs. John Barry, 196
Shell (company), 76
Shelters, 33–38
  conditions in, 37, 46–48
  cost of adoption from, 42
  cruelty in, 44–46
  endowments to, 41
  geriatric services at, 180–82
  registration by, 35
  returnees at, 39
  suggested standards for adoption of pets from, 39–41
  varieties of euthanasia at, 183–87
Simmons, Jay, 61
Sled Dog Association, 132
Smith, Owen, 133
Snow Peak Kennels, 7
Snyder Manufacturing Company, 187
Sobel, Louis, 196
Societies for the Prevention of Cruelty to Animals (SPCAs)
  adoption from, 41
  buying from, 24
  disposal of animals by, 23, 34–35, 185
  Massachusetts, 135, 137, 142
  New York, 42, 46
  Pennsylvania, 36, 46, 54, 119
  tattooing clinics sponsored by, 176
  *See also* American Society for the Prevention of Cruelty to Animals

# INDEX 211

*Sporting Dog Journal,* 142
*Sports Illustrated* (magazine), 149
Stackhouse, Elizabeth, 132
Standard Brands, 61
Standard Poodle Clips Chart, 100
Stander, Matt, 85
Staph infection, 56
"Starters," AKC interpretation of, 156
Stifel, William F., 160
Stock Dog Fanciers of Colorado, 154–55
Stockner, Priscilla K., 56, 167
Stolen dogs, xii, 174–75
*Stud Book Register* (AKC), 163, 167
Sunburn, 91–92
Swanson, Dagmar, 177

Tabu Lhasa Kennels, 124
Tattoos, 174–76
"Teacup poodle," 19
Test of private breeder's litter, 32
Thomsen, Frederick L., 41–42
Thurber, James, 197
Tidypet Indoor Toilet, 78
*Tiger in the House, The* (Van Vechten), 86
Tips
  accessorizing your pet, 86–87
  boarding-kennel, 113
  common training problems, 122
  do-it-yourself grooming, 100–1
  feeding your pets, 74
  how to locate a lost pet, 179
  playing the show/field game, 158
Training, 114–22
  for habit breaking, 114–16
  for obedience, 116–21
Train-O-Mat, 78
Trainor, Bill, 158
Tumors, 56

UKC, *see* United Kennel Club; Universal Kennel Club
Undulant fever (brucellosis), 58–60
United Cat Federation (UCF), 172
United Kennel Club, 170–72
United States Congress
  letters to, 49
  *See also* entries under "House" and "Senate"
United States Pet Registration, 177

Universal Kennel Club, 170–72, 177
University Medical Center (Mississippi), 47
University of Pennsylvania College of Veterinary Medicine, 55, 60
Unkelbach, Kurt, 191–92
"Unwanted Pets and the Animal Shelter," 36
Utility dogs, 27, 131–43
  decline of, 131–32
  transformation of, to racing and fighting, 133–43

Van Vechten, Carl, 86
Veterinarians, 2, 4, 14–15, 51–60
  boarding with, 111
  certification by, 6
  fees of, x, 53–54
  registry and, 178
  tests by, 57–60
Veterinary Version of the Hippocratic Oath, 31
*Visualization of the Standard* (Foley), 84

Wachsman, David, 148
Walker, Alan D., 64
*Wall Street Journal,* 44
Walter Reed Army Institute of Research, Division of Veterinary Medicine, 58
WARDS, 49
Warwick Animal Shelter, 109
Waugh, Evelyn, 188
Weddle, Ruth, 129
Weddle, Sharon, 129
Western Vocational School of Dog Grooming, 95
Westminster Dog Show, 18, 21, 22, 26, 134, 147
Westminster Pit, 134
Whippet Racing, 153
White City (London, England), 133
Whitemarsh Memorial Park, 195*n*
Whittier, John Greenleaf, 197
William Penn Poodle Club, 54
Wright, Duncan, 139
Wyler, Gretchen, 45, 180

Yo Yo (fighting dog), 135
*Your Friend and Mine* (magazine), 135, 139